A Manual on Disaster Management

A Manual on Disaster Management

Edited by

Dr. Parag Diwan

Pentagon EARTH
AN IMPRINT OF PENTAGON PRESS

A Manual on Disaster Management / Dr. Parag Diwan (Ed.)

ISBN 978-81-8274-438-7

First Published in 2010

Published by

PENTAGON EARTH

An Imprint of
PENTAGON PRESS
206, Peacock Lane, Shahpur Jat,
New Delhi-110049
Phones: 011-64706243, 26491568
Telefax: 011-26490600
email: rajan@pentagonpress.in
website: www.pentagon-press.com

Printed at Aegean Offset Printers, Greater Noida, U.P.

Preface

Disaster management is the discipline of dealing with and avoiding or reducing the aftermath of an emergency situation. It is a discipline that involves disaster response such as emergency evacuation, quarantine, mass decontamination, etc. and also supporting, and rebuilding society after natural or human-made disasters have occurred. In general, any disaster management is the continuous process by which all individuals, groups, and communities manage hazards in an effort to avoid or ameliorate the impact of disasters resulting from the hazards. Actions taken depend in part on perceptions of risk of those exposed. Effective disaster management relies on thorough integration of emergency plans at all levels of government and non-government involvement. Activities at each level (individual, group, community) affect the other levels. It is common to place the responsibility for governmental emergency management with the institutions for civil defense or within the conventional structure of the disaster services.

The nature of management depends on local economic and social conditions. Experts have noted that the cycle of disaster management must include long-term work on infrastructure, public awareness, and even human justice issues. The process of disaster management involves four phases, namely mitigation, preparedness, response, and recovery.

Mitigation

Mitigation efforts attempt to prevent hazards from developing into disasters altogether, or to reduce the effects of disasters when they occur. The mitigation phase differs from the other phases because it focuses on long-term measures for reducing or eliminating risk. The implementation of mitigation strategies can be considered a part of the recovery process if applied after a disaster occurs. Mitigation is the most cost-efficient method for reducing the impact of hazards, however it is not always suitable. Mitigation does include providing regulations regarding evacuation, sanctions against those who refuse to obey the regulations (such as mandatory evacuations), and communication of potential risks to the public. Some structural mitigation measures may have adverse effects on the ecosystem.

Preparedness

In the preparedness phase, disaster managers develop plans of action for when the disaster strikes. Common preparedness measures include:

- communication plans with easily understandable terminology and methods.
- proper maintenance and training of emergency services, including mass human resources such as community emergency response teams.
- development and exercise of emergency population warning methods combined with emergency shelters and evacuation plans.
- stockpiling, inventory, and maintain disaster supplies and equipment
- develop organizations of trained volunteers among civilian populations.

Another aspect of preparedness is casualty prediction, the study of how many deaths or injuries to expect for a given kind of event. This gives planners an idea of what resources need to be in place to respond to a particular kind of event.

Response

The response phase includes the mobilization of the necessary emergency services and first responders in the disaster area. This is likely to include a first wave of core emergency services, such as firefighters, police and ambulance crews. When conducted as a military operation, it is termed Disaster Relief Operation (DRO) and can be a follow-up to a Non-combatant evacuation operation. They may be supported by a number of secondary emergency services, such as specialist rescue teams.

A well rehearsed emergency plan developed as part of the preparedness phase enables efficient coordination of rescue where required, search and rescue efforts commence at an early stage.

Recovery

The aim of the recovery phase is to restore the affected area to its previous state. It differs from the response phase in its focus; recovery efforts are concerned with issues and decisions that must be made after immediate needs are addressed. Recovery efforts are primarily concerned with actions that involve rebuilding destroyed property, re-employment, and the repair of other essential infrastructure. An important aspect of effective recovery efforts is taking advantage of a 'window of opportunity' for the implementation of mitigative measures that might otherwise be unpopular. Citizens of the affected area are more likely to accept more mitigative changes when a recent disaster is in fresh memory.

In this Manual on Disaster Management effort has been made to address issues pertaining to these four phases in Disaster Management cycle.

It dwells extensively on processes and efforts that should be adopted and applied for:

(a) Preparedness Planning
(b) Disaster Response
(c) Disaster Communications
(d) Managing the Disaster Aftermath.

This Manual is an assimilation of a lot of public domain material in a structured format so as to be useful to students as well as practioners of science of Disaster Management

New Delhi **Dr. Parag Diwan**
1st September 2009

Contents

CHAPTER 1

Introduction to Disaster Management

The Scope of Disaster Management

The term "disaster management" encompasses the complete realm of disaster-related activities. Traditionally people tend to think of disaster management only in terms of the post-disaster actions taken by relief and reconstruction officials; yet disaster management covers a much broader scope, and many modern disaster managers may find themselves far more involved in pre-disaster activities than in post-disaster response. This is because many persons who work in the development field, or who plan routine economic, urban, regional or agricultural development projects, have disaster management responsibilities. For example, housing specialists planning a low-income housing project in a disaster-prone area have the opportunity (and an obligation) to mitigate the impact of a future disaster if the houses incorporate disaster-resistant construction technologies. In the same manner, agricultural development projects must be planned in such a way that they help stem environmental degradation and thus lower the farmer's vulnerability to losses from droughts, floods, cyclones, or other natural hazards. In fact, in dealing with natural hazards, the vast majority of disaster management activities are related to development projects; only a small portion are related to emergency response.

Of course, disaster management also encompasses the field of emergency assistance and long-term maintenance for refugees and displaced persons. The refugee field of disaster management is highly specialized and requires not only many development skills but also a broader awareness of political, legal, and humanitarian issues.

Figure 1.1, which is based on a conceptual model developed by the Office of U.S. Foreign Disaster Assistance, shows some of the many sets of activities in management of natural disasters. Figure 1.2 depicts the principal sets of activities in management of refugee and displaced persons.

Definition of Disaster Management

"Disaster management" can be defined as the range of activities designed to maintain control over disaster and emergency situations and to provide a framework for helping at-risk persons to avoid or recover from the impact of the disaster. Disaster management deals with situations that occur prior to, during, and after the disaster.

The Objectives of Disaster Management

The objectives of disaster management are:

- to reduce or avoid the human, physical, and economic losses suffered by individuals, by the society, and by the country at large;
- to reduce personal suffering;
- to speed recovery.

When assisting refugees or displaced persons, a fourth objective is to provide protection to victims or persons whose lives or property are threatened by armed conflict, tribal animosity, religious persecutions, etc. The University of Wisconsin Disaster Management Programme defines "protection" as intervention by governments, international organizations, or private relief organizations to protect persons threatened by armed conflict. Intervention for refugees or displaced persons may include provision of sanctuary or a means of escape from conflict, and emergency support to victims threatened by disease, starvation,

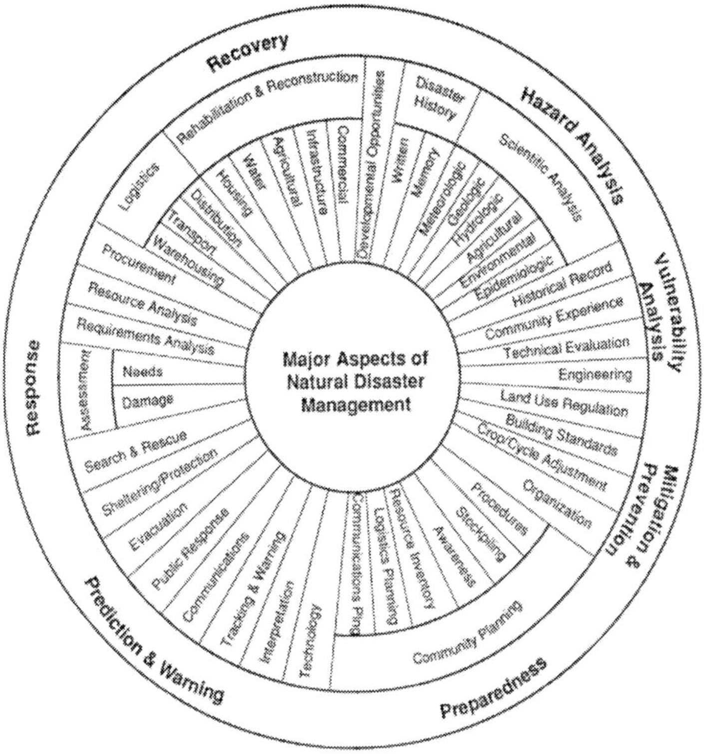

Figure 1.1: Major Aspects of Natural Disaster Management

and exposure to the environmental elements. (This definition may be broader than the usual interpretation by the United Nations and the International Committee of the Red Cross.)

Disaster Managers

The term "disaster manager" is applied to a person who has responsibility for planning and managing pre- and/or post-disaster activities. Disaster managers may be found in a variety of positions in many different types of agencies. The most prominent disaster managers are the personnel in governmental disaster preparedness agencies, national emergency or relief agencies, national reconstruction agencies, and emergency service agencies, departments or ministries. All require disaster management specialists.

Figure 1-2: Major Aspects of Refugee Management

Municipal or provincial governments often have disaster managers. Large cities will often have a director of emergency services; and persons in public health departments, police departments, or public works departments may be assigned additional responsibilities in emergency management.

Intergovernmental organizations often have specialized disaster or emergency management agencies. For example, the United Nations Disaster Relief Office (UNDRO) provides a wide variety of emergency management services to member governments. The United Nations High Commissioner for Refugees (UNHCR) and the United Nations Relief and Works Agency (UNRWA) provide specialized assistance to refugees. Even within the nondisaster agencies of the United Nations, there are often special emergency management offices. Examples include UNICEF, which has an Emergency Unit; the World Health Organization, which has a Director of Emergency Relief

Operations; and the Pan American Health Organization (a regional office of WHO), which has an Emergency Preparedness and Disaster Relief Coordination office that focuses specifically on the Americas. The World Food Programme also has a special Office for Emergency Relief.

Some nongovernmental organizations, both at the local level and at the international level, are specifically organized to provide emergency services. The most prominent of these are National Red Cross and Red Crescent Societies, the League of Red Cross and Red Crescent Societies, and the International Committee of the Red Cross. There are also hundreds of other private relief organizations throughout the world organized to provide specialized assistance to victims. These agencies range in size and scope from small, local ambulance corps to large U.N. agencies with scores of staff and multi-million dollar budgets.

Many nongovernmental development organizations (NGOs) have disaster specialists on their staffs. This is in recognition of the fact that disasters often occur where development agencies have normal programmes, and they cannot avoid becoming involved in post-disaster activities. This is also because of the frequency in which NGO's are called on to assist disaster victims. The specialists help to develop disaster plans for their organizations and to manage post-disaster operations.

Disaster management specialists can also be found outside of the systems specifically oriented towards disaster management or relief. Government ministries, such as agriculture, forestry, public health, defense, and public works, will often have major departments or key personnel assigned to disaster management or mitigation roles. It is common, for instance, to find a public works department employee who has assigned responsibilities for flood control activities. To be effective, that person must exercise responsibility not only in flood fighting but also inland use, settlement planning and evacuation. Thus, the effective disaster manager must have input into a variety of activities.

Key Personnel and Specialists Related to Disaster Management

Many people who serve in critical roles provide useful services in disaster management. While they are not considered disaster managers per se, their technological knowledge and skills and especially their experience warrant recognition of their potential contribution and function in disaster management. The examples are myriad: city and regional planners, watershed management and water resource development specialists, flood control engineers and specialists, code enforcement officials, public health specialists, doctors and nurses, dietitians and nutritionists, economic and agricultural development specialists, social scientists and welfare specialists, clergy and religious/ecumenical personnel, structural engineers, architects, reforestation and range land management specialists, firefighters, police, and development workers in general.

Although the above typically serve as the decision makers, other specialists often have an impact on disaster management decisions. These specialists include representatives from civic groups, academia, and the media, persons from research institutions focusing on disasters or disaster consequences, disaster management consultants, directors of development agencies, city managers, and other government officials.

The Role of a Disaster Manager

Table 1-A depicts the major natural disasters and some of the principal professions and specialists that should be involved in order to meet the needs in each particular phase. (Table 1 Depicts similar information for refugee operations.) This chart shows clearly that scores of different professionals are involved and that the primary role of a disaster manager involves the planning, coordination, and orchestration of actions in each time phase. In order to be successful, a disaster manager must have abroad base of knowledge in many different subjects and the ability to blend this knowledge into workable coordinated programmes to meet the needs of those affected by disaster.

Elements of Disaster Management

A disaster manager must deal with six distinct sets of activities in order to affect successfully the course of events related to disasters. Known as the elements of disaster management, these include risk management, loss management, control of events, equity of assistance, resource management, and impact reduction.

Risk Management. Risk management consists of identifying threats (hazards likely to occur), determining their probability of occurrence, estimating what the impact of the threat might be to the communities at risk, determining measures that can reduce the risk, and taking action to reduce the threat.

In natural disasters, risk management includes:

- hazard mapping
- vulnerability mapping
- estimation of potential losses, which can include:
- losses of housing and physical structures
- agricultural losses
- economic losses
- losses to physical infrastructure (such as roads, bridges, electric lines, etc.)
- development of appropriate disaster prevention and mitigation strategies.

Risk management is accomplished by lessening the effects of the natural hazard or by taking actions in normal development projects that will reduce the risks to an acceptable level. For example, if flooding is determined to be a major risk, the risk can be reduced by physical measures such as dams, flood control embankments, or channeling of the streams. Risk can also be reduced by moving threatened communities from flood plains and/or restricting economic activities in the flood zone to those that could absorb flood losses (such as forestry or agriculture).

Loss Management. Losses in a disaster include human, structural, and economic losses. Loss management addresses each of these through both pre- and post-disaster actions designed to keep losses to a minimum. The most effective loss management activities occur prior to the disaster and are focused on reducing the society's vulnerability to the disaster. Actions include: improving the resistance of buildings and physical structures in the event of disaster providing improved safety for the occupants of buildings or settlements situated in hazardous areas increasing and/or diversifying the network of social support (or coping) mechanisms available to victims and communities in threatened areas.

Table 1-A: Professions Active in Various Phases of Disaster

Types of Disasters	Prevention	Mitigation	Preparedness Planning	Emergency	Reconstruction
Drought	Climatologists Agronomists	Agronomists Agricultural Engineers & Extensionists Water Engineers	Water Engineers Agronomists Nutritionists	Nutritionists Physicians Nurses Social Workers	Agronomists Engineers Water Engineers
Earthquakes		Architects Engineers Contractors	Architects Engineers Physicians Nurses	Physicians Nurses Social Workers	Financial Specialists Architects Engineers Contractors
Floods	Engineers Rangeland Managers	Engineers Rangeland Managers	Engineers Planners		Architects Engineers Planners
Hurricanes		Engineers Architects Contractors Agronomists	Planners Nurses Physicians Meteorologists	Physicians Nurses	Engineers Architects Contractors Agronomists
Volcanoes		Planners	Planners		Planners
Insect Infestation	Entomologists Climatologists Meteorologists	Entomologists Agricultural Extensionists Agronomists	Chemical Engineers	Pesticide Applicators	Entomologists Agricultural Extensionists Agronomists

Table 1-B: Specialists Active in Various Phases of Refugee Operations

Preparedness	Early Warning	Forward Planning	Emergency Response	Maintenance	Durable Solutions	Evaluation
Operations	Political	Operations	Nutritionists	Social	Political	Operations
Scientists			Workers	Scientists	Managers	
Managers		Managers	Nurses		Internation	
	Media			Engineers	al Legal	Medical
Medical	Representatives	Planners	Doctors		Specialists	Specialists
Personnel		Engineers	Engineers	Planners		
	Diplomats	Medical Staff	Planners	Administrators	Diplomats	
Public Health		Communications	Social Workers	Logisticians		
Planners	Communications	Diplomats	Communications	Dieticians		
Engineers		Logisticians	Housing Specialists	Nurses Housing		
Communications		Public Health Sociologists	Sanitarians	Specialists Sanitarians		
Specialists		Food Aid	Diplomats	Vector Control		
Logisticians		Specialists	Food Aid Specialists	Specialists Agricultural		
Food Aid				Specialists		
				Appropriate Technology Specialists		
				Self-help Specialists		
				Teachers		
				Physical Therapists		

Post-disaster loss management focuses on improving the response and broadening the range of support given to victims. This includes facilitating relief delivery and stimulating a rapid recovery. These are accomplished through emergency preparedness, which consists of (1) the estimation of post-disaster needs and development of approaches and programmes to speed relief, response, warning and evacuation of persons known to be at risk from an immediate threat, (2) the provision of emergency assistance to help reduce the impact of losses, and (3) reconstruction, to lessen the economic burden of long-term recovery (see Figure 1.3).

Disaster preparedness refers to a broader range of activities, such as establishing emergency policies, developing evacuation plans, designating emergency shelters, and developing methods for rapid assessment of pre-positioning supplies. Materials planning emergency services, training and drills for emergency staff, training seminars and courses, and broad campaigns of public awareness aimed at preparing communities for the onset of a disaster are other aspects of preparedness. (The Disaster Management Center course, "Disaster Preparedness," explores the subject in detail.)

Another means of improving response is to expand or diversify the portfolio of assistance given to the disaster victims. Shelter, water, food, medicine, and clothing are usually considered as the normal emergency response. The potential range of assistance is in fact much broader. It should include economic assistance, family reunification, assistance to small businesses, rehabilitation of a community's public utilities, emergency assistance to farmers that enables them to harvest the remnants of crops, provision of food to livestock and draft animals, reduction of erosion caused by floods, social and psychological counseling, and literally hundreds of other activities.

Control of Events. The critical element of disaster management is the control of events during and after the emergency. It is important that disaster managers control a situation rather than respond to it. Control is maintained through the following measures:

Anticipation of a disaster and the cause-and-effect

Fig. 1.3: Operational Functions In Disaster Response

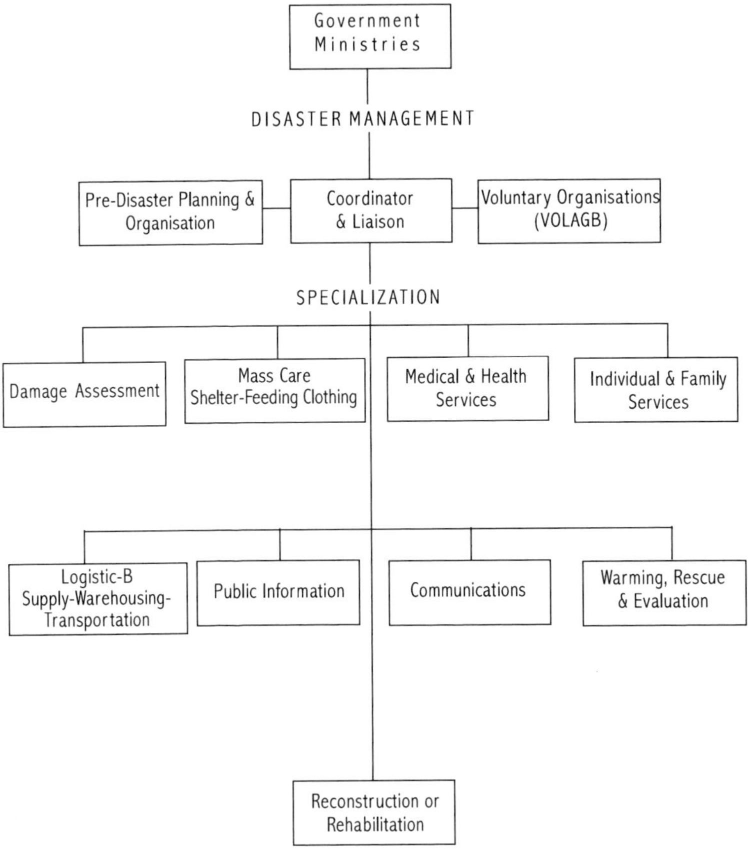

relationships generated by each type of event mitigation, or reduction, of the scope of a disaster. Mitigation is the most important function in bringing disasters under control. The more that can be done to reduce the effects of disaster, the fewer problems a disaster manager will face in the aftermath.

Preparedness. By reviewing the anticipated scope of a disaster, managers can plan adequate responses, develop organizational procedures, and prepare to meet the needs that are going to arise.

Accurate information collection and assessment. Once a disaster has commenced, the manager needs to have reliable data upon which to base priorities and to guide response.

A balanced response. Each type of disaster will require a different set of responses. The disaster manager must review the different strategies and approaches for meeting disaster needs and develop an appropriate mix of responses, so that all sectors of the community can be equitably assisted. More than one approach may be necessary in order to meet a variety of needs in the same sector.

Action. Once a problem has been identified and a response strategy selected, the action must commence immediately. Appropriate action must be phased in a timely manner and undertaken before demands and needs escalate. Action delayed means lost opportunities and a lessening of control, which add to the suffering of the victims.

Leadership. Disaster management should lead, rather than follow, public action. If programmes are timely, the first element of leadership is attained. Rapid response and timely aid give people hope and encourage them to take positive actions themselves to help meet their needs. A delayed response leads to confusion and frustration and may force disaster managers to choose alternative courses that are ultimately less desirable.

Discipline. Disaster managers, disaster management systems and organizations, and all key personnel in the relief and disaster management system must operate in an orderly, precise, and disciplined manner. The appearance of discipline and self-assuredness will reassure the public and promote compliance. The success of a disaster manager relates directly to the leadership exercised and the ability to coordinate the actions required to bring order out of chaos.

Equity of Assistance. All disaster assistance should be provided in an equitable and fair manner. Assuring that all disaster victims are treated fairly and equally is an important element of disaster management. This is especially important at the national level when a variety of different relief agencies, each with different constituencies and demands by their management and donors, are trying to provide assistance. Doctrines of fairness must underlie uniform relief and reconstruction policies in order to insure that disaster victims receive fair treatment and obtain adequate access to the resources available.

Resource Management. Few disaster managers have adequate resources to meet all the competing needs and demands of a post-disaster environment. Thus, resource management becomes a critical element of disaster response. The disaster manager must be familiar with the resources available. He or she must know how to form them into a balanced package of assistance and how to maximize their use to the greatest advantage. For example, in the aftermath of a flood a relief agency may receive seeds that will enable 1,000 farmers to replant the crops that were destroyed by the flood. Yet disaster assessment surveys indicate that 2,000 farmers need replacement seeds. The manager who decides to give away all the seeds and reinvest the proceeds from the crop sales to purchase additional seeds can expand the number of persons serviced and thus maximize the contribution.

Impact Reduction. Disasters can have an impact far beyond the immediate human, physical, or economic losses. In a very real sense, disasters represent a loss of opportunity, not only to individuals, but also to entire societies. They can also be a serious setback to the country's entire development programme. The impact of the disaster on individuals and their society should be reduced to a minimum. For a nation struck by a disaster, this means managing the disaster in such a way that recovery is accomplished quickly and that the recovery efforts contribute to the overall development needs of the country and all its citizens.

CHAPTER 2

Concepts and Terms in Disaster Management

What Constitutes a Disaster?

There are many definitions of a disaster. Among relief organizations definitions vary according to each agency's roles, biases, and capabilities. This course defines a disaster as a situation resulting from an environmental phenomenon or armed conflict that produces stress, personal injury, physical damage, and economic disruption of great magnitude. It is important to note that even though disasters are referred to by the event that caused them, a disaster is not the event itself. For example, an earthquake is a natural phenomenon; if it does not strike a populated area with weak buildings, it is not likely to be a disaster.

Whether an event qualifies as a disaster often depends upon who is doing the defining. To a government, an oil refinery explosion could be a major disaster, but it is unlikely to trigger a massive response from the United Nations or from voluntary agencies (VOLAGS) unless hundreds of low-income families are hurt in the explosion. Conversely, disasters caused by long-term environmental degradation will often draw attention from VOLAGS long before governments mobilize their resources.

It is necessary to differentiate between disasters and accidents. An airline crash is certainly severe and costly, but the number of people affected is relatively small. What separates a disaster from an accident, or incident, is its magnitude of need and of victims involved.

It is also important to differentiate disasters from individual, non extreme or small-scale suffering. For example, hunger is a growing world-wide phenomenon; while it is a major concern, it is often endemic, being addressed with different approaches. Only when hunger becomes widespread and acute, in other words a famine, does the situation qualify as a disaster. This distinction is important because it helps define disasters as a separate set of events and gives a starting point for studying and understanding their importance, their impact, and the proper responses they require.

Natural Disasters

The term "natural disasters" refers to those disasters that are triggered by natural phenomena. These phenomena (such as earthquakes, cyclones, floods, etc.) are known technically as natural hazards.

The term "natural disaster" can be misleading because it implies that the disasters are solely a result of natural hazards-when in fact, human endeavors are a major contributing factor in creating a disaster. For example, if settlements or farms were not located in flood plains, disasters would not result from floods. If housing were built to earthquake- and cyclone-resistant standards, these hazards would be of scientific interest only and not result in disasters. (Natural hazards, their causes and effects, are the focus of the Disaster Management Center course "Natural Hazards.")

In recent years, a special type of natural disaster has begun to occur more frequently. This disaster is environmental degradation. It results typically from poor farming, grazing, or settlement practices, or because of demands for fuel wood. Excessive exploitation of natural resources or improper use or maintainance of lands change the ecological balance; the resulting effects of deforestation, desertification, erosion, siltation, or flooding often bring disaster. Primary examples are increased flooding due to overgrazing or poor farming practices in the upper portions of a watershed, and increased desertification resulting from overgrazing or improper use of water resources.

This type of disaster is a growing concern not only because of the environmental consequences but also because large numbers of people can be displaced. The resulting social disruption can cause massive problems. For example, in the 1970s a massive drought forced thousands of Sahelian farmers and herdsmen to abandon their lands and migrate to urban areas in search of food and work. Few of these urban migrants returned to the rural areas. Because the towns were unable to provide adequate services or decent housing, they now contain large slums with high unemployment.

Man-made Disasters

The term "man-made disasters" usually refers to disasters resulting from man-made hazards. Man-made disasters can be divided into three categories: armed conflict, technological disasters, and disasters that are not caused by natural hazards but that occur in human settlements.

Armed Conflicts and Civil Strife. Disaster management concerns itself with various aspects of armed conflicts and civil strife, including the protection and support of displaced persons and refugees during the conflict; physical and economic reconstruction; and social rehabilitation in the aftermath of the conflict.

Technological Disasters. Technological disasters are usually a result of accidents or incidents occurring in the manufacture, transport, or distribution of hazardous substances such as fuel, chemicals, explosives, or nuclear materials. The catastrophic gas leak at the pesticide plant in Bhopal, India, in 1984 is an example that may be an indication of future industrial disasters in Third World nations ill-equipped to cope with their own rapid development.

Environmentalists fear that such disasters could become increasingly common in industrializing countries that lack the trained workers and government regulators to detect and correct hazards in larger and complex plants. The level of technical expertise among workers in developing countries is not as good as in developed countries. Even when safety regulations and legislation exist, the level of enforcement is often seriously inadequate. Often developing countries believe that environmental safeguards are too costly. Sometimes the working conditions in developing countries make it impossible for companies to impose safety standards. For example, in a plant in a country where the workers do not have shoes it is difficult to require the workers to wear steel-toed safety boots.

The accidents themselves are not much different from the kinds of accidents that occur in industrialized countries, but the likelihood of their occurring and the potential damage is much greater. The death tolls from the resulting accidents could be magnified because Third World industries often are encircled by shantytowns and slums filled with migrants from the surrounding countryside.

In other cases, technological disasters are more economic than physical. For example, large refineries have exploded with minimal loss of life, yet the cost of restoring those facilities can be a major burden substantially affecting the entire economy of a small country.

Disasters In Human Settlements. The principal disaster of this type is urban fire. When fires break out in Third World shantytowns they can have a devastating effect. Flimsy, wooden shanties packed closely together create conditions that allow the fires to spread quickly and burn virtually out of control. As unchecked urban growth continues throughout the Third World, this threat will grow even greater.

Disaster Victim. A victim is a person affected by a disaster. The term "victim" has many negative connotations. It provokes images of helplessness, of people who must be taken care of. For this reason, many agencies use substitute words such as "beneficiaries" or "recipients." Unfortunately, these terms do not adequately describe all the people affected and may not accurately depict the actions taking place. The term "survivors" could be used, but technically the word applies only to those who have escaped a life-threatening situation, whereas any individuals may be drastically affected by the consequences of a disaster even though they were not directly threatened by a loss of life. Victims are not helpless. They are capable of making intelligent choices. When allowance is made for their special need to cope with personal losses and to put personal affairs in order, they can participate effectively in all post-disaster activities. In fact, participation in constructive activity is one of the most effective means of coping, and disaster victims are usually highly active and thoroughly dedicated relief workers. Furthermore, as local people, they are particularly well suited to deal with the needs of their communities.

What's in a Definition?

Definitions are important. An organization's response is often dictated by the strictness or flexibility of the definition used. UNHCR, for example, has a very precise mandate and definition of a refugee. Voluntary agencies and governments, on the other hand, have considerable latitude over those whom they can assist.

While most countries, and international law, do not classify combatants as refugees, some countries and NGOs do. UNHCR and other humanitarian organizations may classify as refugees persecuted people, such as tribal or ethnic minorities, who desire to flee a country but who still remain in their homeland. This classification can provide them protection until they can be relocated to another country. Those Vietnamese under consideration for the Orderly Departure Programme of UNHCR furnish an example.

The term "displaced persons" also refers to people who are forced to leave their homes and homeland as a result of droughts and famines. The Ethiopians who migrated to Djibouti because of the 1984 drought were displaced persons. Several definitions of "refugee" illustrate the differences. UNHCR defines a refugee as any person who,

> "owing to a well founded fear of being persecuted for reasons of race, religion, nationality, membership of a particular social group or political opinion, is outside the country of his nationality and is unable or, owing to such fear, is unwilling to avail himself of the protection of that country; or who, not having a nationality and being outside the country of his former habitual residence as a result of such events, is unable or, owing to such fear, is unwilling to return to it."

The World Council of Churches adds, "systemic economic deprivation" to the list of persecutions, thus broadening the definition. The Organization of African Unity includes the clause

"...owing to external aggression, occupation, etc. ...," which enables people to seek refugee status even though they may personally not be threatened (Robert White, UNHCR).

In armed conflicts displaced persons and refugees are of special concern to disaster managers. Displaced persons are individuals and families forced to leave their homes because of the conflict, but who remain inside their country. Refugees are noncombatants who have sought (or are seeking) safety by leaving their homeland and entering another country.

The laws regarding refugees and displaced persons are vague in many ways. For example, do persons who flee their homes because of extreme economic hardships coupled with human rights oppression qualify as refugees or as illegal immigrants? For the most part, this and other related questions are unresolved, and it is outside the scope of the University of Wisconsin Disaster Management Programme to discuss the fine points of refugee and immigration law. For the purpose of these courses, a refugee will be defined as a person who flees his/her homeland as a result of armed conflict and not for reasons of economic hardship or natural disaster.

Disaster Types

Another means of classification is available in addition to the categories already discussed. Disasters may be classified according to how rapidly they begin and how long they last. In this classification system are two types of disasters: rapid-onset or cataclysmic disasters, and long-term or continuing disasters.

Rapid-onset disasters include earthquakes, cyclones, floods and tsunamis (popularly know as "tidal waves"). Slow-onset, long- term or continuing disasters include civil wars, droughts and famines, and epidemics.

This type of classification is useful because the general approaches that are used to respond to the disasters in each category are very similar. For example, in supporting refugees and displaced persons, feeding programmes similar to those that are required for famine victims are used.

In a cataclysmic disaster, one large-scale event causes most of the damage and destruction. Following this event there may be a tremendous amount of suffering and chaos, and secondary disasters such as landslides may occur. Yet, things soon begin to improve. By contrast, in a long-term, continuing disaster the situation remains constant or may even deteriorate as time passes. In a cataclysmic disaster the damaged area is usually relatively small, while the area affected in a continuing disaster may be extremely large.

The "Relief System"

In disaster management there is much talk about a "relief system." However, no one specific system exists, but rather groups of organizations that provide different types of assistance at different levels. These include governments; intergovernmental organizations, such as the United Nations; Red Cross Societies; international voluntary organizations; international credit institutions, such as the World Bank and the International Monetary Fund; local social and economic groups; and many peripheral organizations such as cooperatives, trade unions, etc., that often become involved when disaster strikes. In any one country or in any one disaster, these groups may band together formally or informally to provide relief to the disaster victims. Some agencies act in the capacity of fund raisers, others act as donors. Some provide funds directly to the victims while others provide funds to other agencies that will help the victims. It is the role of the disaster manager to insure that coordination to the greatest extent possible is carried out.

Certain relief systems have evolved to provide assistance to refugees and displaced persons; other systems have evolved to provide assistance to victims of natural disasters.

Sectors In Disaster Relief

Disaster relief activities typically address a variety of needs. In disaster management this spectrum of human endeavors is classified by sectors. The most common are health, housing, agricultural, economic, and social sectors. These sectors are known as the prime sectors, because they are of prime concern to the disaster victims. A second group of sectors include urban settlements, transportation, lifelines, and critical facilities. These are known as secondary or support sectors, because they have indirect effects on the disaster victims.

Most disaster-related programmes take a sectoral approach. That is, most programmes focus on the problems unique to a particular sector and usually require technicians with skills specific to that particular field.

Intervention

"Intervention" refers to an action taken in order to change the course of events. In disaster management the term's use is similar to the medical sense, i.e., disaster response initiated from outside the affected community is a form of intervention and, as such, must be handled with care because it does come from without. It therefore always runs the risk of being more disruptive than productive.

Other Important Terms In Disaster Management

Pre-disaster planning is the process of preparing, in advance, to meet a future disaster. Pre-disaster planning consists of disaster prevention, mitigation, and preparedness.

Disaster Prevention is action taken to eliminate or avoid harmful natural phenomena and their effects. Examples of prevention include cloud seeding to control meteorological patterns, pest control to prevent locust swarms, erection of dams or levees to prevent flooding, etc.

Mitigation is action taken to reduce both human suffering and property loss resulting from extreme natural phenomena. Measures include land use planning, improved disaster-resistant building techniques, and better agricultural practices.

Preparedness encompasses those actions taken to limit the impact of natural phenomena by structuring response and establishing a mechanism for effecting a quick and orderly reaction. Preparedness activities could include pre-positioning supplies and equipment; developing emergency action plans, manuals, and procedures; developing warning, evacuation, and sheltering plans; strengthening or otherwise protecting critical facilities; etc. (The Disaster Management Center course, "Disaster Preparedness," covers the subject in detail.)

Risk is the relative degree of probability that a hazardous event will occur. An active fault zone, for example, would be an area of high risk.

Vulnerability is a condition wherein human settlements, buildings, agriculture, or human health are exposed to a disaster by virtue of their construction or proximity to hazardous terrain.

Secondary Threats are hazards such as landslides or erosion. Created or triggered as a result of a larger or stronger hazard (e.g., an earthquake, cyclone), secondary threats can occur during the primary disaster event or may happen days, weeks, or even months afterward. After a recent earthquake in Central America, hillsides that had been loosened by the tremors finally slipped five months later when they became saturated with water during the rainy season. The resulting mudslide killed dozens of low-income families who were squatting on the slope.

Secondary threats in the immediate aftermath of a disaster are a major concern of disaster managers. A top priority of assessment teams is to identify secondary threats and evacuate people before secondary disasters occur.

Phases of Disaster Response (Natural Disasters)

The Preparatory Phase. The preparatory phase of disaster response includes all of the activities that help a society and the disaster agencies to prepare for a disaster event. Activities carried out in the preparatory phase include organization, legislation, development of procedures, inventories of resources, and establishment of response plans. These activities are broadly classified as disaster prevention, mitigation and preparedness.

In general, disaster prevention is event-focused. In other words, the objective of prevention is to prevent the disaster from occurring. Disaster mitigation accepts the fact that some natural event may occur, but it tries to lessen the impact by improving the community's ability to absorb the impact with minimum damage or disruptive effect. Disaster preparedness assumes that a disaster will occur; it focuses on structuring the emergency response and on laying a framework for recovery.

Warning Phase. Preceding most disasters is a period of time during which it becomes obvious that something hazardous is going to happen. Certain specialists focus on trying to detect signs of a building threat. By monitoring events, they look for indicators that tell when, where, and what magnitude the event may be. This is known as prediction or forecasting. The objective is to provide disaster managers with enough information so they can give the people at risk adequate notice or warning to prepare for the disaster and, if necessary, to evacuate.

At the present time, warning is possible for droughts and famines, cyclones and most severe weather phenomena, volcanoes, large scale fires, and in some cases earthquakes. Work is also underway in refugee management to develop early warning techniques that will let relief agencies know of impending refugee crises.

Emergency Phase. This phase of disaster response involves actions that are necessary to save lives and reduce suffering. They include search-and-rescue, first aid, emergency medical assistance, and restoration of emergency communication and transportation networks. Some disasters, also necessitate evacuation from areas still vulnerable to further disaster events and provision of temporary shelter, food, and water. Other actions taken during the emergency phase include initial disaster assessment and emergency repairs to critical facilities.

Rehabilitation (Or Transitional) Phase. The transitional phase is a time period when people begin to return to work, to repair infrastructure, damaged buildings and critical facilities, and to take other actions necessary to help the community to return to normal. During this phase, emotional recovery occurs as families and individuals regroup and try to put their lives back in order. In many ways, the rehabilitation period is the most difficult for the victims. Relief agencies must be sensitive to varying degrees of need and must provide appropriate forms of assistance. Emergency relief measures must be discontinued during this phase so that people can begin to regain their self-reliance. (The Disaster Management Center course, "Disaster Response," covers in more detail the subjects of response and rehabilitation.)

Reconstruction Phase. The reconstruction phase of a disaster involves the physical reordering of the community and of the physical environment. During this period people reconstruct housing and other community facilities, and agriculture returns to normal. The actual time span is often very difficult to define. It may start fairly early and may last for many years.

Phases of Refugee Relief Operations

The phases of refugee relief operations parallel in many ways the operations in natural disasters, but there are some significant differences.

Emergency Preparedness is the set of activities taken by organizations to plan and prepare for reacting to a new refugee emergency. These preparations can and should meet any contingency, but they may also focus on a known situation that is predicted to develop into an emergency. Preparedness activities usually include organizing, developing contingency plans, stockpiling emergency supplies, developing procedures, and training staff.

Monitoring and Early Warning is the process of keeping watch on current events in order to predict when political, economic, or social events may deteriorate to a point where information to diplomats may allow mediation before a crisis develops. Diplomats can also provide relief agencies with timely data that will facilitate the development of contingency plans specific to the area of concern.

Forward Planning is advanced planning carried out when an emergency is imminent, e.g., refugees are known to be displaced and moving toward a border. Some of the usual activities include preparations for protecting the refugees and granting them refugee status, as well as alerting agencies that will provide assistance.

Emergency Response encompasses the activities that occur immediately after the refugees arrive in the care of humanitarian agencies. Typically, emergency activities include protection and legal assistance; provision of health services-food, shelter, water, sanitation, and many other basic necessities for survival; and a variety of social services to people with special needs such as unaccompanied minors and widows with small children.

Maintenance refers to the services that are provided to refugees during the period after the emergency but before a permanent solution to their plight is developed. Maintenance operations may include tracing and family reunification, general care and food distribution, a variety of social services such as education and cultural activities, and efforts to help the people to become as self sufficient as possible under the circumstances.

DURABLE (Permanent) SOLUTION is the term used to describe collectively the three long-term solutions that resolve a refugee situation-voluntary repatriation, assimilation, and resettlement to a third country. In this phase, any number of activities can take place including transportation of the refugees, legal assistance, and provision of financial and material aid to the refugees to help them start their new lives. If the solution is repatriation or assimilation, the patterns of assistance often resemble reconstruction and development assistance given to the victims of natural disasters.

Evaluation occurs as a refugee operation ends or as a new phase begins. Evaluation should be carried out by every manager and key members of the staff. The results and lessons learned should become the basis for further emergency preparedness activities.

Key Concepts

Several themes and key concepts of disaster management should be kept in mind. Some of these are:

The Relationship of Disasters to Development. People tend to regard disasters as separate and distinct events having little or no relationship to the political or economic development of a country. In recent years, however, the relationship between disasters and development has become clearer. Disasters are now recognized as one of the major contributors to underdevelopment, and underdevelopment is one of the major contributors to disaster. It has also been recognized that if disaster response is mishandled, many years of progress can be wiped out and the chances for further progress set back. Disasters can alter agricultural patterns, settlement patterns, patterns of migration, work habits, diets, and even basic family structures. If disaster management is well planned and development oriented, a disaster can provide opportunities for accelerating the pace of development. Constructive changes can then be made.

It is extremely important that disaster managers be aware of the impact of disasters and the role that development programmes can play in mitigating disasters and reducing vulnerability.

The Relationship of Various Disaster Activities to the Appropriate Phase of a Disaster

All disaster-related activities are divided into distinct time periods. The length of any one period can vary greatly depending on the type of disaster and other factors. Disaster managers must recognize the different phases and know what activities are appropriate in each phase. For example, emergency activities often include the distribution of free relief supplies. But if this activity is carried on in the later phases of a disaster, there is a danger that dependencies may be fostered and that the relief may provide disincentives to agricultural or economic recovery.

The Relationship of Various Time Phases to each Other. The phases of a natural disaster can be depicted graphically as a continuum, as shown in Figure 2.1. The activities that are carried out to mitigate a disaster closely resemble the activities that would be carried out during reconstruction. They are essentially development activities since they not only reduce the disaster impact but also provide economic or social benefit. By understanding how these activities relate to each other and to development, one can see the close interrelationship between good disaster management and development activities.

How Activities in One Phase Should Set the Stage for the Next. Study of Figure 2.1 and Figure 2.2, the latter depicting the phases of refugee relief operations, will show how activities in one phase relate to the preceding and following phases. For example, emergency response can be facilitated if the operations have been planned prior to the disaster, not during it. As a general rule, each phase and each activity of a disaster lays the framework and sets the stage for activities in the next phase. Therefore, when planning an emergency response, the disaster manager should keep in mind how that activity can help promote faster recovery. Consider this simple example. If a house has been destroyed in a windstorm or flood, there are several options for providing shelter during the emergency. The relief agency can provide a tent that will offer shelter; or it can provide building materials that the victims can use to build a temporary shelter and then later reuse in the reconstruction of their permanent house. The tent solves one need during one phase, but the building materials not only solve needs

Figure 2.1: Disaster Continuum

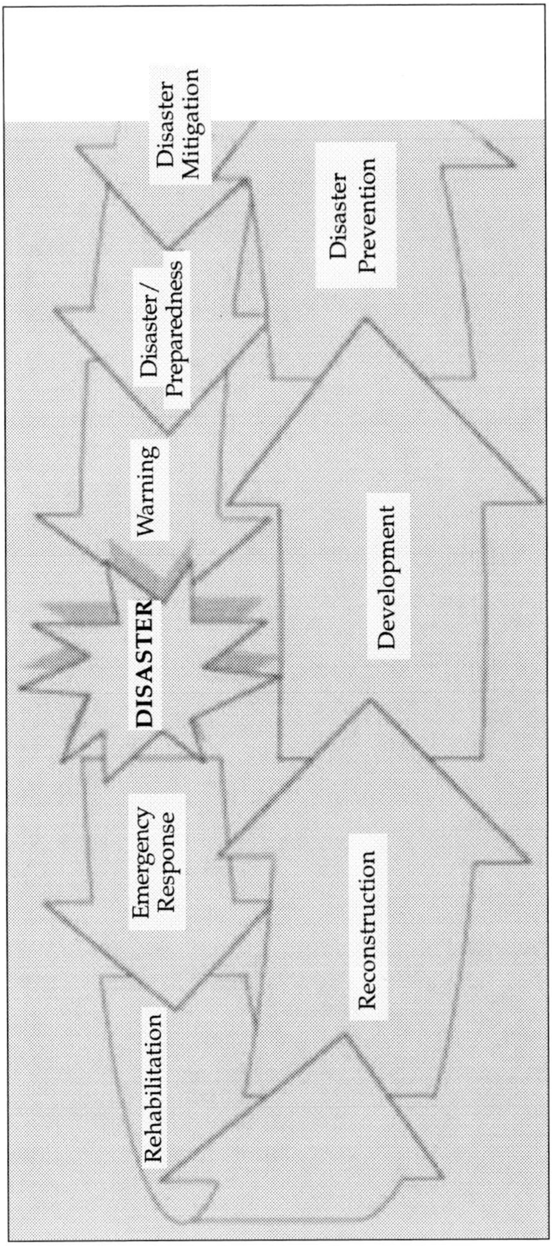

Figure 2.2: Refugee Operations Continuum

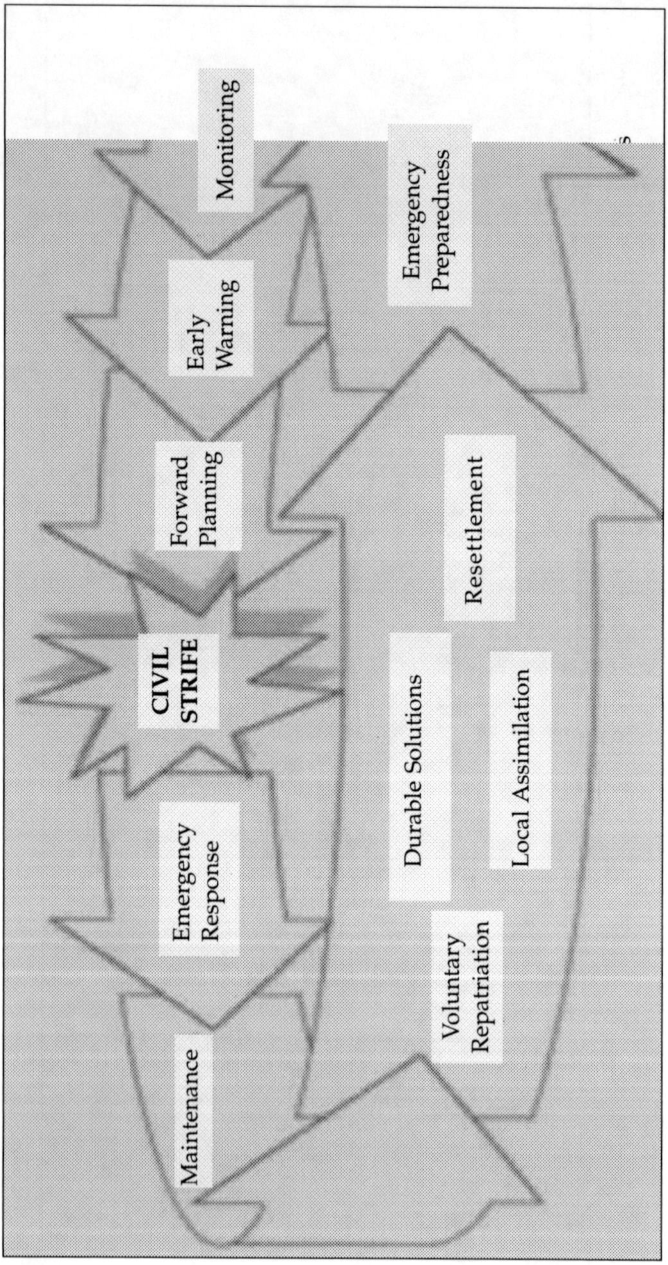

in the emergency phase but also help prepare for activities during the reconstruction phase. By opting to provide building materials rather than tents, the disaster manager maximizes the utility of resources at his or her disposal and paves the way for a speedier recovery.

CHAPTER 3

Introduction to Disaster Preparedness

This chapter describes describe the purpose, extent, limits, and primary activities of disaster preparedness. The following Lessons will provide detailed information on how to plan or execute each of these activities and steps. This Lesson provides an overview of the scope of disaster preparedness activities and demonstrates their inter-relationship with each other.

This chapter will be of help to disaster managers working in or with national governments. People working with inter-governmental agencies and voluntary agencies should find this chapter helpful in their preparedness activities as well. Much of the information or procedures described are of direct application to these other groups.

I. What is Disaster Preparedness?

Formerly, disaster planners thought disaster preparedness only referred to getting ready for an emergency response, but the concept is, in reality much more complex.

"Disaster preparedness consists of a wide range of measures, both long- and short-term, designed to save lives and limit the amount of damage that might otherwise be caused by the event. Preparedness is concerned with long-term policies and programmes to minimize the impact of disasters. The corresponding measures are taken in such fields as legislation, physical and urban planning, public works and building."

Short-term preparedness measures are taken during a warning period before the impact of a disaster event. They must be supported by legislation and be concerned with operational planning; education and training of the population at large, and the technical training of those who will be required to help in a relief operation; stockpiling of supplies; and emergency funding arrangements. These measures must also include vulnerability analysis, and warning system and evacuation planning. The more effectively these tasks are carried out in advance, the more readily will it be possible to take the action necessary during the emergency phase itself and in the later phases of relief, rehabilitation and reconstruction.

Preparedness measures taken during a disaster include sheltering evacuees, maintaining communications and protecting critical facilities and lifelines; and immediately following the disaster, planning and implementing search and rescue, disaster assessment, evacuation and treatment of injured persons, security in the disaster-affected area, restoration of lifelines and critical facilities that have been damaged, and further evacuation of areas threatened by secondary disasters.

The *scope of disaster preparedness*, therefore, goes well beyond the tasks of preparation. As mentioned above it carries into the emergency period of the disaster itself. The initial actions of disaster response should be the reactions of implementing a disaster preparedness plan. That is, a well planned disaster preparedness programme which has been tested and practiced will become a learned activity. The knowledge of what to do in a disaster will be "internalized." Not only will the governmental and non-governmental organizations know what to do and how to act accordingly, but so will the general public.

The *state of disaster preparedness* in a country can be defined as a measure of the willingness and capability of the country and its people to take the various steps needed to safeguard lives and property during any warning period which may be granted, as well as in the post disaster phase.

Preparedness is normally seen as an activity of the planning and engineering disciplines as well as medical, social, and security services. Practical experience has shown that the best organizations to assume responsibility for preparedness are operational agencies. For governments, this means ministries that have their own communications and transport, as well as administrative facilities (for this reason, preparedness is often assigned to military or paramilitary organizations such as civil defense agencies). Additional appropriate ministries are public works departments, housing ministries, and other "operational" agencies.

The organization of these various agencies with their respective services and skills must allow them to work harmoniously together. If one part of the system fails, other elements could be seriously handicapped, and there is, of necessity, a high degree of interdependence between the various components. However, the system should be so designed that if one element does fail, the organization, although weakened, will continue to function and provide the service required. (Fig. 3.1)

What this implies is that effective plans cannot be based on the assumption that the authorities and the emergency services will themselves be untouched in the event. Even if physical facilities are not destroyed or disrupted, personnel may be killed or injured, or suffer the adverse effects of stress, or may simply be prevented from reaching their duty station. Plans which do not allow for these factors may fail just when they are most needed.

II. Relationship of Preparedness to Other Parts of the Disaster Continuum

The disaster-related activities of prevention, preparedness, emergency relief, rehabilitation and reconstruction each occupy a distinct time period in relation to a disaster. The length of time any one period will last can vary greatly depending on the type of disaster and other factors. Nevertheless, it is important that people involved in disaster planning and response recognize the different phases and the appropriate activities that occur in each phase. For example, many emergency activities involve the distribution of free relief supplies. If this activity is carried on in the later phases (for example, during reconstruction), there is a danger that dependency relationships can be established, and the relief may provide disincentives to agricultural or economic recovery.

Figure 3.1: Disaster Continuum

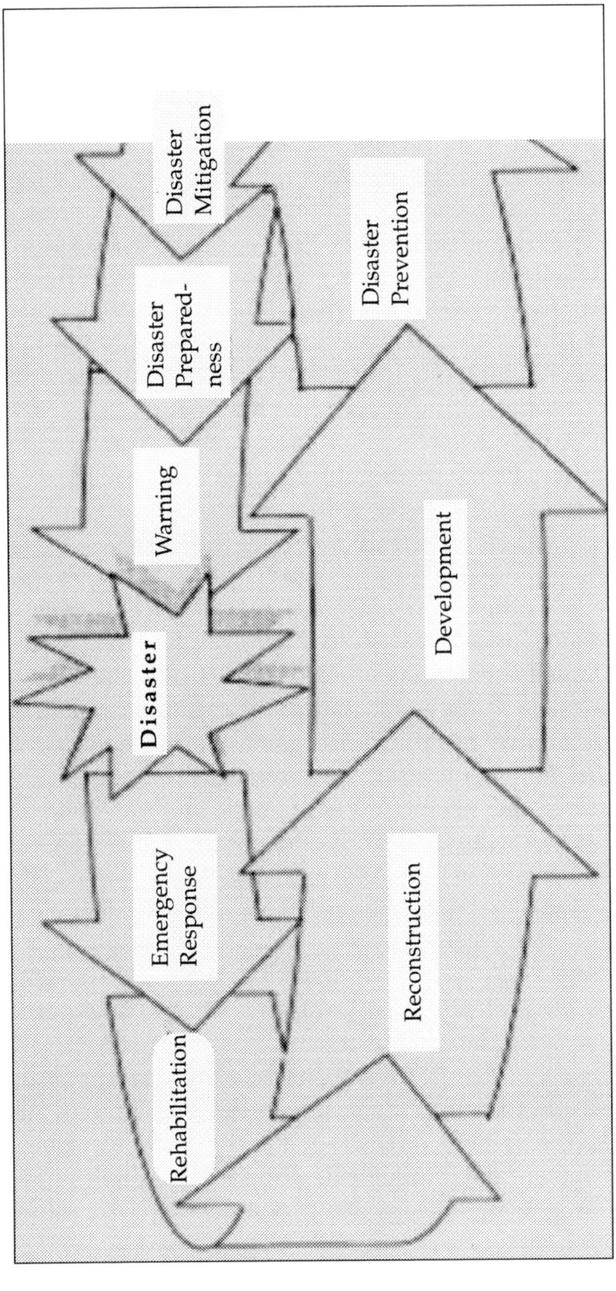

This course on disaster preparedness includes information on the predisaster activities of disaster preparedness and on planning for emergency response. A separate course, called Disaster Response, deals with carrying out emergency response activities as well as planning and implementing the postdisaster recovery activities of rehabilitation and reconstruction. These activities are shown on the disaster continuum on the previous page.

Pre-disaster activities. These activities are normally subdivided into disaster prevention, disaster mitigation and disaster preparedness. In general, disaster prevention is event-focused. In other words, the objective of prevention is to prevent the disaster from occurring at all. Disaster mitigation accepts the fact that some natural event may occur but tries to lessen the impact by improving the community's ability to absorb the impact with little damage or disruptive effects. Disaster preparedness assumes that the disaster will occur and focuses on structuring response and laying a framework for recovery.

Emergency response activities. Emergency response activities are those carried out during the actual emergency or immediately prior to it. This may involve evacuation of threatened communities, emergency assistance during the disaster, and actions taken in the immediate aftermath during the time when the community is rather disorganized and basic services and infrastructure are not fully functioning.

The emergency period is dramatic and traumatic, therefore most attention by the press and international community is focused here. Yet in most disasters (with the exception of droughts, famines, and civil strife), the emergency passes rather quickly, and in reality, only accounts for a very small percentage of the disaster continuum.

Postdisaster activities. Implementation of these emergency response activities is an element of disaster response which, as mentioned earlier, is covered in the Disaster Response course. Recovery in the postdisaster period can be subdivided into two phases. The first begins at the end of the emergency phase and is a transitional phase (often called the rehabilitation phase) when people and community systems try to re-establish a semblance of normalcy. This period is usually characterized by such activities as businesses reopening in damaged structures, farmers returning to reclaim and clear their land, and resumption of basic infrastructure such as water and sanitation systems in urban areas.

The reconstruction phase is marked by large-scale efforts to replace damaged buildings, revitalize economies or restore agricultural systems to their full predisaster production capacity.

The Relationship of Various Time Phases to Each Other

The activities that are carried out to mitigate a disaster very closely resemble the activities that would be carried out during reconstruction. An observer will also notice that the activities carried out in both these phases are essentially development activities as they not only reduce the disaster impact but also provide economic or social benefit. By understanding how these activities relate to each other, one can see where development activities can play an important role in disaster mitigation and response.

How Activities in One Phase Should Set the Stage for the Next

Referring again to the disaster continuum, it is possible to see how activities in one phase relate to the preceding and following phases. For example, emergency response can be facilitated if the operations have been planned prior to the disaster, not during it. As the general rule, it should be remembered that each phase and each activity of a disaster lays the framework and sets the stage for activities in the next phase. Therefore, when planning an emergency response, the disaster manager should keep in mind how that activity can help promote faster recovery. A simple example would be as follows. If a house has been destroyed in a windstorm or flood, there are several options for providing shelter during the emergency. You can provide a tent, which will offer shelter, or you can provide building materials that can be used to build a temporary shelter and then re-used in a permanent house during reconstruction. The tent solves one need during one phase; the building materials solve needs in the emergency phase and set the stage for reconstruction.

III. Formulating Policies for Disaster Preparedness Programmes

Preparedness Planning

Disaster preparedness is a product of planning and of implementing those plans. The planning process results in a preparedness plan that includes:

- identification of the various disaster risks
- identification of the needs of specific communities to protect themselves from that risk
- identification of the resources of the community, its government and the agencies involved in disaster preparedness
- specification of actions to be taken and by whom.
- clear chain of command within which all organizations active in disaster relief are coordinated

Orientation to Preparedness Planning

In providing assistance to disaster victims, many differing approaches and programmes may be used. Unfortunately, different approaches may result in the inequitable or unequal delivery of materials and services. This can cause problems for the local government and for the organizations with long-term commitments to the area.

One of the ways in which these problems can be avoided is by setting uniform policies or guidelines and minimum standards. These provide a method for shaping the emergency response and a basis upon which programme coordination can be affected. Ideally, uniform policies and standards are set as a part of the disaster preparedness process.

Normally, the national government is responsible for developing and implementing policies and standards, but all major organizations, especially those providing substantial relief, should participate in developing the documents.

Policies do not need to be extremely complicated nor long; in fact, simpler and briefer documents increase the chances of voluntary compliance.

Key Issues

There are three key issues to consider when establishing and implementing uniform policies and standards. They are:

Who Sets the Policies

It is the responsibility of the national government to establish and implement policies and standards. A government, however, may be reluctant to develop or enforce these standards for fear of alienating foreign assistance agencies, and thereby reducing or hampering the aid process. In this case, the relief agencies or a consortium of the major donor organizations should get together and work out informal policies and minimum standards which all relief agencies can follow.

Compliance

Unless the government makes compliance a requirement, some agencies will conduct relief programmes contrary to the expressed intent of the policies or provide services below the minimum standard recommended. If policies and standards have been developed by the government but are not enforced, donor agencies can assist by ensuring that projects they fund meet and/ or exceed the standards set.

Restrictive Versus Permissive Policies

It is important that all policies and standards be flexible and permit relief agencies to adapt their programmes to the specific requirements of the communities in which they are working. As a general rule, it is best to develop permissive policies and to set minimum standards, rather than be too restrictive. The objective of policies and standards is to guide reconstruction, not to dictate the precise approach of all relief agencies.

Key Concepts

Linkage to Development Plans

Preparedness policies and standards should be coordinated with long-term development plans and objectives of the government. Preparedness strategies can be a means of helping to attain many of these objectives, and thus, preparedness policies and standards must be compatible with long-term plans and, to the greatest extent possible, contribute toward these ends.

Performance Concepts

The establishment of policies and standards should be based on the level of performance desired. This needs to be done by establishing the level of performance that is expected of each relief sector. For example, plans can be made that establish a minimum amount of food and water that each disaster victim will need for emergency survival.

People and Organizations

Key organizations that should be involved in the development of policies and standards are:

- The national emergency coordinating organization(s)
- Appropriate government ministries
- Appropriate financial institutions
- The National Red Cross Society
- Voluntary agencies
- Representatives of affected trades
- Representatives of the local technical community (architects and engineers)
- Foreign government missions typically involved in emergency relief
- Appropriate U.N. representatives

Roles for Relief Agencies

Important roles which agencies, both internal and external, and governmental and nongovernmental, can play are:

- To encourage the appropriate authorities to develop and implement uniform reconstruction policies and standards as part of disaster preparedness activities.
- To provide technical input to the development of the policies and standards.
- To disseminate information about the standards and encourage periodic review.
- To give funding priority to those agencies that agree to comply with the government's standards and policies.

Lessons Learned

Without policies and standards, relief programmes and the aid they provide will be unequal, confusing, and in many cases, inequitable to the disaster victim.

In order to achieve maximum compliance, as many agencies as possible should be involved in the setting of policies and standards.

Most non-governmental agencies welcome the establishment of standards and policies as it provides guidance to them in programme planning and implementation.

The policies and standards should be based on reasonable expectations of performance and should recognize the capabilities and capacities of the implementing agencies.

The policies and standards must be set prior to the onset of relief, rehabilitation and reconstruction activities. Otherwise, they are unenforceable.

In summary, any disaster or major emergency disrupts normal life, causes breakdowns in (or makes excessive demands upon) the national administration and infrastructure, affects production, and generally means that resources have to be diverted from normal and development purposes to relief, rehabilitation and reconstruction. The people who suffer the most are usually those with the least resilience and with few, if any, resources of their own. The final objective of predisaster planning, using that term in its widest meaning, should be the attainment of postdisaster conditions which will be superior, at least in terms of disaster resistance, to those which existed before. To attain this aim, it will be necessary to seek and obtain the participation and cooperation of the people in the execution of the plans, to encourage self-reliance, and to avoid the creation of a state of dependency or apathy. Technical resources have their place— an important place in predisaster planning, but the wise planner will recognize that people themselves are the most important resource at his or her command.

CHAPTER 4
Prerequisites for Preparedness Planning

The process of developing a preparedness plan that enables quick and appropriate response to a disaster requires considerable groundwork. This chapter identifies the kind of information to be collected and processed to formulate the plan, describes the institutional requirements that are necessary for a plan to be developed and implemented, and outlines the legal and monetary authority that is required for enabling legislation to put the plan into practice.

Information Requirements

A thorough and appropriate disaster preparedness plan is based on a wide range of information. In fact, a great deal of information needs to be collected to describe the scope, content, and purpose of any disaster preparedness plan. The plan can actually be viewed as a document created in response to the disaster related information. This chapter will identified the types of information needed to create an effective preparedness plan and possible information sources.

Hazards, Risk, and Vulnerability

The first step in developing a preparedness plan is to identify the natural hazards of the region, the degree of risk that the population is subjected to and their vulnerability to injury, loss of life or property.

The following sources of information are normally of use when analyzing the threats posed by each type of disaster:

National Records

- Data and advice from specialist departments (such as meteorological service, geophysical observatories, mines and surveys);
- Publications resulting from surveys and studies, both national and international;
- Past experience of disasters as recorded or noted by organizations, the media, and individuals;
- Any available analyses of risks and vulnerability; and Local knowledge.

From these sources, it should be possible to construct a comprehensive assessment of the nature, degree and pattern of the likely threats to different areas of a country, and perhaps to determine the general priority which should be given each threat. However, before the effects of the threat can be fully assessed, certain subsidiary factors should also be considered.

These factors may include:

- Terrain characteristics;
- Geographical distribution of people and property;
- Agricultural and crop patterns in a given area;
- The type of buildings in which people live, work and go to school;
- The specific vulnerability of roads, communications and essential service centers such as hospitals;
- Experience of officials and communities in dealing with disaster;
- Any major environmental changes that have occurred recently like the building of a dam or the silting of a river.

The accuracy of the disaster warning and the length of time between the warning's issuance and the expected onset of the disaster.

Disaster Effects and Required Response

Estimate the effects of the disaster and the requirements of a response. The primary sources to develop these estimates are the same as above. Others include the application of microzonation, mathematical modeling of disaster agent impact, scenarios, gaming, and the use of field exercises. From them the planner can calculate the potential extent of disaster related losses and casualties in terms of geographic area, specific populations, agricultural crops and livestock, industry and infrastructure/lifelines.

The estimate of a disaster's effects can be characterized as a scenario of possible losses and needs. Estimates can then be created that anticipate the resources that are required to respond to the loss. These estimates include not only commodities of food, medicines, and shelter but also the logistical requirements of getting relief to the potential victims.

Resources

Make an inventory of the resources available to a vulnerable community or region. These resources include:

- available stocks of items that will be needed for emergency relief;
- agencies (public and private, domestic and foreign) capable of contributing to emergency relief;
- facilities that can be utilized for emergency relief such as temporary shelters, distribution centers, operations centers, etc;
- public services that will be called on to assist in emergencies such as police, fire department, civil defense forces;
- maps showing population distribution, rivers, roads, tunnels, bridges, train routes, air/sea ports, etc.
- items necessary for meeting logistical requirements such as trucks, warning and other communications systems and equipment, water reserves and equipment for transport and storage, etc.

The inventory which locates and quantifies all of these resources within a disaster prone area may well be one of the most important resources. One of the primary purposes of such a document is that it indicates the level of self-sufficiency of the area surveyed. As a general rule it is preferable to rely on and utilize locally available resources than to import them during a crisis. This is because the local resources—whether food, medical assistance, people, or trucks—are invariably more appropriate, more readily put into service, and are usually more cost effective than imported resources.

An important part of the information gathering process is to correlate the resources with the estimated emergency and postdisaster needs. This will describe the deficiencies within the disaster prone area and quantify those resources that either need to be increased within the area or will be needed from the outside.

Legislation

Research the existing legislation on disaster preparedness, response, and reconstruction issues. It is necessary to identify what is already "on the books," to analyze the adequacy of the current legislation, and to describe what steps need to be taken to update or strengthen the legislation.

Financial Matters and Compensation

In considering the matters to be covered in preparedness legislation, it is important to note what "financial measures" have been included. It is clearly important that authorities charged with the responsibility for directing or carrying out relief operations should not be hampered by any lack of the necessary authority to spend public funds. The detailed arrangements for achieving this end will naturally vary according to the type of governmental structure in each country, but in principle there should be created either a permanent Emergency Reserve Fund or an Emergency Funding Committee which would be empowered to vote the necessary money if the Legislature were not in session at the time an emergency were declared.

Institutional Requirements

It is obvious that a disaster plan and its implementation during emergencies requires a great deal of inter-agency cooperation and interdependence. This places a certain burden on each agency or institution that will be an active participant in disaster response. That is, each agency must have its own "house in order" so that it can meet the obligations of the agency and meet the needs of the disaster victims.

Each institution, therefore, must have its own internal structure that allows it to respond to disasters in the manner required. For agencies that are incorporated its constitution and bylaws need to identify disaster response as a function of the corporation and to make allowances for decision making, raising and disbursing funds or supplies using emergency procedures. These procedures should be coordinated with the overall policies for disaster planning and response as described in the preceding lesson.

Public institutions or governmental agencies also need their charter or governing regulations tailored to allow for streamlined decision making, clear identification of lines of communication and authority, and a complete description of their role in the disaster.

Elements of Preparedness Planning for Emergency Response

Once the information identified above has been gathered, a preparedness plan is developed. This includes six steps. *First* is the prior determination of the objectives to be met in each affected sector. *Second*, the strategies and approaches necessary to accomplish these objectives and plug any gaps that have been identified are determined.

The *third* step is the development of an implementing instrument. This is usually in the form of a disaster preparedness plan, a formal document that sets out the sequence of activities and the responsibilities of each participant.

The purpose of the plan is to place all activities in a comprehensive framework, so that they can be executed in an orderly and sequential manner. Normally, activities are divided into parts, so that resources can be marshaled at each critical place and stage, and disaster managers can concentrate on the most critical activities at the appropriate time.

Plans for a small agency or community may be no more than a brief checklist and description of activities with the assignment of responsibilities noted on the margins, while a national preparedness plan may include a series of documents, including network diagrams and flow charts of activities, subplans (known as specialized plans) for each sector, department, and/or agency, scores of checklists and emergency procedures to be followed, along with a statement of policies. Whatever form a plan follows, it is important that it be written down, both to serve as a reference and to ensure that no activities are forgotten in the haste of the disaster.

To be successful as an implementing instrument, an emergency preparedness plan must meet the following requirements:

- It must present the sequence of activities in a logical and clear manner.
- It must be comprehensive and balanced.
- It must assign specific tasks and specific organizations to be responsible for each.
- It must link appropriate organizations into a cooperating whole and establish mechanisms to bring people, organizations and information together at the critical points.
- It must reflect the policies of the implementing agencies or the national government in a disaster.

The *fourth* step in preparedness is the development of the tools necessary to respond and implement the plan. Tools include the establishment of communications networks; transport capabilities; action plans, procedures, and checklists for specific areas; the establishment of evacuation routes; and the acquisition and strategic placement of search and rescue equipment.

The *fifth* step is the strategic placement of resources to be used in the response. For most agencies, this means stockpiling or working out relationships with suppliers to enable rapid acquisition and delivery of needed relief materials. Other activities may include drawing up lists of materials, personnel, and other resources, and the establishment of contingency funds. For the international relief agencies, stockpiling has become a much debated topic, with many critics pointing out that it is of only limited benefit unless carried out in-country.

Generally, if a resource is of real value, then stockpiling should be encouraged in or close to a threatened community, while insuring its protection from prevailing hazards.

The *sixth* and final step in preparedness is training and drill. A preparedness plan and the tools of preparedness are of little value unless people know how to use them effectively. Performance is enhanced first by training, which means acquainting personnel with the plan and the sequence of activities, as well as with the tools and resources, and instruction on how to use each effectively. Drill includes practice designed to make each activity routine and thereby help reduce time of response, and to help identify the bottlenecks and "debug" the system. Disasters, fortunately, occur infrequently. But between disasters, people and institutions change, it is easy for gaps to develop and for people to forget what has been set out in the plan. Periodic review and drill is the only practical way of keeping the preparedness activities fresh in everyone's mind and adapting the plan to changing organizational structures and to changing needs. (An innovative method of keeping the preparedness plan up-to-date has been formulated in Sri Lanka. Each year at the beginning of the cyclone season, the government holds a "Cyclone Awareness Day." On that day, each government department and non-governmental institution with a disaster assignment is required to review and update its plan and send a notice of any changes to the central disaster coordinating office.) In many countries, it is normal practice for critical facilities, such as hospitals and power generation facilities, to conduct periodic disaster drills, which are analyzed to determine what changes need to be made in the disaster plan.

Without constant drill and training, disaster preparedness efforts will come to naught. Recently, a small island nation that had been stuck by heavy flooding decided to establish a preparedness plan. After several months of painstaking activities, the new plan was prepared and submitted to the government. Only after it was adopted was it learned that a similar plan had been prepared twenty-five years earlier in response to flooding in the same location. Because there had been no provision for drill or updating, it had been forgotten over the years.

CHAPTER 5
General Preparedness Plan

Introduction

Disaster preparedness is the composite readiness of a nation or community to meet an emergency. The previous chapter described the various components of preparedness. One of the components, the preparedness plan, in effect describes or embodies all of the others. It puts in place the means with which to respond to a disaster and to start the process of bringing a community back to normal after a disaster.

There is no such thing as a standard, all-purpose emergency plan. There are, however, certain elements which any plan must contain if it is to be effective. At the outset, it should define clearly and precisely the situation for which it is designed, distinguishing between the nature and magnitude of the threat or threats, and the specific local factors which are expected to influence the possible and desirable actions in response.

A plan must be realistic and adaptable: just as there can be no standard plan there will be no "ideal" disaster. It must therefore lay down what resources the planning area can, and will be expected to, provide, and how and when they will be called forward. Broadly, resources can be grouped into manpower, equipment and finance. This exercise will be based on the expected needs for the type and severity of disaster, and once completed will indicate how much in the way of additional resources will be required from outside the area. Naturally a balance must be sought between the three groups of resources. Manpower will perhaps be of little avail without equipment, or funds for its purchase; equipment will be useless if there is no one to operate it. Resources of any kind can be wasted if their provision and use are not properly coordinated.

In general it should be noted that any complete disaster preparedness and response plan needs to make arrangements in four categories, namely:

- General (or main) plans (which cover overall arrangements for dealing with disaster at any particular level).
- Functional plans (which cover aspects such as communications, search and rescue, emergency shelter, feeding, etc).
- Organization plans (which cover the roles and activities of organizations, departments, etc. in fulfilling their allotted tasks within the context of a general plan).
- Special plans (which deal with a particular or special threat, usually as an adjunct to a general plan; an example could be the threat of a dam collapse which would flood a specific populated area).

This chapter focuses on the contents of the plans at various levels of government, identifies key issues in their preparation, and outlines the steps for developing them.

The National Plan

Plan Elements

The following are the key elements of a national disaster preparedness plan. These plan elements are intended to be illustrative rather than definitive. They call attention to primary requirements and alternatives for disaster planning objectives, disaster preparedness organization, operation procedures, and support for disaster plan implementation. The solutions to these requirements have worked in a number of countries, but they are not the only way to do the job. The plan elements presented herein should be considered and adapted to meet the specific conditions of each country or region according to their requirements and capacity to support a disaster planning and preparedness capability.

This discussion may also serve as a guide to the state or provincial level. Requirements for organization, assignment of functional responsibility, and planning effort must also be identified at these levels. They are similar in character, if not in scope, to the requirements underlying a national plan and organization.

Objectives of a National Plan

A national plan supports the nation's capability to respond to disasters rapidly and effectively, and thereby to minimize human suffering and loss of life and property. By anticipating disasters and acting to minimize their effects, this plan also supports the continuity of the nation's growth and development.

Such a plan identifies the disaster-related organizations, systems, and detailed plans necessary to assure that available resources and skills are mobilized rapidly and effectively to meet essential human needs and to reestablish normal conditions.

A disaster plan is designed to make as much use as possible of existing resources, systems, and organizations and to work within the established government structure.

Scope of National Plan

A national plan, outlined in the following pages, identifies requirements for developing additional, detailed operating plans by agencies assigned disaster preparedness and response roles.

This plan includes the following elements:

- A description of the structure and functions of the national disaster assistance organization;
- A description of disaster preparedness and response objectives and activities, and the assignment of responsibility for them;
- General concepts for preparedness and response operations; and
- Steps for the establishment and funding of the required organizations, systems, and activities.

Organization

The national disaster preparedness system of a country may be organized in several ways. The fundamental principles of agencies designed to prepare for and contend with a disaster or other emergency differ very little from those applicable in other activities of government. Some countries have modeled their organization upon the military example, others rely on the military itself as the lead agency, while other governments have an interdependent relation with voluntary organizations such as the Red Cross or Red Crescent Society to share some of the responsibility.

For the purpose of demonstrating one model this chapter describes a national disaster assistance organization, which is responsible to the Chief of State for ensuring adequate national disaster preparedness and for coordinating disaster assessment and rescue and relief operations. Usually a key cabinet minister is appointed to provide oversight of this organization and to chair a national disaster committee which coordinates inter-ministerial and policy matters relating to disasters. The minister is responsible for overall supervision of the organization which assumes direct control of mobilization and relief operations in the event of a disaster. This is usually achieved under special "enabling legislation", i.e., laws that give the agency authority during the emergency.

Structure

The organization consists of the national disaster committee, chaired by a minister, and a permanent staff headed by a Director. There is also a standby staff of personnel loaned from the ministries and departments that would become involved in an emergency.

The national disaster committee may consist of any of the following individuals:

- Minister of Agriculture
- Minister of Communications and Postal Services
- Minister of the Home Affairs
- Minister of Finance
- Minister of Health and Family Welfare
- Minister of Urban Development
- Minister of Transportation
- Representative of the Meteorological Service

- Representative of the Seismological Service
- Others designated by the Director.

The committee suggests, reviews, and approves detailed disaster preparedness programmes and plans; committee members are responsible for seeing that plans are fully coordinated and supported within their respective agencies.

The permanent staff usually consists of a planning and research section, which analyzes disaster threats and develops plans to cope with them, and an operations section, which controls disaster operations and handles training and public education. In addition the staff may organize and support local organizations for disaster coordination, education, and relief.

Placement of the Organization

The location of the disaster assistance organization in the governmental structure is an important issue. Most planners place the organization in the executive office of the government, i.e. under the Prime Minister or President. The advantage is that decisions can be made at the highest level of government and are more likely to be carried out. Other planners prefer to put the organization in a national planning agency, noting that most preparedness and mitigation activities are a planning function. Others argue that disaster response involves command and control and tend to place the agency in military or para-military (ie., civil defense) organizations. And finally, others feel the best location is in a civilian, "operational" agency, for example, an agency with an emergency logistical capacity to respond to a disaster as well as a long-term role in economic development, such as in the ministries of housing and construction, public works, etc. Almost all planners agree that the organization should not be a social welfare or social service agency.

In reality the placement depends on the structure of the government, its degree of decentralization, the geographic area at risk, and the principle disaster threats that the country or region faces. In practice the two best places for the disaster preparedness organization seem to be within an operational agency or within the executive level.

Responsibilities

The disaster assistance organization is responsible for preparing adequately for disasters and, if a disaster occurs, for mobilizing the necessary resources and coordinating effective disaster assessment, rescue, relief and rehabilitation.

The permanent staff of the organization is responsible for the following disaster preparedness functions:

- Analysis of disaster and the nation's vulnerability to them
- Identification of the likely resource requirements and development of inventories of available resources
- Identification and organization of methods and systems for disaster prediction
- Adaptation or establishment of communications systems and definition of communications procedures for disaster warning and control of post disaster operations
- Promotion of disaster awareness and instruction of the public with respect to disaster warning systems
- Development and coordination with other agencies of contingency plans, procedures, and systems for effective disaster assessment, rescue, relief, and rehabilitation
- Development of plans to expedite the process by airport and port authorities, of waiving normal charges and fees for unloading relief shipments
- Establishment of liaison with private interests, voluntary organizations, and foreign missions to develop procedures for securing quick access to resources such as medical equipment and personnel; food, clothing and shelter; and transportation and heavy equipment.
- Establishment and maintenance of a disaster assessment capability to include aerial reconnaissance and operation of communications systems, and definition, selection, and dispatch of assistance
- Establishment of a disaster control center and other appropriate facilities

- The permanent staff also has the following postdisaster responsibilities:
- Activating warning systems and notifying officials and agencies having disaster response roles
- Coordinating and providing other assistance in disaster assessment, and collecting and analyzing information
- Defining, selecting, and coordinating the logistics of rescue and relief operations
- Securing the release of resources from other government agencies, and from private and voluntary organizations, as necessary
- Assisting the national disaster assistance Director as necessary in monitoring, controlling, and expediting postdisaster operations.

General Operating Procedures

Preparedness

The organizations identified in the national disaster plan maintain a state of preparedness by assuring that resources necessary in case of disaster are accessible and that their duties in the event of disaster can be or are being executed effectively.

Disaster Operations

When a disaster appears imminent and has been forecast by responsible organizations or individuals, the national disaster assistance Director advises the Chief of State and recommends that a State of Alert be declared. Upon such declaration, the Director will mandate a public warning, and implement appropriate contingency plans in anticipation of mobilization.

When a disaster occurs, the Director advises the Chief of State whether to declare a State of Disaster; standing provisions (contingency plans and the like) for mobilizing forces for rescue, relief, and rehabilitation will be implemented. Organizations having resources place them at the disposal of the Director or deploy them according to pre-established plans. Mobilization and rescue and relief activities are carried out according to the same plans through specified authorities.

Emergency operations directed by the national disaster

assistance Director should continue until rescue operations have been completed or can be carried no further, until relief meets pre-established objectives, and until essential services have been restored and public health and safety secured.

Plan Implementation

Successful implementation of the overall plan requires development of detailed contingency plans and administrative procedures and the appropriation of funds.

Detailed Plans

Through its permanently staffed planning and research section, the national disaster assistance organization is responsible for developing detailed contingency plans to meet the effects of likely disasters.

These plans outline the appropriate responsibilities for various government agencies, which then develop detailed, internal plans to satisfy assigned responsibilities. The national disaster committee reviews and approves all plans, to assure a coordinated response from all agencies involved in the overall disaster response effort.

Detailed plans or programmes are developed for maintaining emergency communications systems, carrying out disaster-related public education, and implementing disaster training for government personnel.

Contingency plans to counter the effects of likely disasters should be developed for damage assessment, rescue, relief, and rehabilitation. These plans will address key operational requirements for direction and control of operations, manpower, materials and equipment, logistics, and support and administration.

The organization's permanently staffed planning and research section will be responsible for development of these plans.

Funding

The permanent staff of the disaster assistance organization is responsible for securing funding for programmes established under this plan. The staff normally requests funds for the activities and programmes of the national disaster committee and permanent staff, and for salaries for the permanent staff. Equipment, facilities, and materials necessary to support the activities and programmes of the national disaster assistance organization and other organizations it establishes are then budgeted.

Special disaster funds may also be established; the disaster assistance organization maintains the accounting systems and mechanisms to release emergency funds and to charge disaster operations and materials to emergency fund accounts for disaster assessment, rescue, relief, and rehabilitation.

Costs incurred by other government agencies in planning and preparing for disasters as outlined in this and subsequent plans should be budgeted by those agencies. Costs incurred in supporting operations in the event of an actual disaster as outlined above are charged to emergency fund accounts.

Administration

The disaster assistance organization and its staff, with organizations established by them and other organizations specified in this and resulting plans, act to accomplish planned objectives. They prepare their own internal detailed plans for discharging responsibilities under the national plan and assign specific internal functional responsibilities.

The national disaster committee and the disaster assistance organization's permanent staff are responsible for implementing the national plan and updating it as necessary. The committee assures that appropriate plans are developed and that organizations assigned responsibilities under the national plan are capable of executing them.

Legal Aspects of the Plan

The crisis of a disaster should not precipitate a crisis of legal authority. It is important that legislation be in place that stipulates the procedure and authority for declaring a State of Alert or State of Disaster. This is required to facilitate flexible action and streamlined decision making during an emergency. It may be necessary, for example, to implement orders for certain relief or other emergency action with only a few hours notice.

This legal authority typically empowers the national disaster committee to assume command over many administrative matters during the declared State of Alert or State of Disaster. This will mean preempting certain authorities of operational agencies. The legislation should make the scope and limitation of such transfer of authority clear. The legislation has the further responsibility to ensure that the special emergency powers do not create opportunities for the exercise of that authority in repressive ways over the population.

Legislative Aspects of Financial Matters and Compensation

Where central government places limits on the expenditures which may be incurred by regional or local authorities, or on the amounts which may be raised by them by means of local taxes or through the money market, legislation may be necessary to exempt from these restrictions expenditures made by local authorities in the course of discharging their emergency responsibility. The legislation may introduce less onerous restrictions, or may have the effect of giving automatic ex post facto approval to expenditures. This kind of legislative action is a long-term preparedness measure, and it should not be forgotten that routine stockpiles or the testing and maintenance of equipment, also cost money. It may be possible to include expenses of this nature in the regular budgetary process, and so to subject them to the normal control by central government, but it might well be considered more satisfactory to have them regarded in the special category as being related to the discharge of emergency responsibilities.

Financial arrangements during an actual emergency operation may on the other hand be made by regulation or decree under the provisions of a proclamation of a State of Emergency. When regulations of this kind are drafted so as to be ready for immediate use in the event of an emergency, they would usefully include provision for price controls at wholesale and retail levels, waivers of customs duties on relief supplies and of landing fees for aircraft carrying them, and compensation for people who render personal services to, or whose property is used by, emergency relief authorities. It may also be necessary to consider the question of compensation for those whose property is destroyed or damaged in the disaster itself or as a necessary concomitant to the relief operation.

Compensation for loss or damage may be paid by insurance, either private or official, or from central funds, or in the case of oil pollution from funds established under the terms of international agreements. Private insurance policies often include protection against earthquake risks as well as the more usual fire and flood, but compensation for damage caused as a result of war or civil strife or commotion will not always be given under standard policies.

The government, the insurance industry and the insured persons or organizations themselves are all involved in this aspect of predisaster planning.

Regional Government Plans

Although the above discussion suggests that the proposed model for a disaster plan is applicable at regional and local levels, there are, indeed, important differences that need to be taken into account.

Identification of Main Capabilities and Limitations

A primary consideration at intermediate or regional levels of government is a critical identification of the main capabilities and limitations which affect disaster preparedness arrangements at such levels. Here, much will depend on the three following fundamentals:

- the national policy, especially the degree to which it governs or influences regional level policy and action;
- the dictates of legislation; and
- the national disaster preparedness plan and the extent to which it covers regional level activities.

Capabilities and Limitations

From these three fundamentals, certain practical aspects of capability and limitation ensue. They are:

- the degree to which delegation of overall government authority passes to regional level and thus the division of responsibility (national-regional) which results;
- the extent to which resources (for example, transport, equipment, medical supplies, trained personnel) are concentrated at or controlled from the national level; this, in turn, has a major bearing on the degree and flexibility of action which can be taken at the regional level;
- the total dependence, in some cases, of regional level authorities on certain national systems; for instance, dependence on the national broadcasting system for the key requirement of communicating with the public: this may have significant repercussions (and perhaps limitations) because of possible conflicting needs and priorities as between national and regional levels themselves;
- the ease (or difficulty) of access to or communication with national and other levels, especially during times of crisis pressure; and
- the effects of distance and remoteness, especially in relation to remote island areas.
- It follows that identification of main capabilities and limitations along the lines indicated above has a considerable bearing on the disaster preparedness policy which should apply at the regional level of government.

Definition of Regional Level Disaster Preparedness Policy

As has been stressed previously, regional level policies obviously have to be compatible with the national policy. However, they are not necessarily or usually identical. Regional level policies tend to be confined to preparedness, local operations, and immediate relief; whereas other aspects such as mitigation and recovery measures are normally directed from national level.

Regional level policies are also conditioned by dependence on the national level for the initiation of certain important disaster preparedness actions. For instance, the provision of an aircraft capability for postdisaster survey.

This modified definition of regional level policy is important since it helps to clarify areas of responsibility, requirements, and scope of operational action.

Community Plan

This discussion about the contents of preparedness plans at the national and regional level is necessarily general. It may be easier to be more specific about details at the community level. Table 3-1 is an example of a table of contents of a hypothetical community preparedness plan. For small communities and villages it is obviously too extensive and sophisticated but for larger communities it may be used as a model of topics that do need to be accounted for.

Many of the line items from this table of contents have been previously discussed in this or preceding Lessons. Others warrant additional attention here. These following topics, each a facet of the plan preparation process, are borrowed or adapted from Disaster Planning by Harold Foster.

Disaster Scenarios

Each disaster plan should include a section devoted to simulations of probable disasters, which includes predictions of the type and extent of damage, the nature and scale of probable casualties, and the various needs and responsibilities that these circumstances generate. Once such information has been refined by the disaster planner it can then be used to ensure that the steps outlined in the remainder of the disaster plan are adequate to meet likely disaster-generated requirements. These scenarios are used only to check the appropriateness and effectiveness of the disaster plan. The raw scenario information should not be referred to during an emergency situation, as it is based on conjecture and could lead to confusion.

Every disaster plan should include a detailed listing of all emergency-related personnel, their addresses, and business and private telephone numbers, if any. In addition, the names, addresses, and telephone numbers of alternates, capable of serving in their place should they be incapacitated or unavailable, must also be included. Where extensive telephone systems exist, this information can be used to develop a telephone fan-out system;

each individual being obligated to call two or more others in an emergency, so rapidly alerting the entire network. Such fan-outs should be designed with some overlap so that, should one link fail, the entire section dependent upon it does not remain uninformed. Care must be taken to keep all names, addresses, and telephone numbers current.

In the absence of a telephone network, or if the network fails in the emergency an alternate method of communication linkages needs to be designed. Some alternatives would be for officials to meet at a predesignated meeting point or to send messengers between officials. Both of these systems have drawbacks, however. The former may lead to a congregation of senior officials in an area where many of them may not be most needed. This may be especially so if the specified meeting point has been destroyed or is seriously at risk. Messenger systems are slow and may put the couriers into grave danger. Other means of electronic communication such as mobile/satphones should be considered.

Table 5.1: Defining and Coping with Disaster-Related Needs

Agent demands: What is the demand?	Who is responsible for meeting the demand?	How is the demand to be met?
• Warning • Pre-impact preparations • Search and rescue • Care of injured and dead • Welfare • Restoration of community services • Protection against continuing threat • Community order • Response demands—food, shelter... • Communication • Continuing Assessment • Mobilization • Coordination • Control and authority		

Operation of Warning Systems

For some disaster types, for example, earthquakes, there is little or no time in which to issue warnings. Most disaster types, however, either increase in magnitude or proximity and can be detected prior to impact. As a result, disaster plans must permit an optimum pre-impact response so that potential life and property losses can be reduced. Warning networks and disaster plans must be coordinated so that there is an effective, rapid, and logical organized response to warning.

Pre-impact Preparations

The length of forewarning, the time between detection and impact, varies greatly from hazard to hazard. Many disaster agents, however, may be preceded by a pre-impact period of days, weeks, or even years. During this phase preparations for impact should be made. Such steps might include canceling the leave of trained personnel, accelerated maintenance of emergency equipment, and stockpiling of supplies. Impact might be reduced by such measures as sandbagging, drawing down oil tanks and reservoirs and barricading windows. Consequences might be mitigated by the evacuation of people and belongings from threatened areas during the pre-impact period.

Emergency Evacuation

Where warning time permits, evacuation is often the most important response to threat. The movement of large numbers of people from an area at risk, with the minimum of stress, involves careful preplanning. Several factors must be borne in mind. Since hazards differ in their physical characteristics and scale of impact, so too must evacuation procedures. Before any evacuation is begun, care must be taken to ensure that there is, in fact, time to complete it, since residents may be more vulnerable if impact occurs during their evacuation. It is therefore essential to know how long an evacuation is likely to take and whether it can be accomplished in the time available before impact. This problem may be particularly acute if many members of the community are unable to leave unassisted. A disaster plan may require detailed and individual evacuation plans for certain facilities such as hospitals, schools, and prisons.

The choice of routes is crucial. It is unrealistic to assume that any one road or system of roads or railways will be an optimum evacuation channel for every hazard. Evacuation routes should then be chosen for each threat, so that the population is channeled to areas of progressively lower risk. With some hazards such as flooding, this may involve an attempt to rapidly gain in altitude. For others, such as chemical leaks, prevailing winds may be the major determinant behind choice. Evacuation routes must be easily accessible from the high risk locations. They should also be linked to alternative transportation corridors, to be used should primary routes be blocked, and free of potential bottlenecks such as bridges or tunnels that may be easily damaged. Disaster plans should include maps showing all such clearly designated evacuation routes. There is merit in including these in the telephone directory to increase public awareness. Estimates should be made of the time required to evacuate the threatened population. Obviously, this should be less than the time elapsing between the issuing of a warning and the impact of the disaster. Where this is not likely to be the case, attempted evacuation may not be a viable safety strategy.

Naturally it is not enough simply to evacuate an area. Alternative facilities must be available elsewhere. While many evacuees are likely to stay with friends or relatives outside the threatened area, some may not be able to do so. Shelter accommodation providing meals and other facilities must therefore be available in the receiving area.

The following points on Emergency Evacuation should be emphasized:

> it is important that the responsibility for decision making on evacuation is clearly defined and that members of the community know which department, organization or individual holds this authority.

The system or arrangements for notifying the community must also be clearly defined and understood.

Self-evaluation by communities is often a very unwise and hazardous undertaking.

Movement capability is often a very important and restrictive factor, especially in developing countries.

Shelters

In the planning of shelters for evacuees, several factors must be given careful consideration. Obviously location is of paramount importance. Shelters must be sited in low risk areas yet should be easily accessible from threatened regions. To determine suitable locations, macro- and micro-scale vulnerability analysis must be carried out to determine the scale of impact of a variety of potential disasters. Such analysis will often indicate that different shelter locations are optimal for each hazard or group of hazards. To accommodate this situation, a variety of buildings might be designated as shelters to be used in specific disasters. Some of these may be within the boundaries of the municipality or region involved in compiling the disaster plan. Some may be required outside its jurisdiction and are best established by reciprocal disaster agreements with other municipalities. Such buildings must be evaluated from the point of view of their structural integrity in the face of various threats, such as fires or earthquakes, as well as the facilities they offer in coping with the demands of evacuees.

Ideally, such shelters should be capable of accommodating evacuees on the scale that they can reasonably be expected and should be staffed with personnel trained in providing social services. Buildings designated as shelters should be capable of storing food, clothing, and medical provisions for long periods and be equipped with communication facilities suitable for collecting and transmitting personal statistics about evacuees. Provision should be made to inform relatives and friends of the safety of the individuals concerned. Any disaster plan should also include a section dealing with the care of special evacuees from prisons, retirement homes, and other institutions that will require unusual services. See Table 5.2 for a summary of shelter requirements for various hazards.

Many of the problems associated with disaster stem from a lack of coordination among the varied groups and institutions that attempt to respond. Typically each views the situation in terms of its own capabilities and perspectives. Many of these difficulties can be avoided if predisaster planning has included the establishment of an emergency operations center. This should be clearly designated and recognized as such, equipped with a wide range of materials, and staffed by personnel representing all agencies involved in meeting disaster-related needs. This center should also be the site from which overall control of emergency activities is undertaken.

Table 5.2: Disaster Shelter Requirements

Hazard	Pre-Event Shelter	Post-Event Shelter	Requirements
Earthquakes	N.A.	Limited temporary refuge usually in urban areas	Earthquake resistant construction, fire resistant
Cyclones	Evacuation shelters	Limited mass shelters for homeless Some emergency mass shelter for flood victims	Cyclone resistant construction Avoid churchs, schools, long-span buildings for emergency buildings unless certified by an engineer These buildings may be suitable for post-disaster shelters.
Floods	Emergency shelter	Temporary refuge	Located above highest possible flood levels

Disaster Control Center and Subcenters

It is essential that, because of its key role in response, such a building is structurally very sound, sited in a minimum risk location, and unlikely to become isolated. It should not be chosen simply because of its convenience for city personnel or its low cost purchase or equip it. An alternative emergency command center should also be designated and made capable of functioning as such should the primary building cease to be operational.

Communications

Communication provides the basis for coordinating an effective disaster response; without it other emergency-related demands cannot be met. Information is a critical aspect of every disaster; data are required about the magnitude, frequency, and location of impact, about victims, evacuees, materials, damage, the state of essential services, the capabilities and number of personnel, volunteers, and numerous other factors. Information must flow during and after a disaster or coordination and effective response become impossible. There must be links between and within disaster-related organizations so that needs and orders can be communicated. They must also exist between such institutions and the public so that warnings can be issued and information on the safety or otherwise of those affected can be provided. Unfortunately, disasters often damage existing communications networks while the convergence of people and information from outside may overload those that continue to function. For these reasons, disaster planning must place heavy emphasis on maintaining existing channels and on providing additional novel alternatives such as citizen band radios, taxi telecommunications, and other potential means. Certain telecommunication links must be preserved for emergency messages only.

Public Information

Few disaster plans make suitable arrangements for disseminating disaster-related information to the community organization, the mass media, and to the public. Consequently, varying and conflicting reports of an emergency sometimes occur and receive extensive coverage. To avoid this type of unfortunate development, the responsibility for making public statements should be limited to a specific individual such as the safety plan coordinator, whose work should be supported by the development of a public information subplan. Media releases should be carefully prepared to make sure that no erroneous information is given out or misimpressions created.

Search and Rescue

Many disasters result in damage to buildings and the trapping of population that requires a search and rescue response. The basic demands are for the location, rescue, and transportation of victims, often in an injured state, to places of safety where their immediate needs can be accommodated. This task often requires specialized equipment such as boats, planes, helicopters, mobile hospitals, bulldozers, and other technology together with the qualified personnel to operate and maintain them. A well-prepared disaster plan will therefore list all the sources and locations of such materials and individuals and will ensure that they are put into a state of readiness in the preimpact period, when time permits. Where obvious gaps occur in personnel or the availability of search and rescue equipment, a programme of training and acquisition should be provided for in the disaster plan.

Community Order

Since confusion may follow the initial disaster-agent impact, it is essential that community order be maintained. Disaster plans should make provisions for the control of the perimeter of the affected area, guarding property, patrolling danger areas, directing traffic and communications, and ensuring that scarce community resources are utilized most effectively. In all cases, the ultimate authority and chain of command must be carefully established prior to the development of threat.

Medical Facilities and Morgues

The treatment of the injured and the handling of the dead are normal demands associated with most disasters. Typically, the hurt must be moved as rapidly as possible from the impact area to locations where supplies and medical personnel are capable of providing relief. Often priorities in the treatment of individuals must be established. This may involve soliciting information on case histories and determining the possible extent of injuries in the field. Such paramedical responses may often mean the difference between life and death for the more seriously injured victims. This information must be recorded in a legible manner and colored tags can be used to establish hospital treatment priorities.

Fatalities also create a disaster demand. The dead must be removed from the disaster area to some permanent or temporary morgue where they can be identified and the cause of death established and certified. Bodies can then be released to relatives and funeral arrangements finalized. These procedures require the mobilization of a wide range of individuals, from coroners and dentists to fingerprint experts and morticians. Any disaster plan should therefore include details of all such hospital and morgue facilities together with information and telephone numbers of the necessary personnel.

Restoration of Community Services

The impact of a disaster frequently results in the disruption of essential community services, such as electricity, gas, telephone, water, transportation, and refuse disposal. The restoration of such facilities, even if only on a temporary basis, is extremely important since search and rescue, the care of casualties, and cleanup operations are often hindered by their absence. The rapid restoration of essential community services should therefore be stressed in disaster planning. Ideally, priorities should be established and responsibilities designated so that crucial services are restored with a minimum of delay.

Protection Against Continuing or Secondary Threat

Initial disasters are often compounded by secondary hazards. These include broken gas mains and power lines, polluted waters, and fires. Any disaster plan must therefore ensure that the community is protected from such secondary, yet related threats. All potential high risk locations such as dam sites, power stations, and sewage works must be rapidly checked and damage contained. Unless such threats are quickly detected they may ultimately prove more destructive than the primary disaster.

Continuing Assessment of the Total Situation

Assessment of the actual damage caused by a hazard and of the effectiveness of responses to it are crucial. This is because without it confusion will result and organized action will be suboptimal. Assessment, therefore, is an essential prerequisite of adequate decision making. Unless a clear overview of the entire situation is available, urgent needs will go unrecognized. The significance of assessment is continuous, since the situation is likely to alter rapidly as secondary threats develop and new sources of assistance become available. Without a detailed overview, it is impossible to set priorities and to gauge the likely effectiveness of selected strategies. For this reason the task of collecting, portraying, analyzing, and assessing disaster-related information should be laid down in any disaster plan. This assignment must be realistic and should allow its accomplishment quickly, so that the ongoing assessment is available to decision makers actively responding to the disaster situation. The need for good assessments is so vital that the Disaster Management Center has developed a course on the topic, entitled "Disaster Assessment."

Testing the Plan

There are many aspects of disaster response that can only be tested by rehearsal. As a consequence, every plan should be subjected to appraisal through game simulations and field exercises. Following each such test and after an actual disaster occurs the plan must be evaluated and changes made to accommodate deficiencies.

Revision

Every community is in a state of flux. New industries are established, old businesses close, and construction and demolition constantly change the pattern of land use. Materials and equipment are acquired and disposed of and individuals leave and enter the community, bringing changes to the skills and experience available in an emergency. As the fabric of a society alters, so too do both the risks it faces and its potential for responding to them.

To make sure that new information is utilized by those involved in plan implementation it is useful to publish the document in ring binders so that revised procedures can be inserted and obsolete pages discarded with the minimum of effort.

Distribution

Discussions over the distribution of disaster plans normally focus on the conflicting need for awareness and for confidentiality. Typically, the community disaster plan contains information that would be of great value to many organizations and individuals in an emergency. It also includes data, such as details of communication channels, police procedures, and expected casualties in particular disaster situations, that should not be widely distributed. This is because such confidential information may allow unauthorized individuals to interfere with emergency procedures or cause unnecessary stress within the community.

To overcome this potential conflict between the desire to know and the need to keep confidential, municipalities might consider producing both comprehensive and abbreviated versions of their disaster plan. The distribution of the former might be restricted to those involved in official response in an emergency. These individuals should be listed in an appendix to the document itself. The abbreviated version of the disaster plan, from which confidential details have been deleted, might be far more widely distributed, being made available to the media and the general public. If this approach is not considered feasible certain details, such as the significance of warning signals, evacuation routes, and shelter locations, should be published in the telephone directory and be made available in other easily accessible public places.

Responsibilities for Disaster Preparedness Activities at Village Level

The above activities and responsibilities may seem overwhelming for a small village. In fact many of them can and are done informally. Nevertheless, the following items are included to demonstrate an appropriate perspective for village level considerations.

Whether the existing local government organization as it stands is used for disaster preparedness purposes, or whether some form of subcommittee of that organization is used, its responsibilities tend to be generally along the following lines:

To keep the community informed, through public meetings and other means, of precautions to be taken, including methods of warning, etc. (special emphasis to be made prior to any clearly defined seasonal threat such as cyclones):

- To allocate responsibilities to persons in the community, as necessary.
- To institute periodic inspections to ensure that precautions are being taken.
- To ensure that equipment required for disaster purposes is available, or can be made available, and is serviceable.

- To ensure that emergency food supplies are available.
- To nominate special wardens or safety officers.
- To designate immediate relief tasks (survey duties, provision of food and temporary shelter, assistance in clearance, etc.): these tasks need to be planned beforehand and made compatible with plans of the next senior level of government.

Preparedness Measures at Local Level

Detailed community preparedness measures will clearly be determined by specific local circumstances, and particularly the nature and extent of the threat. However, some useful aspects for consideration are:

- Development of a first aid capability within the community (probably sponsored through Red Cross, Red Crescent, school programmes, primary health care systems, etc.) always composes a valuable local preparedness asset;
- If drought is a possibility, water conservation measures should be considered, wherever these may be possible;
- Measures for safeguarding or emergency garnering of crops may be possible in some circumstances.

International Support Arrangements

Categories of Assistance

International support arrangements may cover a wide range of possibilities and it is therefore advisable to have a prearranged system for dealing with them. Support and assistance can usually be divided into four categories: direct participation in disaster preparedness operations; for example, the use of aircraft for survey and assessment, emergency transport, etc. urgent emergency relief (provision of emergency food and medical supplies, shelter, etc.) long-term programmes; for example, various forms of assistance in national reconstruction projects. Preparedness and mitigation programmes prior to and after a disaster strikes.

Relationship with Agencies

The number of international agencies (government and non-government) which have to be dealt with may be very large. Also, many different contact-points may be involved; overseas governments will normally deal through diplomatic channels and non-government organizations will tend to work through their in-country counterparts. Therefore, it is advisable to use a national office or department for focusing and coordinating support activities, if this is possible.

The utilization of the diplomatic corps (especially where it can function as a form of committee under the dean of the corps) is a very valuable way of centralizing that particular part of assistance activity.

Steps for Developing a Disaster Programme

So far, this chapter has been primarily devoted to describing what needs to be done to create various disaster preparedness plans. This section will show how to create a plan by outlining suggested series of steps that can be taken.

Phase I: Preplanning

Determine which phases of a disaster to work in (ex. Mitigation, Preparedness, Emergency operations, Recovery, Reconstruction).

- Determine which ministry of office to place the National Emergency Committee in.
- Establish goals and objectives.
- Establish policies to shape methods for reaching objectives.
- Identify Action Plans required.
- Identify data requirements necessary to develop Action Plans.
- Identify staff needs for developing plans.
- Develop preliminary budget.
- Establish Budget and Analysis Routines
- Establish schedule.

Phase II: Development of Preparedness Plans

- Hire planning staff and coordinator.
- Hire consultants.
- Assign work tasks.
- Acquire data (including existing disaster plans in each ministry or department).
- Identify problem areas (geographic and inter-ministerial).
- Establish preliminary coordination links between ministries.
- Prepare preliminary Action Plans.
- Decide on format for presentation (Workbook, Checklists, etc.).
- Send preliminary plans to ministries for review and comment.
- Identify mitigation actions that can be taken as a part of normal activities.
- Determine staff requirements.
- Develop memos of understanding between ministries and departments.
- Determine legislation needs.
- Formulize Action Plans.
- Assemble total Preparedness Programme.
- Present to government and public.

Phase III: Development of Emergency Response

The Disaster Management Center course, Disaster Response, covers this phase in detail.

Phase IV: Development of Recovery Plan

This phase is beyond the scope of this course and is the start of more traditional development planning.

CHAPTER 6
Introduction to Natural Disaster Response

Introduction

What is Disaster Response?

Disaster response is the sum total of actions taken by people and institutions in the face of a threat or occurrence of a disaster. These actions commence with the warning of an oncoming threatening event or with the event itself if it occurred without warning. Disaster response also includes aspects that must be in place prior to a disaster, i.e., the implementation of disaster plans and procedures. Response thus overlaps with disaster preparedness. The end of disaster response ostensibly comes with the completion of disaster rehabilitation programmes. In a real sense, however, the end never comes, as a major disaster so alters a community that it is forever changed; transformed rather than recovered.

This chapter is about what to do in case of a natural disaster. It introduces the scope of disaster response activities and the interrelationship of response with the other time phases of the disaster continuum. It also attempts to "set the record straight" regarding the myths that surround disaster response, myths that have caused the perpetuation of inappropriate responses. Lastly, a case study of a disaster is presented. It does not focus on the successes and failures of the emergency response programmes; rather, it evokes a reflection on the long term impact of all of the post-disaster actions. This sobering perspective illustrates how actions taken immediately after the disaster can affect the community and its ability to recover and cope with future disasters.

The purpose of this chapter is to present basic information about disaster response activities provide a structure for decision making immediately before a disaster, during an emergency and in the recovery period that follows provide guidance to people who become involved in the disaster response process so that the results of postdisaster efforts will improve the conditions of the community that existed before the disaster, reducing future disaster vulnerability and the scarce resources that are available after a disaster will be used to their maximum potential.

This chapter emphasizes specific actions to take and identifies the appropriate context for those actions. Instead of extended discussions on each topic of importance the book typically presents lists of recommendations or conclusions. What it may lack in smooth reading it compensates for in compact, distilled information.

These are disasters which occur with little or no warning, such as earthquakes and tropical cyclones. Many of the principles, recommended actions, and guidelines within this book are general in scope and apply equally to rapid- and slow-onset disasters. On the other hand there are so many unique aspects to slow-onset disasters, primarily drought and famine, that the Disaster Management Center will devote a separate course to that special topic.

Scope of Natural Disaster Response

Disaster response picks up where disaster preparedness leaves off. This relationship is described in the next section of this chapter. Nevertheless, response activities should be considered as inseparable from the planning for them. This means having preparedness plans in place, standing operating procedures developed, stockpiles identified, emergency facilities and their capacities lined up, and legal authorization and emergency funds to implement post disaster activities in place.

The first activity of a response programme, however, will be disaster warning. This will produce public announcements about what actions to take as final preparations and what to do immediately after the disaster has struck. In some cases evacuation will be called for.

After the disaster has struck, response will continue with search and rescue for the victims and an immediate assessment of the damages and needs. Further assessments will be made as the emergency passes and as more information becomes available. Emergency recovery and long-term rehabilitation programmes will be initiated in the various sectors of health, food, shelter, public services and facilities and others. The implementation of these programmes will require the operational support of communication and information flow, logistics and supplies and other resources. These programmes will be linked to the long-term development of the community, either indirectly, or by design, as this book encourages.

Lastly, but perhaps most importantly, disaster response includes the integral involvement of the community population in the planning, and as disaster victims in the implementation of the response programmes.

Relationship of Response to Other Parts of the Disaster Continuum

The Relationship of Disasters to Development

There is a tendency among people working in development to regard disasters as separate and distinct events with little or no relation to the development process. In recent years, however, the relationship between disasters and development has become clearer, and disasters are now recognized as being one of the major contributors to underdevelopment. It has also been recognized that, if disaster response is mishandled, many years of development activities can be wiped out or the chances for further progress set back. Disasters can alter agricultural patterns, settlement patterns, patterns of migration, work habits, diets and even basic family structure. On the other hand, if the response is well planned and takes a development approach, a disaster can provide opportunities for accelerating the pace of development, and constructive changes can be made.

The Relationship of Various Disaster Activities to the Appropriate Time Phases

All disaster-related activities are divided into distinct time periods. The length of time any one period will last can vary greatly depending on the type of disaster and other factors. It is important that people involved in disasters recognize the different phases and the appropriate activities that occur in each. For example, many emergency activities involve the distribution of free relief supplies. If this activity is carried on in the later phases (for example, during reconstruction), there is a danger that dependency relationships can be established, and the relief may provide disincentives to agricultural or economic recovery.

In general, disaster activities can be divided into three broad categories: predisaster, emergency response, and post disaster recovery activities. These phases of a disaster can be depicted on a graph as a continuum, as shown in Figure 6.1.

Pre disaster activities. These activities are normally subdivided into disaster prevention, disaster mitigation and disaster preparedness. In general, disaster prevention is event-focused. In other words, the objective of prevention is to prevent a specific type of disaster in a specific geographic area from occurring at all. Disaster mitigation accepts the fact that some natural event may occur but tries to diminish the impact by improving the community's ability to absorb the impact with as little damage or as few disruptive effects as possible. Disaster preparedness assumes that the disaster will occur and focuses on anticipating the event, structuring response and laying a framework for recovery.

Emergency response activities. Emergency response activities are those carried out during the actual emergency or immediately prior to it. This may involve evacuation of threatened communities, emergency assistance during the disaster, and actions taken in the immediate aftermath during the time when the community is rather disorganized and basic services and infrastructure are not fully functioning.

Because the emergency period is both dramatic and traumatic, most attention by the press and international community is focused here. Yet in most disasters (with the

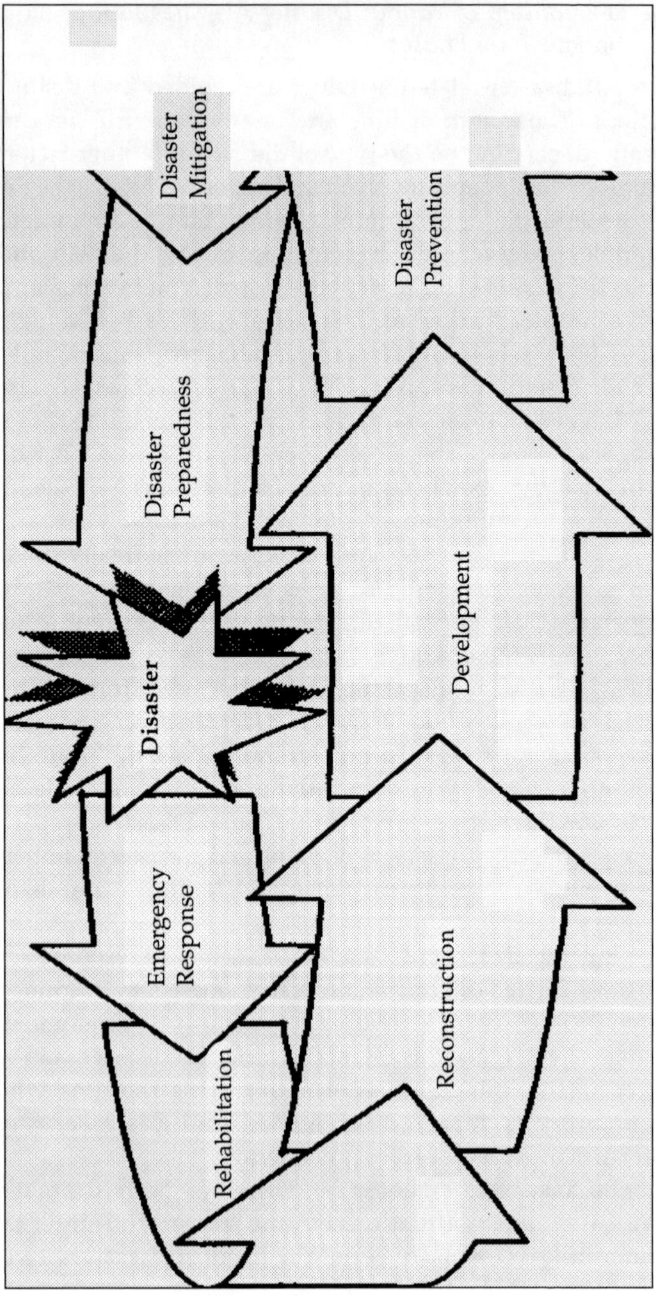

Figure 6.1. Disaster Continuum

exception of droughts and civil strife), the emergency passes rather quickly and only accounts for a small percentage of the overall disaster response.

Post disaster activities. Post disaster recovery can be subdivided into two phases. The first begins at the end of the emergency phase and is a *transitional phase* (often called the rehabilitation phase) when people and community systems try to re-establish a semblance of normalcy. This period is usually characterized by such spontaneous activities as businesses reopening in damaged structures, farmers returning to reclaim and clear their land, and resumption of unaffected or lightly damaged basic infrastructure such as water and sanitation systems in urban areas.

The *reconstruction phase* is marked by large-scale efforts to permanently replace damaged buildings, revitalize economies or restore agricultural systems to their full predisaster production capacity.

The Relationship of Various Time Phases to Each Other

The activities that are carried out to mitigate a disaster very closely resemble the activities that would be carried out during reconstruction. An observer will also notice that the activities carried out in both these phases are essentially development activities as they not only reduce the disaster impact but also usually provide economic or social benefit. By understanding how these activities relate to each other and to development, one can see where development activities can play an important role in disaster mitigation and response.

How Activities In One Stage Should Set the Stage for the Next

The disaster continuum shows how activities in one phase relate to the preceding and following phases. For example, emergency response can be facilitated if the operations have been planned prior to the disaster, instead of being improvised during it. As a general rule, it should be remembered that each phase and activity of a disaster lays the framework and sets the stage for activities in the next phase. Therefore, when planning an emergency response, you should keep in mind how each activity can help promote faster recovery. A simple example would be as follows. If a house has been destroyed in a windstorm or flood, there are several options for providing shelter during the emergency. You can provide a tent, which will offer shelter, or you can provide building materials that can be used to build a temporary shelter and then re-used in a permanent house during reconstruction. The tent solves one need during one phase; the building materials solve needs in the emergency phase and set the stage for reconstruction.

Disaster Myths

Popular literature and legend perpetuate many inaccurate concepts about natural disasters and human behavioral response to them. They have generated many myths that have caused much disaster response to be poorly conceived and misdirected. The following is a collection of such myths, the presentation of which seeks to assist in correcting their inaccuracies.

Panic Flight:
"People will panic in the face of great danger."

Numerous investigators have observed that panic flight (i.e., the competitive mass behavior of individuals involved in fleeing from an imminent threat, thereby increasing the danger to themselves and others) is rare in natural disaster situations. Only in unique disaster situations are found the conditions necessary for emergence of competitive norms and the existence of panic flight. Popular and journalistic accounts of panic flight often involve a large dose of literary license in reporting orderly evacuation. As Allen Barton notes, "All these authors come to the conclusion that the rate of extreme non-adaptive behavior in disasters is generally very low, even in impacts as intense as the Hiroshima atom bombing."

The most widespread myth about disasters is the belief that people will panic in the face of great danger. It has been inferred that most individuals espouse this belief due to its perpetuation through the mass media. Popular film portrayals of mass behavior in the face of imminent threat picture "crazed hordes" fleeing from the approach of such varied phenomena as tsunamis, fires, earthquakes, floods, nuclear holocaust, meteors, flying saucers,

Grog, Kronos, and Godzilla. As noted, news accounts sometimes erroneously report panic flight or may be misinterpreted by the public as indicating such behavior.

Looting Behavior: ***"Looting generally occurs after a disaster."***

Looting, the appropriation of private property for private use, has been found to be rare in natural disasters. Studies report that there are few verified cases of looting in the field studies of disasters.

However, the myth suggests that most people believe that looters roam over a disaster site pillaging the homes and businesses of the victims. Disaster victims themselves have been found to readily believe and in turn to disseminate rumors of looting. Such stereotypes may be partly explained by the dramatic picture of post-impact behavior presented in movie and television versions of fictional disasters. In addition news accounts sometimes erroneously report rumors of looting as fact, or such reports note that mechanisms to prevent looting have been instituted, omitting that no looting has, in fact, occurred. Furthermore, since looting has been so widely publicized in civil disturbances, one might infer that individuals will believe that it is common in other, superficially similar community emergencies.

Post-Impact Crime Rates: ***"The crime rate normally rises during a disaster."***

Studies from the Disaster Research Center have found that the crime rate of a community usually drops during the emergency period of a natural disaster. While one could argue that fewer crimes are committed during the immediate post-impact period as a natural concomitant of the altered social system, it is more likely that the reduced crime rate is a result of altered law enforcement practices that result from changes in the value priorities of the community. Traffic violations, drunkenness, vandalism, and other misdemeanors are ignored as the local social control agencies turn their attention to other problems, such as handling the massive human convergence that often inundates the disaster site.

However, since most people believe that antisocial behavior is common immediately after disasters, it is often also incorrectly inferred that the crime rate normally rises during a disaster.

Evacuation:

"There is often a wild panic and disorderly flight in the face of a disaster."

Even when an evacuation is ordered, the majority of inhabitants often do not leave. Those who do flee in such cases are primarily transients and tourists—not the people who live there. It appears that the major problem in an emergency is getting people to move, rather than preventing wild panic and disorderly flight. Many individuals refuse to evacuate areas until they are forced to do so either by the physical effects of the agent or the legal efforts of local authorities. An exception to this was the evacuation from the volcanic eruption of Mount St. Helens in the United States. In this case most local residents did heed the warnings.

Disaster Shock:

"The shock of a disaster leaves the victims dazed and disoriented, unable to cope with the immediate task of recovery."

One of the most consistent findings of disaster response studies is that the initial search-and-rescue activity, casualty care, and restoration of essential services are accomplished by the victims themselves with the assistance of those in the immediate area. The rate of non-adaptive behavior on the part of victims is tow; in most circumstances only a few exhibit any shock reaction, and this state is usually short-lived. Actually, the immediate post-impact period is highlighted by intense activity, the emergence of new groups, and adaptive behavior. Empirical evidence suggests that only a small proportion of the victims are in a state of shock and unable to care for themselves and that the great majority perform with unusual effectiveness and stamina, often heroically.

Accuracy and News Reports of Disaster:
"News accounts of disasters are generally accurate."

A major generator of myths about disaster response is the mass media. Media accounts are often not very accurate with respect to the extent of physical damage, human loss, or social disruption. Initial accounts have frequently overestimated the number of dead and injured. News films and photographs focus upon only the most extreme, not the average rate of damage or the destruction. As a result the public is given a false impression of the overall extent of devastation. We have noted that myths of looting, panic, shock, and crime are often spread by the media. Reporters have preconceived notions of what happens in a disaster, and in the absence (or even in the presence) of contrary evidence they report the images which support their notions. Part of this issue may be that news reports focus upon the unique or extreme events of disaster but present them as if they were representative examples.

It would appear obvious that individuals with insight into disaster response would be cognizant of the inaccuracies and bias in news accounts. It is believed by the investigators, however, that most of even these experienced people believe the media accounts, and that as a result the myths are perpetuated.

Shelter Utilization:
"Disaster victims generally seek shelter in mass public shelters."

A consistent finding in the literature on disaster response is that, of those individuals who evacuate their homes, the great majority do not use formally established shelters, but find shelter with friends, relatives, neighbors, or provide for their own lodging.

Victims' Initial Search for Help:
"Initial search-and-rescue efforts are conducted by formal disaster rescue organizations."

In general, disaster victims react immediately to their plight. Individuals first seek help from family and friends, then from larger groups such as churches. If these groups are unresponsive or unavailable, victims will look to more impersonal official organizations—the police and welfare departments. Only as a last resort will they turn to the special disaster agencies like the Red Cross or civil defense organizations.

Disaster victims are also credited with most of the search and rescue of their fellow victims who have been marooned by flood waters or trapped by debris.

Human and Material Convergence:
"Any or all forms of material aid sent to a disaster site will be useful."

Investigators have found that the massive convergence of people, supplies of food, clothing, and materials:

- often provides unneeded and unusable materials
- requires for their management the services of personnel and facilities which could be otherwise allocated to more essential uses
- often causes conflict among relief agencies or among various segments of the population
- increases congestion in and near the disaster area
- in some cases, disrupts the local economy.

CASE STUDY

In its essence, this self-study course is about how to provide humanitarian assistance in response to a disaster. A premise of this book, and one that appears to be almost universally shared, is that people who are temporarily deprived of their ability to support themselves as a result of natural disaster forces beyond their control deserve the support of unaffected communities that have needed resources to share.

This self-study course makes many references to the necessity of providing disaster assistance in positive ways. The following case study traces the impact of postdisaster aid. The long-term implications of even the emergency relief programmes have proven to be highly significant. A primary implication is that all programmes need to be designed and implemented so that the negative consequences of relief are anticipated and minimized.

Unanticipated Repercussions of International Disaster Relief

Summary

Following the Peruvian earthquake of May 1970, the devastated provincial town of Huaraz received massive disaster relief aid. The reconstruction process rapidly transformed the economic and social structure of the community by causing a short-lived boom which raised the expectations of the population. Once the relief agencies withdrew, the demand for goods and services fell sharply and the people were forced to readjust to a less prosperous life. It also appeared that their capacity to respond to future disasters had not been significantly improved. This case study highlights the need for research into the long-term consequences of disaster relief.

Introduction

Natural disasters have changed in the last few decades. The forces of nature remain as they were, of course, but the social and cultural dimensions of extreme situations are being altered by demographic trends, technological innovations, relationships within and among nations, and other variables affecting risk, vulnerability, response, and recovery. Such quantitative changes in the disaster process are due in part to rapid urbanization, population growth, and lack of sufficient human and material resources in the Third World.

A major qualitative difference in natural disasters is the relatively recent appearance of multinational relief programmes made possible by technological and organizational developments since World War II. An earthquake, storm, or other catastrophic event is no longer of local concern alone, even in the most remote region, for news of calamity can now be quickly transmitted through sophisticated communications networks. Resources can be mobilized and delivered to a stricken area in one or two days, and scores of governments, international agencies, and private organizations may become involved in efforts to provide emergency supplies and service. The process, moreover, does not end with rescue and relief, for the affected communities may become targets of accelerated, externally supported long-range reconstruction and development programmes.

International disaster assistance is by no means a minor aspect of the disaster process. One report conservatively estimated that nearly $7 billion was spent between 1965 and 1975, and the figure would undoubtedly be far greater if funds for postdisaster projects were included in the estimate. This means that significant resources are concentrated in relatively small, economically poor geographic regions, and the infusion of wealth cannot be wholly without effect. Whereas chronic deprivation in these regions underlies collective stress, sudden abundance does not necessarily bring only benefits to the recipients. Massive aid can lead to distortions of the socio-economic conditions and an increase in vulnerability of a population to further disaster and further dependency.

This analysis sheds some light on multinational disaster relief by examining conditions in the Huaraz area of Peru following the earthquake of 31st May 1970. Huaraz, capital of the Department of Ancash, was one of hundreds of communities destroyed in the north-central part of the country; it subsequently became a primary recipient of international assistance. Located north of Lima in the Andean valley called the Callejon de Huaylas, the departmental capital was once a typical provincial town of about 30,000 inhabitants and served as the principal commercial center in an almost exclusively agricultural area.

Disaster and disaster relief transformed the city. The rubble of adobe homes was shoveled into dump trucks to be hauled away, and on the dusty field left behind was built a new Huaraz with wide, paved streets and earthquake-resistant houses. Reconstruction brought millions of dollars into the area, provided jobs for many laborers from nearby farming communities, and spurred a period of economic expansion as unanticipated in its scale as it was welcomed by the residents. New businesses appeared and prospered, while many older establishments recovered quickly from the earthquake and grew at an extraordinary rate for several years.

Post-earthquake prosperity in Huaraz and satellite communities illustrates one of the significant changes brought about by large-scale multinational relief. The situation in the Callejon de Huaylas seems to have been the direct result of external aid, and the correlation between prosperity and disaster-related programmes carries with it some disturbing implications regarding long-term repercussions of international disaster assistance.

Disaster and Disaster Relief

The earthquake triggered the worst natural disaster in the history of the western hemisphere. In less than a single minute hundreds of communities along the coast and in the highlands of north-central Peru were leveled, tens of thousands of people perished and hundreds of thousands more were injured and homeless. Devastation was very nearly complete, and eight out of 10 structures in an area of more than 80,000 square kilometers were rendered uninhabitable. The Callejon de Huaylas was among the most severely affected regions. Settlements towards the southern end of the valley lay in ruins as 95 percent of all buildings collapsed, and death tolls were tragically high, particularly in urban centers.

Four days after the earthquake, the first helicopters succeeded in crossing the Cordillera Negra, the western wall of the valley. Relief teams of doctors and nurses were among the first to follow, and the devastation they observed exceeded their worst expectations. The smell of death lay over the larger towns, and the hospital in Huaraz was overflowing with injured victims requiring immediate attention. The more critical cases were evacuated to the coast, but others had to wait long hours before being attended.

The Peruvian government did not have to wait long for international assistance, and the response of the world community corresponded in scale to the emergency. Nearly 70 nations offered some kind of aid—cash donations, medical services, supplies or technical assistance—and 52 countries became directly involved in relief operations. From the United States alone came representatives of 42 public and private agencies, and many other organizations or groups channeled resources through these active agencies or through Peruvian institutions.

There are no precise figures for the monetary value of all emergency goods and services in the affected area during the first months. But a study completed by the U.S. Agency for international Development placed reported international and private donations at over $70 million before October of 1970, and another $10 million was provided by various sources (CRYRZA, 1971). The Peruvian government also received a number of loans from such institutions as the International Development Bank ($35 million) and the International Bank for Reconstruction and Development ($30 million). Japan extended a loan of $17 million for the installation of electric power lines from Lima to Chimbote, while Germany lent another $180 million for electrification projects. In at least one case, the city of Huaraz, the unusual supply of goods, services and capital contributed to relatively short-lived economic expansion, or what might appropriately be called a disaster boom economy.

The Disaster Boom Economy

Repercussions of multinational assistance can best be described in the context of the economic conditions in the Callejon de Huaylas prior to the 1970 earthquake. As mentioned earlier, the region was almost exclusively agricultural, with 221 of 226 settlements directly dependent for subsistence on the cultivation of potatoes, corn and other tubers and grains. Only a fraction of foodstuffs ever found its way into the market system, for nine out of 10 families owned less than one hectare of land and produced little more than enough to meet the immediate needs of the household. Agricultural production, moreover, was kept at low levels by limited arable land, simple technology, and the absence of credit; and per capita yields were actually declining in some communities because of population growth and deteriorating soils. Mining brought some wealth into the valley, but a relatively small percentage of the population was employed by the mining companies. Thus the Callejon de Huaylas was rather marginal to the Peruvian economy as a whole, lacking any significant amount of resources which could profitably be exploited to lift the area to a position of economic parity with other regions of the country. The valley was poor and seemingly destined to remain so.

After the earthquake Huaraz was chosen to become a showcase of modernity and efficiency, a symbol of careful planning and management. Tens of millions of dollars were earmarked for projects in the city, and the amount of money spent increased each year between 1970 and 1974, with only a slight decrease in 1975 (Figure 6.2). Much of the money went toward reconstruction of homes, schools, government offices, and other private and public structures. By 1975, 684 apartment-like houses were completed at a cost of nearly $12 million, and more were to be built with funds from the International Development Bank and the Peruvian government.

Huaraz was physically transformed, and its new metropolitan aspect was in sharp contrast to the provincial ambience of predisaster years. More was changed than outward appearance, however, and the signs of prosperity were unmistakable to anyone familiar with the city before the earthquake. The number of hotels had tripled. Restaurants quadrupled in number. Several new stores opened to sell goods which once had been considered luxuries affordable only to the well-to-do: television sets, stereo components, bicycles and kitchen appliances. The presence of such items was not in itself unusual, but the increased number of stores providing the commodities indicated greater demand for them. Records of 34 varied commercial establishments were examined, and total annual income for the sample is summarized in Figure 6.3. Recovery was remarkable as the volume of total receipts increased exponentially from 1970 through 1975.

Disaster aid spurred the economy in several ways. Relief organizations brought their own vehicles, but maintenance was sought in local repair shops. By 1975, one automobile mechanic experienced a 10-fold increase in revenues over 1969 levels, and other garages saw substantial if less dramatic growth because of the presence of national and international agencies. The same agencies also purchased some supplies and materials from Huaraz merchants, as did construction companies contracted by the Peruvian government.

The high priority assigned to the promotion of tourism also affected the business community directly and indirectly. Tourist-oriented enterprises such as gift shops were eligible for low-interest loans, and government consultants provided technical assistance and advice. Construction of new paved roads, improved transport facilities and new hotels encouraged tourism, and the Peruvian government increased its advertising campaign to lure visitors to the Callejon de Huaylas, the "Switzerland of

Peru". An organization of businesspeople interested in promoting the tourist trade unofficially estimated that the number of visitors to Huaraz in 1975 was approximately three times that of 1969, a substantial increase which brought additional capital into the area.

The rebuilding of Huaraz, however, was perhaps the single most important factor contributing to rapid economic expansion. ORDEZA, the central coordinating agency created by the Peruvian government, supervised all construction activities in the earthquake zone, and more than 18 percent of its entire budget (two-thirds of its budget for the Huaraz area) was set aside for projects in and around the departmental capital. Some materials were purchased locally, but another aspect of reconstruction was probably even more significant in stimulating the economy, namely the employment of laborers from Huaraz and satellite farming communities. The precise number of people hired for construction jobs between 1970 and 1975 could not be ascertained, but ORDEZA officials estimated that between 1,000 and 1,200 individuals were on payrolls for various lengths of time during the period.

Many of the construction workers, especially those from the rural sector, had never before received regular salaries, a fact which helps to explain certain features of the economic boom. Clearly, a few businesses profited from direct transactions with relief organizations, while others depended on the patronage of tourists and persons temporarily assigned to relief agencies. The growth of some commercial establishments, however, was not as obviously due to the presence of outsiders or the influx of disaster aid. Retailers, for instance, sold furniture, radios and kitchen appliances at an unprecedented rate. Such commodities were not often purchased by tourists or by individuals who anticipated working but a short while in the region. Rather, most customers were reported to be residents of the area. Merchants whose own businesses were flourishing could afford to spend more, and wages paid to construction workers meant that more people were participating actively in the cash economy than before the disaster. The market for household goods and other items consequently expanded. Subsistence farmers who obtained employment during reconstruction of Huaraz could, and perhaps for the first time in their lives did, purchase goods previously beyond their means and considered "luxuries."

Thus multinational disaster assistance in north-central Peru did not end when the immediate needs of disaster victims were met. Long-term programmes of reconstruction, recovery, and development continued to bring large amounts of external resources into the area long after the initial emergency diminished in intensity. Ironically, merchants were the social group most severely victimized by material loss due to the earthquake but seem to have been the chief beneficiaries of the economic boom, although the benefits of disaster-related aid were not limited to any particular socioeconomic stratum. On the contrary, the remarkable growth of commercial establishments reflected a more general prosperity enjoyed by many individuals in both the urban and rural sectors. Poverty did not miraculously disappear in the Huaraz region, of course, but the effects of the disaster boom economy were far-reaching.

Other Implications of International Aid

Rapid economic growth triggered by a massive input of aid might easily be considered a positive feature, even a goal, of

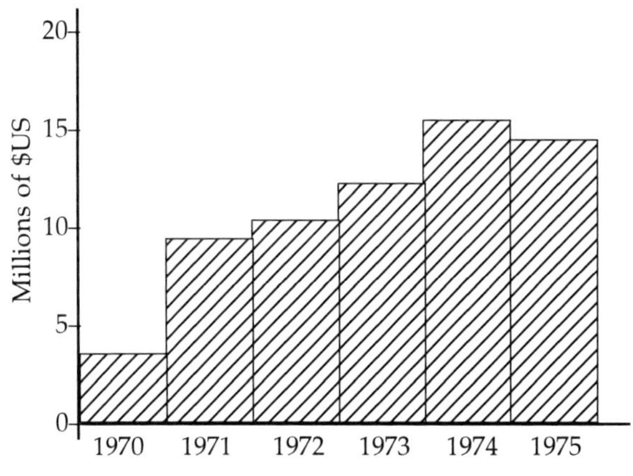

Figure 6.2: Total Aid to Huaraz Region 1970-75

Source: Fig. 1 from DUDASIK CASE PAPER, p. 33.
Total National and International Disaster Aid to the Huaraz Region, 1970-1975.

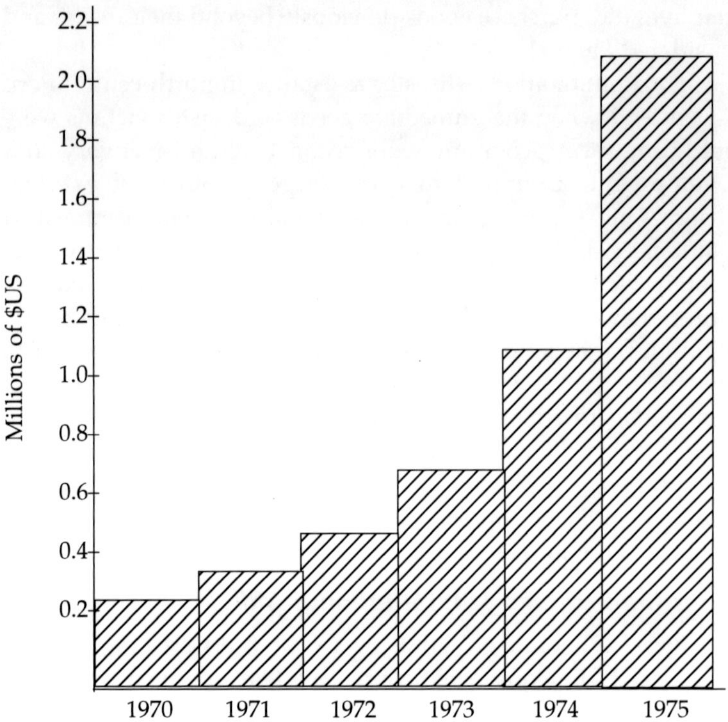

Figure 6.3: Combined Annual Revenues of 34 Huaraz Businesses 1970-75

Source: Fig. 2 from DUDASIK PAPER p. 33.
Combined Annual Revenues of 34 Commercial Establishments in Huaraz, 1970-75.

multinational disaster relief. Without question, segments of urban and rural populations in the Huaraz area profited from the economic boom, and even a temporary improvement in the standard of living could hardly be viewed as lamentable. Still, short-term gains may obscure long-term costs, and this possibility justifies a certain amount of speculation despite the paucity of longitudinal disaster research. The following remarks are therefore offered more as suggested areas of future research than as conclusions confirmed by existing data.

The city of Huaraz, like every human community, is a system whose social and cultural elements are functionally interrelated.

With shared beliefs, values and codes of behavior, the people of the capital order their relationships and daily activities to satisfy a range of personal needs and wants while, in a larger sense (and ideally), contributing to the common good. The community in effect reflects the cultural strategy for meeting individual and collective needs, and every behavior pattern is an integral part of the overall scheme.

Huaraz maintained a steady state of cultural and economic equilibrium prior to the 1970 earthquake. Although poverty was widespread, pressures for change at the local level did not greatly surpass the community's capacity to absorb change, control deviance and perpetuate established patterns of thought and behavior.

The earthquake adversely affected the steady state in several ways. First, many material resources required for needs-satisfaction were destroyed or buried in the rubble. Second, the death of thousands of persons represented a loss not only to surviving loved ones but to the community system as well. Third, physical and psychological traumas incapacitated a significant number of survivors, further disrupting normal interactional networks. Finally, social disorganization was accompanied by cultural distortion as world and woridview failed to approximate one another as closely as before. Many cultural cues were not appropriate to the disaster situation, and no longer was there always a clear correspondence between what could be done and what should be done.

Despite the degree of disruption, adaptive reorganization of activities began to restore, insofar as possible, the more vital aspects of the community system. Before outside assistance arrived, groups formed to recover bodies and rescue victims, to administer first aid and transport the injured, to search for and stockpile supplies, to control looting, to reunite separated family members, and other necessary tasks. The world community provided urgently needed goods, services and capital, compensating in part for the diminished capacity of the affected community to meet individual and collective needs. The infusion of aid continued after the period of extreme crisis, however, and the amount of resources in the post earthquake system eventually exceeded predisaster levels.

The resulting situation in Huaraz was an example of what might be called overload. Even had the earthquake not occurred, the departmental capital did not have the means to handle the extraordinary amount of resources pouring into the region and the disaster further reduced its ability. The required expertise, experience, and organizational complexity lacking in Huaraz was provided by national, international, and other-national institutions. A new entity took form, a dualistic relief system comprising the community as one constituent part and the outside organizations as the other. In a dominant position were the disaster agencies which represented an externally imposed, loosely integrated component controlling the allocation and distribution of almost all resources. The prerogative of local institutions was usurped by these external power groups whose concepts, assumptions, values, and goals were by and large inconsistent with the world-view of the disaster-stricken community.

Subordination and dependence had other dimensions. Multicultural dominance, for example, at times distorted patterns characteristic of Huaraz and other stricken communities, paradoxically adding to collective stress in the attempt to render assistance. In some cases, behavior codes were at odds, and relief agents were able to enforce their own principles because of their control of resources. Oliver-Smith describes a situation in Yungay, an urban center north of Huaraz, where emergency supplies were distributed freely and without regard to the established social hierarchy. Not only was egalitarian distribution a contradiction of local norms, but "the fact that aid was extended at all to rural people was, from the urban perspective, an indication of changed statuses," and the perceived threat evoked hostility and aggression. Similar kinds of tensions existed in Huaraz and other communities of north-central Peru where relief agents acted in accordance with preconceptions, assumptions, and values incongruent with those of the victim populations. The political process was likewise affected because external organizations, possessing power derived from differential access to resources, almost completely appropriated the decision-making, decision-implementing and social control function of the dualistic system.

Clearly, the presence of relief organizations and the massive inputs of aid had unforeseen effects on recipient communities, but what were the consequences of the eventual diminution of disaster-related goods, services, and capital? Because the boom economy was dependent on disaster programmes, the decrease in external resources was reflected in the incomes of the 34 commercial establishments studied. As Figure 6.1 shows, the amount of aid flowing into the Huaraz area in 1975 was about 6 percent less than that of the previous year. Business revenues, which had expanded exponentially between 1970 and 1975, subsequently slackened in their rate of growth and increased only 18 percent in 1976, the last year for which data are available.

There is not enough information to project a statistical trend, but the situation is nonetheless clear. The construction activities in Huaraz reached their peak in 1974 when most of the streets, private homes, and other projects neared completion. Many unskilled workers were not rehired as the frenetic pace of rebuilding began to abate. Also, the majority of international and foreign relief agencies were gone or preparing to leave the earthquake zone. In short, businesses in Huaraz were losing a significant number of customers, and the increase in tourism was not sufficient to offset the loss. By the end of 1978, nine of the 34 establishments in the sample had closed their doors, and, according to personal correspondence with informants in Huaraz, at least two others have since gone out of business.

Prior to disaster, residents of Huaraz had come to expect a certain level of needs-satisfaction, and collective stress inherent in the community reflected the degree to which expectations were or were not met. For example, many material items such as radios, watches, or bicycles were highly valued but few people could afford to purchase the commodities. Although denial entailed deprivation, the frustration of unattained goals could be reduced by adjusting priorities, and society itself provided some assistance in this regard. Chronic deprivation gave rise to beliefs which helped the individual rationalize and tolerate socioeconomic realities. In rural communities making up the larger Huaraz system, for instance, all valued things in the universe were thought to be limited in quantity, so that personal accumulation of wealth was considered somehow improper, even antisocial. One person's gain, after all, could only mean another's loss (the "image of limited good") is discussed by Foster, 1965). The individual was taught not to strive for more than one's share, and fortuitous bounty— perhaps an unexpectedly abundant harvest—was to be shared with family and friends or distributed during festivals. Similarly, religious tenets reinforced belief in the ascendancy of spiritual matters and the insignificance of the material world.

Many people who obtained employment in reconstruction projects enjoyed a substantial increase in personal income, and some goals previously denied could be attained. Increased sales of radios, bicycles, kitchen appliances, and other commodities indicated that a portion of salaries went towards such items, and merchants confirmed that customers were generally from the Huaraz area, not outsiders. Members of an affluent society where material needs-satisfaction beyond subsistence is taken for granted may find nothing unusual in the sequence of events; in fact, the ability of the people of Huaraz to satisfy their desire for goods may be perceived as a benefit of relief and development programmes. This interpretation, however, overlooks the importance of the new patterns. The essence of the situation lies in the probability that "changing expectancies about the degree to which given goals may be obtained by changing behavior leads to changes in behavioral (sic) directions." In other words, once individuals experienced higher levels of needs-satisfaction, expectations were altered. Ownership of material goods assumed a higher priority with respect to traditional behaviors of self-denial and redistribution of accumulated wealth.

In the rural areas especially, farmers who previously participated in reciprocal arrangements of sharing and mutual aid now demanded money for labor in order to continue their involvement in the cash economy of Huaraz. The weakening of reciprocity networks not only affected patterns of production and distribution in the farming communities, but also hastened the erosion of social solidarity which was derived in large measure from interpersonal bonds reinforced by nonmonetary exchanges. Diminishing social cohesion, a continuing decline in per capita agricultural production, rising expectations and other factors yet to be studied stimulated migration from the countryside to the urban center. Not all such changes can be traced directly to multinational relief and consequent relative deprivation, but the infusion of aid apparently had an impact on many facets of the socio-cultural system.

The Callejon de Huaylas is resource-poor, and diminished aid almost certainly means that higher expectations associated with the disaster boom economy coincide with fewer means to fulfill new individual and collective needs. Readjustment of priorities is possible, but more likely is a state of increased discontent and frustration, the precondition of further alterations in social and cultural elements. Disassembling the dualistic relief system exacerbated the situation by removing human as well as material resources, and the loss of expertise represented by external organizations will affect the efficacy of planning, decision-making and management of the change process. One solution to the problem, continued administration of local programmes by national institutions, seems to be the path chosen by the Peruvian government. ORDEZA, now called ORDENOR, has remained a component of the Huaraz system.

To summarize, the evolution of multinational disaster relief has changed the very nature of natural disaster by introducing new variables into the process. Scholars have studied various aspects of extreme situations, but most research has been conducted in the United States and other industrialized nations while the majority of large-scale catastrophes occur elsewhere. Consequently, little is known about the advantages and disadvantages of emergency aid to less developed countries, although humanitarian motives justify such assistance while political realities make involvement in the aid game imperative. Still to be determined is the effect on victim populations.

Research in north-central Peru indicates the possibility that short-term benefits of disaster aid may have unintended long-term costs. The entry of national, international, and other-national organizations into the Huaraz area brought into being a dualistic relief system which interrupted adaptive adjustment at the local level, placed power in the hands of personnel alien to the region, and distorted social and cultural patterns. Wider streets and earthquake-resistant buildings reduced the vulnerability of the urban center to physical destruction, but there was little positive change in the capacity to respond to crisis without turning to outside assistance. Huaraz will probably again be almost exclusively dependent on external aid when a future disaster occurs. Moreover, new needs and expectations did not decrease as the boom economy waned. Relative deprivation insures continued collective stress.

Relief programmes of the sort found in north-central Peru have frequently been called secondary disasters" because of the many problems encountered in rendering assistance to victim populations. By and large, attention has been focused on the immediate difficulties of interorganizational coordination, needs assessment, distribution of emergency supplies and other dimensions of global response to local crisis. This analysis suggests that truly effective disaster relief involves more than the solution of short-term problems, and that a sudden increase in resources is less a panacea than a potential source of greater stress in recipient communities. Cessation of all relief is hardly a viable option, but more longitudinal, cross-cultural research could more clearly define the consequences of aid, make possible the functional articulation of periodic disaster assistance and ongoing development programmes, and reduce the possibility of further victimizing the victims of natural calamity.

CHAPTER 7

Disaster Response Planning

Implementing Disaster Response

Preparedness Planning

The previous chapter, referred to the activities of disaster response as picking up where disaster preparedness leaves off. The two are, of course, closely interrelated. The Disaster Management Center course Disaster Preparedness discusses the scope of that topic. This chapter will not review preparedness activities, but rather it will describe the transition between the two.

The tools of preparedness should be in place before a disaster response is called for. Assuming some form of preparedness measures have been taken by the disaster manager, his or her ongoing role is to periodically review these plans or other preparedness measures to ensure that they are current.

Standing Operating Procedures

Implementing a disaster response programme should be achieved under the discipline of a predetermined approach. The preparedness plan should therefore include a standing operating procedures manual. These procedures are commonly known as SOPs and include the following:

- A description of the organization of the emergency operations center, including a command center, operations room, communications center, and support services the identification of activities of the emergency operations center during the initial hours and days of

the emergency, describing the various phases of the emergency
- Checklists of responsibilities and actions to be taken by each member of the organization
- A description of the warning and alert system public information and message control procedures
- A list of documents and aids which are propositioned in the emergency operations centers to assist the response actions, including the preparedness plans, data on the country's communities, roster of key local government officials, maps and other demographic data.

Elements in Place

Another of the immediate responses to a disaster will be to access the resources that will be necessary to support the emergency operations and recovery. These resources include not only the people that administer and implement the response programme but also the machinery and materials that are required to support them. These include:

- tools for search and rescue
- communications equipment
- road clearing and repair machinery
- medical supplies
- food supplies
- building supplies for sheltering
- ground transport and air support

Many of these supplies are traditionally conceived of as stockpiles. Some of them, in fact, may come from reserves formally designated as emergency stockpiles. But in practice such reserves should come from the resources, such as commercial stocks, already in place. They are referred to here as elements in place, a form of *active* stockpiling. That is, rather than a stock of food or medicines isolated from the market for emergency use only, the reserve will be taken from the stocks that exist in the market and that can be quickly diverted for emergency use. These can be later replaced from donors or other suppliers. Such a system can be implemented when disaster preparedness agencies keep track of the status of the supplies and equipment that are important to the disaster response. This approach to providing supplies usually is more effective than the massive, post disaster influx of supplies. It also does not tie up capital on stocks that may have a limited shelf life or never be used.

Institutional Requirements

Preparedness plans generally identify what to do in case of an emergency. Much of this book describes how to do it. This section reminds government coordinators and other disaster managers to evaluate the relief organization's capability to do it.

Many disaster response operations have floundered or failed because the relief agency was not capable of meeting its task. In order to increase the probability of success and quality of response each participating relief agency should meet minimal criteria.

Experience. A relief agency should be directed by people with disaster response experience. In some areas where disasters occur at lengthy intervals this requirement may not be directly met. However, partial equivalence for experience is training and drills.

Adequate Staff. Relief operations are by their nature inefficient and labor intensive. Inefficiency is a by-product of the one-of-a-kind nature of many disaster events that also may render unusable the typical tools of standard operations such as telephones, electricity, and roads. Disaster relief becomes labor intensive to compensate for the failure of such infrastructure and to reach the often sizable victim populations. Therefore the agency must have the capability of supplying enough staff, many on a temporary basis, to meet the emergency needs.

Equipment. A relief agency that accepts responsibility for certain disaster response activities, such as search and rescue, must have immediate access to all the tools and equipment necessary to implement these tasks. This equipment can either be fully under the control of and readily redeployed by the agency at all times, or the agency can have agreements with equipment suppliers to furnish it during declared emergencies. This may be particularly true for large, costly items such as cranes and bulldozers.

Funds. Almost everything costs money. Even supporting volunteer labor may require considerable expense. The best-made paper plans with the necessary trained staff will not be able to implement their programmes without the required resources. For the government this may mean legislation that authorizes special procedures for procuring emergency operations funds. Voluntary agencies rely on donations and fundraising. Obviously there must be a commitment of the funds necessary to implement the whole programme.

Legal Authority. If it's not legal it may not be possible. This criteria is so important that the following section is devoted entirely to it.

Legal Authority for Emergency Operations Support

Effective operation of disaster response plans requires that sufficient legal powers exist for their execution. The conferment of responsibility without authority is worse than its opposite.

It is clear that there is no commonly accepted practice for deciding which matters should be treated in legislation and which should be contained in disaster plans. Legislation for disaster prevention is not touched upon here. An approach to the problem of legislating for disaster preparedness and response is found in the "Guidelines for Disaster Prevention and Preparedness in Tropical Cyclone Areas." This approach recognizes that preparedness means both a readiness to undertake relief operations and an ability to begin the reconstruction process at the earliest possible moment; it also recognizes that as the phases of prevention, preparedness, relief, and reconstruction form the "disaster continuum," they merge into one another so that some activities may be underway concurrently.

The "Guidelines" recommend that legislation for disaster preparedness, especially in countries without a preparedness organization, should direct:

- the monitoring of natural phenomena, the issuing of warnings, and the directing of response actions
- the conduct of emergency measures (e.g., flood fighting and evacuation)

- the operation of measures related to protection, rescue and relief
- measures to educate and inform the population, including school children, of appropriate emergency responses
- measures to restore buildings, installations, and equipment
- health measures, including epidemic control, public health, and sanitation
- measures to preserve social order, for emergency transport, traffic control, and crime prevention
- measures for rehabilitation
- financial measures
- the definition of authority and responsibilities and, if required, the establishment of appropriate agencies.

Legislation should (and typically does) include as a minimum the procedure for declaring a state of emergency. Legislation should identify the emergency-related duties of authorities that form part of the nonnal structure of government as well as those of bodies specially established to prepare for and deal with emergencies. The powers those authorities will enjoy and related financial provisions are additional considerations to include.

Some countries, finding it appropriate to couple arrangements for a state of war with those for a natural disaster and emergencies created by accidental events, will cover the whole in a single act of the legislature. Others may prefer to employ a very short act which gives the government officials wide powers to operate by regulation, with or without the need to lay those regulations *ex post facto* before the legislature for ratification. The decision as to which legislative formula to adopt will probably be dictated—or at least influenced—by the kind of counter-disaster organization which is favored.

Exhibit 7.A

Analysis of Civil Defence Act, New Zealand, 1962, as amended, April 1977

Title
Short Title
Interpretation
Act not to derogate from certain other Acts

PART I

ADMINISTRATION

Secretary for Civil Defence
Director of Civil Defence
Deputy Director and other officers
Officers to act under direction of the Director
Functions and powers of Director
Delegation of powers of Director
National Civil Defence Committee
Functions of National Civil Defence Committee
lla. Power to appoint subcommittees
Planning committees
Preparation and approval of national civil defense plans
Obligation to conform to operative plan

PART II

CIVIL DEFENCE REGIONS

Civil defence regions
Regional Commissioners
Functions and powers of Regional Commissioners
Deputy of Regional Commissioner
Director may authorize Regional Commissioner to act for another Regional Commissioner
Regional Civil Defence Committees

PART III

DECLARATION OF NATIONAL EMERGENCY OR OF CIVIL DEFENCE EMERGENCY

Declaration of state of national emergency
ANALYSIS

Declaration of state of civil defence emergency
State of civil defence emergency may be declared in district not affected by emergency
Declaration of state of dvil defence emergency may be limited in purpose
Communication to Parliament
Duration of state of national emergency
Duration of state of civil defence emergency
Extension and termination of state of civil defence emergency

PARTIV

DUTIES AND POWERS OF LOCAL AUTHORITIES

Local authorities to plan for civil defence
Local authorities may unite for civil defence
28a. Time limit for preparation of plans
Local Controller of Civil Defence
Group Controller of Civil Defence
30a. Regional Controller of Civil Defence
Joint plans
Plan to be submitted to Regional Commissioner for approval
32a. Plan to be submitted to Regional Council in certain cases
33. Objection to Regional Commissioner's decision
33a. Obligation to conform to operative local or joint plan
34. Operative plans to be available for inspection
34a. Review of operative plans
34b. Confirmed plan to become inoperative if modification not made within 6 months
Effect of change in boundaries of districts or constitution of new districts
Local authorities may unite in contracts for civil defence purposes

Repealed
Powers of local authorities
38a. Specific functions and powers of regional councils

Assistance by Regional Commissioner to local authorities
Powers of local authorities in case of national emergency or civil defence emergency
Power of delegation
Powers of Chairman and other officers in urgent cases
Contracts by Chairman or other officers of local authority or Local Controller in urgent cases
Minister's power of direction
Repealed
45a. Compensation for loss of or damage to personal property
45b. Right to compensation restricted if person entitled can claim other compensation or damages
46. Financial provisions

PART V

MISCELLANEOUS PROVISIONS

Protection from liability
Requisitioning powers
Evacuation of places and buildings
Closing of roads and streets
Removal of vehicles, etc.
Entry on premises
Civil defence police
53a. Civil defence traffic officers
53b. Local authority traffic officers to have extended authority during national emergency or civil defence emergency
54. Absence on duty not to affect employment rights
Regulations
Obstruction or personation of officers
Penalty for offences
Consequential amendments
Repeal

Exhibit 7.B

Commonwealth of Dominica Emergency Powers Ordinance

Chapter 245

EMERGENCY POWERS (HURRICANE, EARTHQUAKE, FIRE OR FLOOD)

An Ordinance to make provision for the welfare and the safety of the community in cases of hurricanes, earthquakes, fires or floods.

(16th July, 1951)

This Ordinance may be cited as the Emergency Powers (Hurricane, Earthquake, Fire or Flood) Ordinance.

(1) It shall be lawful for the President, after the occurrence in this Island of any hurricane, earthquake, fire or flood, to declare by proclamation in the Gazette that a state of emergency exists.

No such proclamation shall be in force for more than one month, without prejudice to the issue of another proclamation at or before the end of that period.

Where a proclamation of emergency has been made, the occasion thereof shall forthwith be communicated to the Legislative Council, and if the Legislature is then separated by such adjournment or prorogation as will not expire within five days, a proclamation shall be issued for the meeting of the Legislature within five days and the Legislature shall accordingly meet and sit upon the day appointed by that proclamation, and shall continue to sit and act in like manner as if it had stood adjourned or prorogued to the same day.

Where a proclamation of emergency has been made, and it is impossible to communicate the occasion thereof to the Legislative Council owing to the dissolution or the expiring of the term of the Legislative Council and members of a new Legislative Council have not yet been elected, a proclamation shall nevertheless be issued for the meeting of the Legislative within five days, and thereupon notwithstanding the provisions of any Act or Ordinance to the contrary, the members of the late Legislative Council shall assemble and the Legislative Council shall stand revived and shall sit as the competent body of the Legislature but only for the purpose of considering such proclamation of emergency and the Legislature shall accordingly meet and sit upon the day appointed by that proclamation.

3. (1) Where a proclamation of emergency has been made and so long as the proclamation is in force, it shall be lawful for the President to make orders securing the essentials of life to the community and for the preservation of the health, welfare and safety of the public.

(2) Orders made under this section may, without . prejudice to the generality of the power conferred by subsection (1) of this section, provide—

- for the requisitioning of all forms of transport:
- for requisitioning and regulating the supply and distribution of food, clothing, water, fuel, light and other necessities of life, and for fixing maximum wholesale and retail prices in respect thereof;
- for the requisitioning of private lands, buildings and premises;
- for conferring on any person the right of entry on or passage through or over any private lands, buildings or premises;
- for the demolition of any building or other structure deemed to be dangerous;
- for the disposal of the dead and for dispensing with inquiries under the Coroners Ordinance, and from the provisions of the Registration of Births and Deaths Ordinance;
- for the payment of compensation in respect of anything done under any order made under this Ordinance.

Any order so made shall be laid before the Legislative Council as soon as may be after they are made, and shall not continue in force after the expiration of seven days from the time when they are so laid unless a resolution is passed by the Legislative Council providing for the continuance thereof.

The orders may provide for the trial by Courts of summary jurisdiction, of persons guilty of offences against the order; so, however, that the maximum penalty which may be inflicted for any offence against any such order shall be imprisonment with or without hard labour for a term of three months, or a fine not exceeding four hundred and eighty dollars, or both such imprisonment and fine, together with the forfeiture of any goods or money in respect of which the offence has been committed: provided that no such orders shall alter any existing procedure in criminal cases, or confer any right to punish by fine or imprisonment without trial.

The orders so made shall have effect as if enacted in this Ordinance.

The expiry or revocation of any orders so made shall not be deemed to have affected the previous operation thereof, or the validity of any action taken hereunder, or any penalty or punishment incurred in respect of any contravention or failure to comply therewith, or any proceeding or remedy in respect of any such punishment or penalty.

No action shall be brought against any person for anything done in good faith in the exercise of any powers conferred by any order made under this Ordinance.

CHAPTER 8

Disaster Response Roles and Responsibilities

The Relief System

Defining the System

The relief system consists of donors and interveners. At the upper levels of the system, those who collect and channel resources to those active in the field are collectively known as the donors. Interveners are the organizations that carry out the activities in the affected countries. In the middle levels of the system, some organizations are both donors and interveners (for example, AID). An organization that is a donor in one disaster may be an intervener in another. Generally, however, roles are firmly established.

What is generally referred to as the International Relief System can be divided into five tiers: the first three represent the international level, the fourth the regional or country level, and the fifth the project level. Into these tiers are fitted a complex network of organizations, each of which has a specific role or resources to offer following a disaster. If the system is viewed theoretically as a multi-tiered funnel for collecting resources and channeling them into a disaster-affected community, it is possible to visualize the workings and interrelationships at each level.

The Five Tiers

Starting at the top are the individuals and companies that contribute funds or material; these are the primary donors. It is not practical for donors to deliver directly to the victims; therefore, they must donate to an organization that either works in the community or can in turn pass on their gift to an organization that is on the scene. The organizations that receive the gifts, including churches, governments, and foundations, form the second tier.

The second-tier organizations have a number of options for distributing the donations. They can pass them on to the groups in the next level, composed of the international relief and development organizations (known collectively as voluntary organizations or volags), or to international intergovernmental organizations such as the United Nations or the Organization of American States (OAS), or they can bypass this level and give directly to the fourth tier, the local government and non-governmental organizations. In practice, most funds are passed directly from second-tier to third-tier groups.

Figure 8.1 shows the tiers, the patterns of donations, and the interrelationships of the various organizations. For example, churches normally give to volags in the third tier rather than to lower levels in the system. Governments donate to all levels, depending on the disaster and the political implications of the aid. Foundations contribute to volags, international organizations, and sometimes directly to local nongovernmental organizations, but almost never to the local government. At the third tier, volags and international organizations often support each other. For example, many volags give money directly to specialized UN organizations such as UNICEF, while many of the UN organizations (such as UNHCR) contract the volags to carry out their programmes. Similarly, volags often donate to regional organizations and vice versa, even laterally to other volags.

The volags serve as a conduit for funds to three of the groups in the fourth tier. First, they support their own field offices and the projects that their staffs develop. They also fund other intemational volags or the local nongovernmental organizations in the affected country. Often, too, they provide funds to missionaries through organizations in the third tier or Disaster

Figure 8.1: Disaster Response System

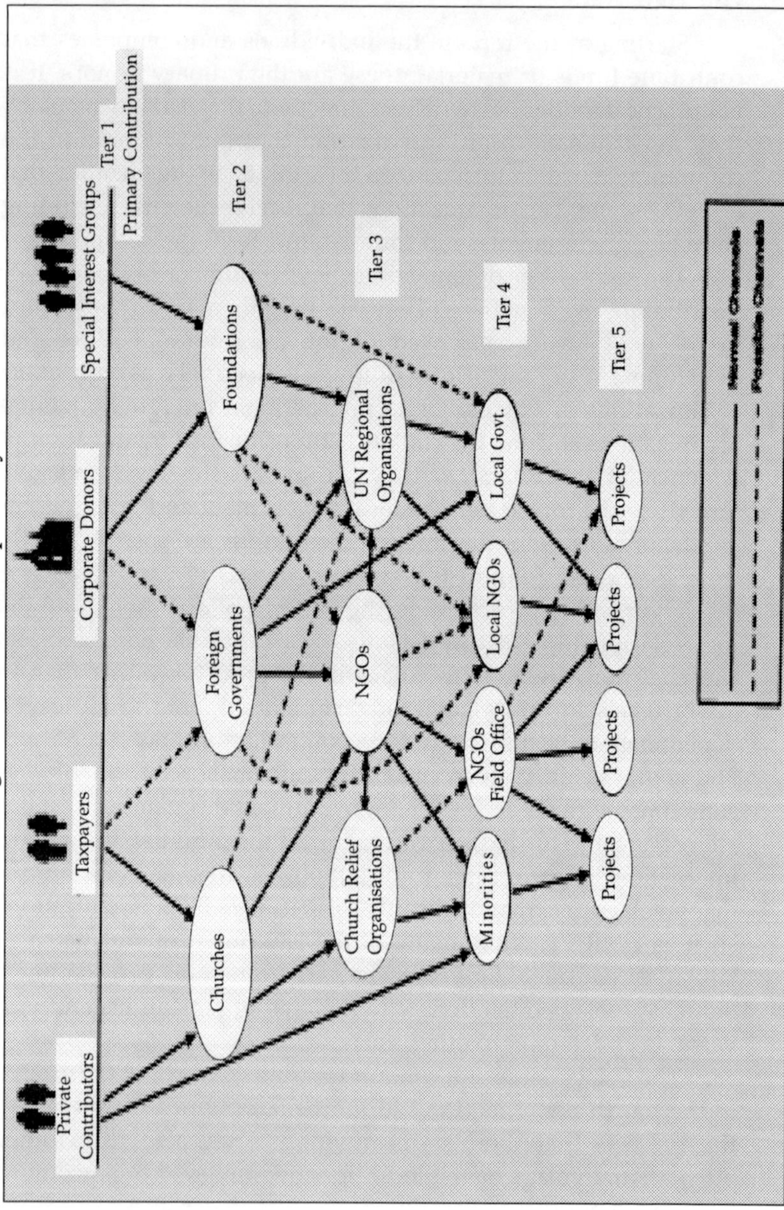

Response System Relationships and Funding Channels in the Relief System directly to those in the fourth tier. Volags often also fund each other in the third tier and the UN or regional intergovernmental organizations. In fact, volags have a record of funding just about every type of organization in both the third and fourth tiers, except local governments. Thus, in effect, volags often become not only operating agencies but also de facto foundations.

The fourth tier represents the first group of organizations in the affected country. It comprises the host government, local nongovernmental organizations, and the offices or field representatives of the foreign volags and missionaries. Their interrelationships are not as complex as at the international level, for here there is a competition for funds. Here too the decisions are (or should be) made on how the funds will be spent inside the country, and such decisions are critical for the outcome of the overall relief and reconstruction programme.

The final level through which the resources must go before reaching the victims is the project level. This fifth tier represents the operational level at which the funds and relief materials are dispersed or distributed and the point at which the victims' needs are resolved.

Most of the organizations in tiers 2 through 4 are both recipients and donors. In terms of the relief system, all organizations in these tiers, and many in the fourth tier, are collectively known as donors.

The International Media

Another major element of the relief system is the international media, which carry the major burden for mobilizing world concern for disaster organizations. The press is often the first to acknowledge a disaster and to provide the first evaluation of relief operations during and after the event.

Relief Agencies

General Roles Filled by Assisting Groups in Disaster Relief.

Principle

The success of a relief and rehabilitation operation depends on the correct and logical distribution of roles. Ideally this allocation should be undertaken by the local government authorities who are best qualified to decide who should do what, when, and where. However, if the local administration lacks the organizational capacity and resources to assume this responsibility, the priority must be to strengthen it.

The Role of National and Local Governments in Reconstruction

Second in importance after the surviving community's own role is that of national and local governments. Local government has the key task of allocating roles for all assisting groups. In undertaking this, it is likely to need assistance from the national government. In spite of the obvious risk of delegation of authority, this pattern of management has been found to be much more effective than centralized control. Local direction is frequently difficult for outside groups to accept, but it is vital to successful cooperation between survivors and assisting groups.

The Military

National military organizations in affected countries are often called upon to set up emergency tent camps for disaster victims. Because military-style camps are too rigid in layout, too uniform, too large, too dense, and often too far from original homes and work, they are the source of unforeseen problems: either they remain half-empty, or they breed environmental and social ills. In the administration of emergency shelter programmes, military organizations seek uniformity and conformity. This concern for order is simply too much to expect from a civilian population stricken by disaster. The period immediately after a disaster is a time when people need to get together and develop a collective response. A military hierarchy of decision-making inhibits this organic social process.

The military nevertheless can play an important, positive role in the emergency phase. It has great potential for rescue and relief since it possesses certain unique advantages over all other agencies, such as the capacity for rapid, disciplined action, pre-established emergency stockpiling facilities, and considerable logistical resources. The military's most effective roles in relief operations include:

- opening up roads and re-establishing telecommunication links
- providing emergency water supplies and sanitation
- transporting and, in some situations, distributing emergency relief supplies and personnel
- assisting survivors in search and rescue operations
- demolishing structures which threaten to collapse
- stockpiling essential demolition equipment, building tools, and vital building materials
- undertaking aerial surveys of damage.

The Role of Local Professionals

Local professionals have the potential to fulfill important technical assistance roles in the post-disaster phases. However, their involvement is often limited because of professional and social barriers between the liberal professions and the low-income groups who form the majority of those affected by disasters, and who frequently live in unsafe buildings and/or on hazardous land.

The Role of the Private Sector

The private sector includes enterprises operating on widely differing scales, from the small artisan to the large corporation. Overall reconstruction policy determines who will receive relief resources and thus who in turn may prosper, and it is therefore important to recognize the encouragement that can be given to small or medium-scale enterprises. Governments have a key social role in the way they administer credit, grants or loans to the business sector. The evidence suggests that a major bottleneck in disaster recovery is the lack of "cash flow" to get goods moving. A constraint on the rapid delivery of key building materials in some disasters has been the monopolistic practices of a few large stock suppliers and producers of building materials.

The Role of Experts

In many developing countries there is an acute shortage of local expertise on many aspects of reconstruction following disaster. Expertise is needed for:

- contingency planning (preparedness)
- damage survey methods
- preparation of building codes for hazard-resistant construction
- appropriate modification techniques to rebuild low-income housing and make it more hazard-resistant (this will include both traditional housing as well as some "modem" housing) education of local architects, engineers, builders, and carpenters, in hazard-resistant construction organization and management of reconstruction programmes.

The Role of External Voluntary and Relief Agencies

In addition to the primary, altruistic motivation of emergency relief, there are extraneous pressures on voluntary agencies which may be harmful to their purpose. These include:

- the need to impress their contributors with a rapid and visible response
- the need to raise funds
- competition with rival agencies
- the need to avoid offending the susceptibilities of the local administration
- in some instances, the limitation of their role to a specific "relief role", thus encouraging them to restrict their perception to an artificially narrow frame of reference.

However, they have certain inherent advantages which are particularly apparent when they operate in close rapport with local counterpart agencies. These include:

- the capacity to operate very rapidly
- a grass roots link to the local social and political structures
- flexibility of approach
- prior experience of disaster management (often these groups will have greater experience than all the other assisting groups including, in some instances, the central government).

The Role of Donor Governments

Similar to the constraints on voluntary agencies, the altruistic motivation of emergency relief provided by donor governments is often tempered by the politics of bilateral aid. However, donor governments have the capacity to fulfill important functions throughout all three postdisaster phases. They are particularly well placed to provide long-term capital and technical assistance for reconstruction and to link such assistance to firmer disaster preparedness and prevention policies.

The Role of International Agencies (United Nations System)

The effectiveness of international agencies may be reduced by extraneous pressures harmful to their central purpose, including:

- the need to demonstrate their value to ensure their future growth and funding
- competition among UN agencies where there are overlapping responsibilities
- oversensitivity to the tendencies and preferences of requesting governments.

However, their distinctive contribution lies in:

- the ability to mobilize large-scale assistance from a multiplicity of sources
- the reduction of the need for bilateral assistance (where there may be strings attached to assistance or such assistance is politically impractical)
- a unique coordinating role that no other agency or government can undertake alone
- access to international expertise.

The Role of the Red Cross/Red Crescent

The Red Cross/Red Crescent is a unique part of the structure of international relief and deserves more elaborate examination here. In a sense, it does not fit within this section, for it is not really a private organization; in fact, it is not an organization at all. The

Red Cross is a movement of individuals who provide their services and funds, organizations that serve its purposes, and even governments that sit in its governing councils and support its activities financially.

The movement is composed of three distinct elements:

The International Committee of the Red Cross (ICRC): Founded in 1863 in Geneva, the ICRC is often referred to as the guardian of the Red

Cross principles. Its primary purpose is the "protection," through implementation of international law and humanitarian principles, of war wounded, prisoners of war, and civilians, in both international and internal conflicts. But it can also, in these situations, assume responsibility for major relief operations. Increasingly in recent years, the ICRC has concerned itself with political detainees.

Soon after the ICRC was founded, governments were invited to form *National Red Cross Organizations;* since that time, 122 countries have done so. These "societies," as they were called, constitute the second element of the movement. Instead of protection, they concentrate on relief, public health, and welfare; some of them have broadened their fields of activity to provide services to virtually the entire population of their respective countries.

In 1919, about 60 national Red Cross societies formed a federation, the *League of Red Cross Societies,* which is the third element of the International Red Cross. The secretariat, or headquarters, of this federation has begun to assume certain international responsibilities and functions on its own in addition to (though not necessarily independent from) the concerns of the individual national Red Cross societies. The relief coordination activities described above are examples of this.

Policy Guidelines for Allocating Responsibility to Assisting Groups for Disaster Response and Reconstruction

Policies to Avoid

The centralization at the national level of authority and decision.

Permitting an anarchistic situation to develop, where various agencies perform their own tasks in an uncoordinated manner.

Allocating key roles to assisting groups which are unfamiliar with the local situation, or which lack local counterpart groups with which they can effectively collaborate.

Any policy that encourages partiality of aid distribution rather than the basis of need.

Policies to Adopt (See Table 8.1)

The government should assume responsibility for the allocation of roles and subsequent direction and coordination of all assisting groups, while making full use of those groups' particular expertise and operational capacities. In the allocation of roles, the following considerations should be borne in mind:

- Avoid mechanical clearance of rubble (bulldozing) where buildings materials can be salvaged, especially where the possibility exists that victims may still be trapped in the rubble.
- The government should allocate all roles for reconstruction to appropriate assisting groups.
- Local professionals can be extremely useful but are often psychologically and socially removed from the needs of low-income families. Their attitudes and commitments may need to be changed.
- The local private sector, particularly small enterprises, can play a major role, but they must be protected from cartels and monopolistic practices.
- Local experts should be used in preference to foreign personnel. However, not all the expertise required can be found locally or some may tend to implement policies in conflict with those recommended.
- Voluntary agencies have a flexible, grass roots capacity which can be a vital asset in providing assistance at local levels.
- There is a noticeable lack of effective project management programmes, with a consequent need for training at all levels.

The United Nations

The following is an overview of the various United Nations agencies that become involved in disaster relief operations.

The Office of the United Nations Disaster Relief Coordinator (UNDRO)

In December 1971, the UN General Assembly created the Office of the United Nations Disaster Relief Coordinator (UNDRO). The Office was to be "a focal point in the United Nations system for disaster relief matters." The resolution mandated two primary functions for UNDRO:

1. To mobilize, direct, and coordinate external aid provided (by the UN system) in response to a request from a disaster-stricken state.
2. To promote the study, prevention, control, and prediction of natural disaster, including the collection and dissemination of information concerning technological developments, and as part of this latter function, to assist in providing advice to governments on predisaster planning.

Recognizing that the coordinator in Geneva would need status within the UN system to deal with the collection of specialized agencies involved with disaster, the resolution created the position of coordinator at the level of undersecretary-general, reporting directly to the secretary general.

The United Nations Development Programme (UNDP)

The creation of UNDRO in 1971 altered somewhat the traditional relief roles of the other UN agencies— notably that of the central UN development agency, the United Nations Development Programme (UNDP).

The UNDP, headquartered in New York, maintains resident representatives in most developing countries and on a regional basis for some others. By agreement with UNDP, these officials also represent the United Nations Disaster Relief Coordinator. They provide a channel for requests from governments for disaster-related matters. When disasters strike, with assistance as necessary from staff dispatched by UNDRO, the UNDP resident representative leads the United Nations in-country team in the assessment of emergency needs and local coordination of aid from the United Nations system and other international sources. The UNDP can also furnish some financial aid in emergencies and, as may be indicated, can adapt country programmes to the needs of rehabilitation and reconstruction following a disaster. In addition, the UNDP directs its attention to projects designed to prepare for or prevent disasters, such as the construction of dams and irrigation works which reduce floods, the formulation of master plans for cities, and the establishment of building research centers.

United Nations Children's Fund (UNICEF)

UNICEF, established in 1946 and based in New York, assists programmes for health, education and welfare for children and mothers in most developing countries. For emergency relief, UNICEF provides mainly material assistance. Normally this takes the form of children's foods, drugs and vaccines, potable water, and vitamin capsules. Long-term measures to meet the needs of children and young mothers have overriding priority in the allocation of UNICEF resources.

While UNICEF's main interest after a disaster lies in the medium-term restoration and long-term development of services to children and mothers, it provides substantial emergency assistance for these vulnerable groups as well. The executive director of UNICEF disperses cash reserves for rapid use in emergencies, and can divert funds from regular programmes to emergency operations with the agreement of the government concerned.

Food and Agriculture Organization (FAO)

FAO was established in 1945, to serve as the organizing and coordinating agency to plan and execute development programmes within the whole range of food and agriculture, including forestry and fisheries. In relation to both relief and short-term rehabilitation, FAO specialists help to assess needs in the agricultural and food sector. In addition, it is concerned with ensuring the availability at all times of adequate world supplies of basic foods, particularly to avoid food shortages in the event

Table 8.1: Ideal Roles for Assisting Groups Relative to Shelter Provision
Roles of Assisting Groups

Activities	Inter-national Agencies	External donor govt.	External voluntary Agency	Experts disciplinary Groups	Private Agency	Local Municipality Architecture Organisation	Local Military	National Govt.	Local Adminis-tration	Local Voluntary Groups	Surveyors
	Phase I—Immediate relief period (Impact to day 5)										
Search-and-rescue operations							✓		✓	✓	✓
Clearance of rubble (recycle materials									✓	✓	✓
Re-establish communications							✓		✓		
Coordinate external assistence	✓							✓	✓		
Provide emergency shelter					✓				✓	✓	✓
Re-establish damaged infrastructure (water sewers, etc.)							✓		✓		
Assess unmet needs of survives	✓	✓	✓			✓	✓		✓	✓	✓

Phase 2—Rehabilitation period (day 5 to 3 months)

Providing essential building materials		✓	✓		✓		✓		✓	✓	
Provide expertise for safe housing construction	✓	✓				✓		✓			
Release safe land for new housing								✓	✓		
Re-establish damaged infra-structure	✓	✓					✓		✓		
Rebuild damaged and destroyed homes	✓	✓			✓				✓	✓	✓
Assess damage to housing	✓					✓	✓		✓	✓	
Coordinate external assistance	✓								✓	✓	
Re-establish local economy								✓	✓		✓
Provide cash inputs to survivors			✓					✓	✓	✓	
Clearance of rubble (recycle materials)									✓	✓	✓

(Contd.)

Table 8.1: (Contd.)
Phase 3—Reconstruction period (3 months onwards)

Activities	Inter-national Agencies	External donor govt.	External voluntary Agency	Experts disciplinary Groups	Private Agency	Local Municipality Architecture Organisation	Local Military	National Govt.	Local Adminis-tration	Local Voluntary Groups	Surveyors
Re-establish damaged infrastructure					✓			✓	✓		
Formulatge building codes for safe-construction	✓					✓		✓	✓		
Provide expertise for safe housing construction	✓		✓			✓					
Device contigency plans for future earthquakes	✓			✓		✓		✓	✓		
Develop stockples of essential building materials					✓			✓	✓		
Rebuild damaged or destroyed homes					✓				✓		✓
Devise any new plans for destoryed towns	✓			✓		✓		✓	✓		

of widespread crop failures and natural and other disasters. Long-term rehabilitation measures are covered by normal programmes outside of emergency relief. FAO and the WFP are based in Rome.

World Food Programme (WFP)

WFP, established in 1963, is a joint UN-FAO effort to stimulate economic and social development through provision of food aid including emergency relief supplies. The food is supplied, as an incentive to development self-help schemes, as part wages in labor-incentive projects of many kinds, particularly in the rural economy, but also in the industrial field. The food is also provided in support of institutional feeding schemes where the emphasis is mainly on enabling the beneficiaries to have an adequate and balanced diet. WFP also purchases and ships food stuffs.

Requests for WFP emergency food assistance should be transmitted through the resident representative of the UNDP, the official representative of WFP in each country. This does not preclude a direct communication from the government to the executive director in Rome.

Quite apart from its interest in provision of emergency food aid, WFP's normal programme activities relate, among other things, to sponsorship of pilot projects using food as an aid to economic and social development, particularly when related to labor-intensive projects and rural welfare.

World Health Organization (WHO)

WHO, headquartered in Geneva, was established in 1948 to promote and protect the health of all peoples. An emergency is defined by WHO as a situation which implies unforeseen serious and immediate threats to public health. In emergencies WHO coordinates measures undertaken by various organizations and donor governments in the health field. It acts as the directing and coordinating authority on international health works. In emergencies it also provides technical assistance, health teams in campaigns against diseases, mother and child care, family planning, nutrition and health education and other related activities. WHO acts in close collaboration with UNDRO, the League of Red Cross Societies and other specialized organizations providing assistance in emergencies. At the country level its representatives assist the local authorities in assessing the requirements for personnel, medical supplies, and equipment to prevent or minimize health hazards to disaster victims. WHO can furnish technical personnel and limited amounts of emergency supplies, and can also assist in measures of disaster prevention and rehabilitation.

The United Nations High Commissioner for Refugees (UNHCR)

UNHCR was established in 1950 in Geneva to provide international protection for refugees, to seek permanent solutions to their problems by facilitating voluntary repatriation and resettlement as well as by providing supplementary aid and emergency relief to refugees as may be necessary. When a natural disaster occurs in a country whose inhabitants include refugees within the sphere of competence of UNHCR, the office may make assistance available. Such assistance may take the form of emergency aid or, if necessary, of a project aiming at facilitating the settlement of the refugees. Under later resolutions of the General Assembly the High Commission may also be called upon to act as coordinator for international assistance in other situations of human distress, and especially those involving displacement of population.

Coordination

Introduction

Coordination is one of those aspects of disaster response that everybody agrees is important for everybody except themselves. Nevertheless, it is essential and is primarily the responsibility of the affected national government to direct. This coordination must be based on policies and procedures described in the following section.

Guidelines

General Considerations

1. The need for coordination in disasters is based on the

necessity for cooperative action by all involved in order to:

- effectively and efficiently meet needs
- avoid waste and duplication of efforts
- ensure that resources are distributed equitably and to areas of greatest need
- ensure that the methods and goals of one programme do not conflict with those of other programmes.

2. Coordination must not only take place at every administrative level (such as between ministries or between the different groups of people in a village) but also between administrative levels (such as between village-level and district-level administration, or between district offices and headquarters).

Elements of Coordination

There are several common operational components involved in the establishment of a cooperative working relationship, whether at local, national or international, organizational or individual levels:

Operating Guidelines—procedures for coordination must be defined and agreed upon by all parties.

Roles—the roles, responsibilities, authority and privileges under which each party will operate should be well defined, in writing.

Priorities—priorities must be clearly defined and accepted as the basis for action by all parties.

Data Collection and Reporting—effective coordination is largely dependent upon an effective data collection and reporting system:

information source—who is expected to provide information must be clearly defined

communication methods—how information is to be transmitted must be understood by all parties

definition—what information is needed must be clearly defined.

Time Considerations—time requirements for all functions should be identified and accepted by all.

Factors Which Inhibit Coordination

Disruption of communication facilities and lack of an adequate emergency system.

The difficulty of establishing an accurate and/or commonly agreed upon assessment of the damage and needs.

The difference of opinions on what is needed, how it should be provided, and what the priorities should be.

The tendency for parties to relate to particular target groups or problems without viewing them from the perspective of the broader needs or the resulting implications.

The tendency of some groups to decline to coordinate for private gain in visibility.

Political differences among relief agencies.

The capability and inclination of an agency to implement their programme in a more accelerated time frame than others.

Factors Which Improve Coordination

- Clearly outline and agree upon coordination roles, functions, and contributions, etc., as part of preparedness planning establishing the host government's central role.
- Establish a physical location for the coordinating center and for each functional operation, such as transport or supply depots.
- Clearly define objectives and review frequently to monitor progress.
- Closely monitor the effectiveness of actions, and carry out periodic reviews.
- Establish an atmosphere of respect for the mutual sharing of goals by all parties.
- Identify gaps or overlaps in functions.
- Written communications will be more reliable than verbal.
- Establish a chain-of-command for every operational project.
- Remain flexible to meet diverse needs.

Minimize the number of coordination meetings.

Coordination committees should include representatives from both private and governmental sectors, including local leaders (such as village elders), religious leaders, and local politicians.

Careful preplanning and the development of written statements of understanding between private voluntary disaster relief agencies and the national government will eliminate much of the potential confusion about roles and activities.

Model District Coordinating System

Responsibilities

Coordinating Committee Functions

- establishing priorities
- developing policy guidelines
- planning
- overseeing system and problem resolution.

Coordinating Center

- centralized collection of data produced by all participating agencies
- liaison between parties and between administrative levels
- implementing decisions of coordinating committee
- directing relevant agencies to specific needs
- issuing policies and instructions
- solving problems.

Vehicles Section

- pooling government vehicles
- requisitioning private vehicles
- assuring fuel supply and fuel control
- providing vehicles as necessary.

Food and Stores Section

- assessing local food stocks
- setting up distribution system

- setting up warehouse for donated materials
- requesting needed supplies
- encouraging local markets to open as soon as possible.

Finance Section

- procuring cash for local purchases
- disbursing funds as needed
- performing all accounting tasks.

Relief Section

- assessing damages and needs
- establishing supply depot and distribution system
- making arrangements for relief payments:
- sending out public notices of pay schedules and eligibility
- establishing an appeal procedure.

Raising with higher levels, external agencies, and visitors, and reporting to the donating organizations and the media.

Emergency Response Guidelines for Governmental and Non-Governmental Agencies

Some of the medical and social effects of large natural disasters are briefly discussed here. Included are sets of statements which are intended primarily to help the staffs of governmental and local agencies determine their actions in the first hours after a major disaster.

The main objective of this section is to present a framework, based on existing field research, which can be used to shape the investigations of governmental agencies and those attempting to provide support for both governmental agencies and groups of survivors. The summary statements contained here are based on research studies by a variety of workers in several large earthquakes during the past decade, but are applicable to most sudden impact disasters.

Despite the apparent confusion and complexity of events, and the differences in the societies in which disasters can occur, certain outcomes and patterns of response tend to recur. In particular, populations tend to behave in the same way; the types of relief needed will be similar; and the priorities will vary little.

This does not mean that a relief response can be administered "blind" over long periods. Operations can only be effectively managed on the basis of observed, *actual* needs. However, it does mean that a fairly clear "model" of the outcome of a disaster can be set out, against which the character of real events can be discriminated. In effect, we can set out a framework of the "expected" to give structure to the investigations and observations of someone attempting to make sense of what is happening locally.

What to Look for as a Relief Agency Coordinator of Disaster Response Activities if No Prior Plans or Preparations Have Been Made.

General Approach

Find out what resources you have already and identify those you are willing to expend. Identify tasks that appear to be vital and urgent, that are not being done and which you can do. Identify activities *that are already in progress* in the community that are worth *reinforcing*. Recognize that certain limited tasks are so likely to be necessary and so urgent that they are worth doing automatically once a disaster occurs. If it is in any way possible, attempt to do the following.

Obtain at no cost or purchase and transport specific medical items to hospitals and clinics in and around the damaged areas within 24 hours. If the disaster is large, literally tons of medical supplies of all sorts will eventually arrive. However, the small packages of appropriate supplies which reach clinics during the first life-saving hours will make the real impact on casualty survival. Determine whether hospitals, clinics, or first-aid centers have unmet needs for auxiliary power, fuel, tents, water storage, or engineering assistance, and whether your organization can help to fulfill these immediately.

Additional Opportunities for Intervention over the Next 72 Hours; Some Areas to Investigate

Support for the Local Community Response

Making sense of local events: Most of the activity in the area will be "unorganized" in the sense that there will be little coordination or central control. A natural response of many observers is to believe that some sort of "order" should be brought to the area. Anyone following this approach, however, may well be rather quickly frustrated. Closer investigation usually reveals that the public's response has its own inherent logic and internal organization; a more effective approach is to find the order that already exists and reinforce it.

However confusing it initially appears, the behavior of the public can be assessed largely in terms of the following activities:

- search and rescue
- movement of the injured to points where medical attention is known to be available
- acquisition of shelter, warmth, and a place to sleep
- acquisition of water
- acquisition of food
- retrieval of possessions
- arrangements for the dead
- contact with family members outside the area.

People will usually be in the open in large numbers. In more developed societies, there will be a tendency to sleep in cars in bad weather. A variety of private vehicles will be used for casualty transport. Search and rescue will be carried out by small groups of family members and *ad hoc* neighborhood groups in the first hours. In many urban areas, the distribution of collapsed buildings will be patchy; concentrations of destroyed structures will be found in older areas, with more localized, individual building collapses in between. Accordingly, the intensity of spontaneous rescue activity may vary from street to street.

What to do: In general the public's response will best be helped by assisting existing administrative efforts to restore basic, services; but certain types of aid given directly to the public in the first few hours and days can greatly reduce suffering and speed up the rate at which some families can stabilize their own condition.

Plastic sheeting: The distribution of plastic sheeting to any groups of homeless people obviously in need of improvised shelter is perhaps the most effective direct assistance that can be given in the first hours after a disaster where survivors are exposed to adverse weather conditions. Plastic sheeting can be used to make simple tents, to extend the use of vehicles as shelter, to cover damaged roofs, to protect possessions stored in the open, to make waterproof clothing, and to store water. For any organization with stockpiles, the aim should be to get stocks into the community as fast as possible, without too much regard for selectivity of beneficiaries. Large amounts usually arrive eventually from international donors, but these tend to be lost for days or weeks in the confusion often after the need for them has been largely satisfied through local solutions.

Other support: It may be possible to provide other support in the immediate neighborhood of the organizations's own facilities. Consider all the following, but bear in mind that the possibilities for widespread and large-scale lifesaving are usually limited. It is often best to concentrate on a well-defined, local area.

Lighting for continued search and rescue at night (bearing in mind that lighting may save more lives if concentrated at hospitals or first-aid centers).

Hand tools: crowbars, manila rope, steel wire rope, saws, chains, shovels for provision to search-and-rescue teams.

Flame-cutting equipment and operators for assistance in rescue.

Vehicles for use as ambulance transport.

Support for Government and Essential Services

Objectives and Criteria

The overall aim should be to reinforce the most sensible elements of the organized response. As a general rule, the following criteria may assist in making a decision:

- Deal with the highest priority problems first.
- Concentrate on things the public has demonstrated that it is not capable of doing for itself.
- Restore the services and procedures that will help members of the public do what they want to do better.
- Give people the things they actually want. Ask as widely as possible.

Suggested Activities

As a guide, aim to do the following, in the order given:

Reinforce first any form of casualty management activity. By visiting hospitals and clinics, investigate as quickly as possible the needs for items you can supply immediately (in particular power, fuel, tents, lighting, water storage, clean water, food, and engineering assistance).

Reinforce any form of organized repair of piped water and sewerage networks by the people normally responsible for this task. Investigate the needs for emergency assistance in water delivery by road-tanker and special needs for repair equipment, fuel, generators, and lighting.

Reinforce any attempt to survey:

- the extent of the damaged area, and the presence of specific hazards;
- the number and location of casualties;
- damage to services: transport, power, water, telecommunications;
- the towns and villages with the greatest housing damage.
- Assist efforts to clear access routes to damaged areas.
- Assist efforts to distribute plastic sheeting and tents.

Activities to Avoid

In general avoid assisting in the following:

- Indiscriminate distribution of blankets and clothing (restrict efforts to established relief centers where a *known* need exists while simultaneously being cautious not to create a magnet for others seeking free relief).
- Distribution of water purification tablets. They are usually ineffective and lead to a false sense of confidence in the quality of the water supply
- Immunization campaigns against typhoid, tetanus, hepatitis or cholera; also any immunization programme in which recipients are not individually identified and documented. (For an explanation, see also the Chapter 5 section on health.)

Spraying of buildings or people with disinfectant.

The rapid removal of rubble, except from dangerous structures and access routes (rubble may well be an excellent source of rebuilding material for the poor). Bulldozing of rubble will *not* affect disease rates.

Guidelines: What Might the Authorities Reasonably Be Expected to Do in the First 72 Hours?

The following list describes administrative activities that are likely to be both feasible and effective in the immediate aftermath of destructive disasters. These activities are premised with four aims:

Precise and specific support for sectors of population that most need help, in particular injured persons needing in-patient treatment.

- Removal of risk for large numbers of people;
- restoration of water supply
- provision of clean water at those places where large numbers of displaced people settle (e.g. camps).

Restoration of a framework in which administrative organizations can coordinate their response: repair of telecommunications and transport.

Provision of a framework within which survivors can re-order their own affairs:

- a clear road network for moving food and supplies
- opportunities for the homeless to move to the houses of relatives and friends (e.g. a restored bus service)
- an energy source for food processing
- where they exist, re-opening of banks and post offices
- assistance in re-opening food stores and markets.

A Rational Response by the Government of Less Developed Countries

First 24 Hours

Attempt to establish the geographical boundaries of the damaged area through the use of telephone, radio, and over flight by available light aircraft or helicopters. Initiate assessment.

Establish contact with military and police units in major towns, and ensure that accessible hospitals receive available high-priority medical items, generators, lighting, tents, and radio communications.

Establish contact with military and police units in major towns, and ensure that priority is given to *moving* high-priority medical items, generators, lighting, tents, and radio communication equipment to accessible hospitals. If necessary, air traffic control equipment, generators and emergency airport lighting should be provided at airports. During the next 72 hours, priority should be given to tarpaulins, plastic sheeting, generators, tents, repair equipment for electric power, water, and telephone systems.

Organize vehicles and fuel supplies for moving out incoming relief stocks.

From 24 to 48 Hours

Give priority to the continued provision of medical stocks and services to accessible hospitals, restoring police, military, and public services communications, and restoring broadcasting where necessary.

Ascertain what activities are being carried out by water authorities in large urban areas and what capabilities they may have for assisting in provision of clean water to high-risk areas, particularly urban slums; e.g. vehicles, fuel, military personnel, generators, tools, and lighting.

Using whatever units are available, including light aircraft and helicopters where possible, continue to survey access routes between main urban centers and the damaged area. Attempt to pinpoint the most concentrated areas of severe damage.

Distribute first to staff of hospitals the incoming supplies of tarpaulins, tents and food. Thereafter, distribute available stocks initially in "high-risk" areas, e.g. cold, wet, high altitude.

Identify and clear route blockages between damaged areas and centers capable of providing relief services.

From 48 to 72 Hours

Make available the necessary vehicles, fuel, road-clearance equipment and personnel to assist the restoration of electric power to water pumping stations, hospitals, radio stations, and airports.

Where helicopters are available, begin a more detailed survey of inaccessible areas, moving in medical teams where possible.

Thereafter concentrate on moving tents and blankets to damaged high-risk areas (mountain areas where a real risk of exposure exists). Distribute plastic sheeting and tarpaulins as widely as possible in other damaged areas. Make a systematic distribution of tents to field units of police and emergency services.

As early as possible, distribute food to the staff of public services and their families.

Provide the media through the public information officer status reports on the disaster response.

Specific Recommendations for Relief Agencies

The following are recommendations made by a private voluntary relief agency for future implementation based on an evaluation of its performance in a major relief operation. They may serve as a guide for other agencies but will need to be carefully edited to reflect the unique characteristics of each agency. Many of these recommendations also serve as a preview of issues in disaster response which are addressed throughout this disaster text.

- A relief agency should attempt to define financial parameters for a programme as soon as possible, and in any case not later than the time when the needs have been assessed. This facilitates rational and cost-effective programme planning.
- A relief agency should ensure that recipients of relief aid are involved in continuing evaluation of the relief effort. Recipient participation in evaluation can often provide opportunities and the stimulus for better community organization.
- A relief agency should take steps to facilitate a more ready exchange of ideas, information and experience between the aid organizations which commonly assist in disaster situations abroad.
- A relief agency should take steps to ensure that its entire field staff is adequately oriented in basic

principles of disaster preparedness and emergency programme planning.

- A relief agency should support its representatives, particularly those in disaster response situations, with legal and organizational credentials which enable them to establish local bank accounts and conduct business on behalf of their agency. Local legal advice should be obtained regarding business principles in the particular country.

Prior to a disaster a relief agency should establish a definite plan which systematically develops working relationships with local ecumenical agencies, church groups, and government contacts in disaster-prone countries. Information regarding these contacts should be compiled and retained both at the field level and at headquarters with periodic updates.

Pressure from a relief agency for results and expenditures does not ensure adequate planning and systematic programme development. In fact, such pressure may have been inimical to those ends, especially in view of the substantial amount of time needed to stimulate, organize and integrate community involvement.

When planning a disaster response relief effort, a relief agency should consider channeling funds through individual, grass roots and local groups as well as large counterpart church groups. In other words, in a situation where a large counterpart does not exist, a relief agency should consider channeling funds directly to projects and through local national intermediaries.

To facilitate a relief effort, the possibility of immediate establishment of an independent relief agency office should be carefully considered. This is recommended even when a strong local counterpart organization already exists. Although the purpose of this field office would be to work directly with the counterpart organizations, the independence would facilitate objective assessment and better quality of assistance to the counterpart organization.

Should a relief agency field office be established, sufficient personnel, equipment, and communication facilities should be provided to permit efficient operations.

The views of a variety of both grass roots tocal leaders and ordinary intended beneficiaries should be carefully incorporated in the relief agency planning process used for a disaster response, particularly in the area of actual distribution and use of resources.

When community development objectives are included in a project, the implementation plan should include indicators to show whether and how success is being achieved.

A relief agency should ensure that after any future disaster in which it becomes involved, adequate support in programme planning should be made available to its representatives in the field. The services of an experienced consulting firm in emergency relief and reconstruction activities may be required for brief periods at the beginning of the planning operations.

A relief agency should consider itself as a potential supplier of a wide range of resources and not exclusively as a source of financial assistance. Examples include expertise and international resource contacts. Projects involving the construction of houses require much more time than is initially apparent for reasons such as land tenure, installation of infrastructure (roads, water, etc.) or availability of building materials. If a relief agency engages in housing construction, adequate staffing will probably be the most important variable in determining success.

Housing construction should not be detached from community development goals. Plans to facilitate and encourage the development of a community should receive emphasis equal to the construction and should be initiated at the beginning of, or preferably prior to, the construction itself.

If repayment is contemplated in housing or other programmes, the relief agency should be absolutely committed to beneficiary adherence to the plan. To help ensure this, repayment plans should be established in consultation with beneficiaries *before* the programme plan is finalized. The plan should include a written contractual agreement covering all aspects of the relationship between the agency and the beneficiary, and most importantly, the use and administration of funds. Both community and agency controls should be included to cover the use of funds repaid. The relationship between legal ownership documents and the repayment plan should be specified. Repayment requirements so established should be enforced.

A relief agency should recognize that prospective homeowners are more likely to fulfill their financial obligations and contribute to the community if they are involved, from the beginning, in the planning of a programme which affects them. Programmes planned without community involvement to provide unduly speedy, agency perceived "solutions" often do not fully reflect the interests of the intended beneficiary and sacrifice the potential for active community participation.

Expenditure deadlines imposed by other funding agencies on projects implemented by a relief agency should be accepted only if adequate time is available for the responsible completion of the project. In any case, acceptance of such deadlines should not require the elimination or undue curtailment of thorough research and planning.

Large-scale construction projects should be operated semi-independently of other relief agency programme aspects unrelated to the disaster to maintain the perspectives of the local programme.

Projects involving municipal or local technical standards should use locally recognized and licensed professional people and/or firms in the design, specification, quantification, and scheduling and installation phases.

As an international organization operating in a foreign country, a relief agency should retain the services of a permanent, locally recognized and licensed engineering firm to assist communities in the operation and maintenance of any urbanization systems installed by the relief agency.

Careful attention should be given to the recruitment and management of volunteers used in a disaster response. Qualifications for prospective volunteers should be established in the field and respected by the recruiting agency in home office. A coordinator should be appointed at the relief agency and a second coordinator located in the field to handle communications and details related to volunteers, including their supervision. Particularly important skills are language proficiency, technical expertise, teaching ability, and team work.

Before embarking on the project, volunteers should be oriented to the history of the country, its culture, important religious beliefs, the disaster and previous activities of the relief agency. A careful briefing of all components of the affected area's relief programme would be useful for the volunteers. The orientation recommended could occur in the home office country or on the site; it should not be left to chance nor assumed to be a minor part of the programme which can be absorbed without appropriate staffing arrangements.

Volunteers should be used only in situations which do not hinder the relief programme effectiveness and when the tasks they perform could not be carried out by available members of the local community.

A relief agency should take steps to ensure that evaluations of past relief operations are made available at the earliest stage to agency officials concerned in the planning and implementation of the disaster response strategy.

If it has no pre disaster in-country activity, the likelihood of an agency's mounting a successful post disaster operation is greatly reduced. Many projects that have failed in the past stem from this lack of an adequate base. Immediate relief operations are generally best handled by local survivors, the military, and the national government. An expatriate agency can fill in cracks but can also waste vast sums of money in this phase. False assumptions abound, one of the most common being the assumed need to bring in vast quantities of food, and another to mount massive inoculation programmes against cholera et al. These have been shown to be highly expensive and largely unnecessary.

The overall emphasis of all rehabilitation programmes should be to return to a state of "normality." Attempts are often made to upgrade standards of building (i.e., indigenous to concrete block housing) in the post disaster phoenix-from-ashes syndrome. Such projects have nearly always been unsuccessful. Projects that demonstrate improved, disaster-resistant construction techniques may be an appropriate model.

Any rehabilitation/reconstruction project must be considered for its developmental value. That is:

- Is it too big a step forward?
- Has it emerged from the victims themselves?
- Is it synchronized with other sectors under development (i.e., health/nutrition/ literacy/ housing)?

Often agencies approach rehabilitation/reconstruction operations with a relief mentality (i.e., free handouts, us-doing-it-for-them, "adoption" of villages). But this has proved to be a classic error whose normal legacy is either a dependency relationship with the donor/recipient, or dissatisfied aid recipients.

One of the key elements in a reconstruction programme after a disaster is equity. Unlike normal development work where there may be isolated housing projects, in postdisaster situations there are numerous (often competing) agencies. One "high grade" project which provides disproportionately greater assistance to a select group can cause intense local dissension.

The victims of most disasters are the very poor. The relief workers (whether local or expatriate) are almost always from an elevated social group. This state of affairs encourages false assumptions being made over local cultural values. Many projects of this nature have resulted in the imposition of middle class values or house forms or eating habits incompatible with the social needs of the victims' community.

The disaster acts as a scalpel—it exposes raw nerves of local problems such as poverty, administrative weakness, or entrenched patterns of local exploitation. Many donors adopt a "phoenix-from-ashes" approach when they seek to use the new construction to right these wrongs. In actuality the pre disaster problems will remain and only be compounded by the new problems that occur with reconstruction. This is not to say that the weaknesses in a society should not be addressed, but experience has shown that it is unrealistic to believe that major changes can occur merely as a result of a rebuilt village.

Relief officials are vulnerable to accepting unreal views of local problems. Local politicians and officials, to promote their own vested interests, will project all their problems as being induced by the disaster. However, it will gradually emerge that most post disaster problems were in existence prior to the disaster.

CHAPTER 9

The Tools and Methods of Disaster Management

Disaster management uses a variety of different tools, programmes, and methodologies to lessen the impact of a disaster and to provide the managers with means of guiding relief and reconstruction activities. This chapter is a three-part exploration of these tools and methods as they pertain to (1) prevention and mitigation, (2) preparedness, and (3) post-disaster management.

Tools and Methods Used In Prevention and Mitigation

The primary focus of disaster management should be to prevent disasters and/or to mitigate those that do happen. Disaster managers can generally use four sets of tools. They are:

- Hazard Management and Vulnerability Reduction
- Economic Diversification
- Political Intervention
- Public Awareness.

The first two apply exclusively to disasters caused by natural phenomena, while the latter are used to try to mitigate impending refugee situations.

As a general rule government, intergovernmental organizations, and the larger VOLAGS carry out hazard management programmes. This is because many of the hazard management activities involve vast areas and require large amounts of resources. At the community level, however, small agencies and communities can undertake a variety of activities with little outside assistance. Planting windbreaks and building flood embankments are examples of such activities.

The role of the disaster manager in hazard management is usually to insure that development plans and programmes incorporate hazard management activities. For example, a country's office of disaster preparedness may help make the various ministries aware of the flooding problem and may carry out studies in conjunction with other ministries. The actual management of a watershed to prevent or reduce flooding is usually the responsibility of river authorities, or of ministries of forests, agriculture, human settlements, and/or rural development. These activities are often carried out with the help of the central planning office and/or rural and urban planning departments.

The range of specific tools for mitigating environmental hazards are:

- Planning
- Building regulations, including zoning, building codes, performance standards, and improved urban design
- Strategic development or investment of sites and services
- Economic incentives
- Housing education, i.e., the training of home builders to improve the quality and performance of housing code encouragement, i.e., the use of building inspectors to advise and encourage homeowners to utilize disaster-resistant construction techniques (rather than simply to enforce codes)
- Financial incentives as an inducement to builders to use hazard-resistant construction techniques
- Insurance
- Environmental management, for example, reforestation and rangeland management in watersheds
- Immunization campaigns to reduce the threat of disease.

All the tools listed above require a technical understanding of the threats and the possible solutions. The selection of a particular set of approaches must be determined by the financial capacity of a government or PVO as well as by their administrative capacity. For example, the adoption of building codes would depend upon the capacity of the government to enforce compliance. In a case where rapid urbanization and small metropolitan budgets would not permit enforcement, housing education or code encouragement could be chosen as an alternative.

Several of these tools deserve more discussion in the context of disaster mitigation in the Third World.

Planning Strategies

Various strategies that can mitigate the impacts of hazards can be adopted through normal planning. Among these are:

- Adjusting normal development programmes to reduce losses. For example, certain varieties of crops that are more wind-or flood-resistant can often be introduced in areas prone to floods or cyclones.
- Economic diversification. In regions where the principal or sole source of income is threatened, planners should attempt to diversify the economy and introduce economic activities that are less vulnerable, or not as vulnerable to the same types of disaster.

Diversification is extremely important where economies are based on a single cash crop. Small island countries that depend on exporting bananas, palm oil, or other tropical agricultural products are vulnerable to extensive damage in a cyclone. Such countries could diversify into fishing, light manufacturing, or other activities, for example. Diversification will help protect the economy against natural disasters and also against unanticipated price fluctuations on the international market.

- Developing "disaster resistant" economic activities within a region. Some economic activities are relatively unaffected by certain types of disasters. For example, warehousing is more suitable than manufacturing for locating in flood plains. Coconut palms are more suitable than citrus or other fruit trees in cyclone-prone coastal areas. Efforts should be made to identify and to encourage the development of enterprises that are less vulnerable to the hazards.

Regulations

Planners can use three sets of regulatory controls for hazard management. These are land-use planning and zoning; building codes and performance standards; and land-use and building standards.

Conventional land-use controls regulate function, density, and location of activities, the rate of development, and limits of growth. "Zoning" may be defined as a division of land into districts or land-use zones; the prescription of regulations within these zones depends on how the zones are to be developed. Zoning ordinances are usually divided into broad land-use categories, such as agricultural, residential, industrial, and/or commercial uses. Sub-zones may include such designations as reforestation areas, range-land management zones, and watershed management zones.

Zoning has a broad function in the reduction of vulnerability, since vulnerable areas can be controlled or set aside for certain types of development. For example, a hazardous area can be zoned permanently for agricultural or recreational use, thus minimizing concentrations of a population or a built environment on this site.

Land-use controls and regulations can be an effective tool for reducing vulnerability, but they are not a universal cure. Controls must be relevant to local conditions and must be formulated with a realistic assessment of the actual risk.

Building codes are used to control the built environment within an area. Economic concerns often dictate that hazardous areas be developed. To offset the threat and mitigate potential damages, building codes can be formulated to guide construction so that buildings and other man-made structures are as safe as possible.

Building codes and land-use zoning are often criticized as being ineffective in less developed countries, since enforcement is difficult and most growth is unregulated. Furthermore, codes and zoning are considered "passive" regulatory instruments; their enforcement often creates an adversary system between the public and the government. If development occurs in an area where it is not permitted, governments are usually powerless to reverse the situation. Enforcement activities may give rise to corrupt inspection officials who institute a system of bribery to overlook nonconforming uses or structures.

Because of these criticisms, planners have recently proposed an alternative that appears more workable in many of the developing countries. This is known as performance standard zoning and building regulation. In this approach, flexible standards are developed and adopted. They permit a variety of uses and construction as long as certain basic, minimal standards of safety and health are met. The standards usually permit people to use a variety of approaches to attain the desired standard. Rather than strictly enforcing the standard, the government makes a commitment to provide technical and planning assistance to persons in order to enable them to reach the highest standard possible. This type of approach is called an "active" approach. While it may be more expensive, a higher degree of compliance can usually be attained. Furthermore, governments become advocates and advisors rather than adversaries.

Strategic Development or Investment

Planners are often able to encourage development away from hazardous areas by investing or creating a favorable environment for investment in less vulnerable regions or communities. This strategy is often difficult to implement in regional development. Most hazards are not site- or area-specific; they can threaten wide areas. For example, earthquake zones often extend for thousands of miles, and relocation of threatened settlements or enterprises is often not possible. Furthermore, hazards that occur infrequently are usually not considered in economic development planning.

Strategic investment has proven successful in agricultural sectors. For example, regional planning authorities in India have been successful in extending irrigation, land reclamation activities, and regional farm-to-market roads onto coastal plains that might otherwise have been developed with more intensive forms of economic activities. By developing the coastal plains with large, plantation agriculture relying on fewer laborers, the authorities have substantially mitigated human losses from hurricanes.

Economic Incentives

Governments are often able to extend a number of economic incentives to people and organizations in order to encourage development away from hazardous areas. Examples of incentives include provision of land, loans, grants, favorable credit, favorable taxation, technical assistance, or a combination of these.

In an effort to reduce human and agricultural losses, the government of Bangladesh recently initiated a programme to provide small plots of irrigated land to landless peasants; these persons normally worked as sharecroppers on hazardous floodplains in the lower Brahmaputra delta and on low-lying, offshore islands threatened by hurricanes and storm surges. Low-cost loans for initial land development were made available through cooperating private sector institutions, and relocation grants were provided by the government. Once people had arrived in the new areas, technical assistance for farming was provided by government agricultural extentionists.

Public Information and Education for Hazard Management

Effective hazard management requires an informed public, especially those at risk. In hazard management this is called public awareness. Public awareness campaigns disseminate information about the types of hazard, the effects of a hazard, the measures available to reduce the impact, and the actions to take when the hazard strikes.

Typical Public Awareness Activities include:

film and video programmes that illustrate and describe the hazard and the risk and demonstrate what can be done to prevent or mitigate losses radio programmes school curricula and booklets that include lessons and projects about hazard mitigation comic books (perhaps based on the films or video programmes) made available for general distribution posters placed around the community to act as a general reminder of the issues presentations on the subject made to public groups or private organizations (e.g., neighborhood councils) brochures and handouts distributed door-to-door or at public event, fairs, etc. features or articles in local media, especially periodicals.

It is crucial to promote disaster awareness in areas where risk and vulnerability are high and people are indifferent to potential hazards.

Public awareness activities can help motivate the public to initiate precautionary measures. Such activities can influence decision making at all levels. However, public awareness will not be successful unless it is continuous and highly visible.

A public awareness programme for disaster mitigation describes or demonstrates techniques that can be taken to keep a disaster from happening. These can include cultivating drought-resistant food crops, making structural improvements to buildings to withstand the forces of earthquakes or high winds, and siting buildings or agricultural land out of floodplains.

Public awareness is also an important disaster preparedness tool. Preparedness awareness activities are designed to inform the public about what individuals can and should do to protect themselves and their property. Disaster preparedness activities naturally vary with each type of disaster. In the case of high winds, people would be encouraged to board up windows, batten down loose objects, etc. In the case of flooding, evacuation routes would be identified for the public. If a communicable disease epidemic threatens, information about its mode of transmission and means of control would be important.

Timing for a public awareness programme in disaster preparedness depends on the type of disaster. For predictable and seasonal hazards such as flooding and high winds, a programme of public awareness should be initiated immediately before and during the season. For slow-onset disasters (e.g., drought), implementation should begin as soon as there are indicators of its development. For non predictable events (e.g., earthquakes), issues of preparedness need to be brought continuously to the public's consciousness.

Economic Mitigation

The purpose of economic mitigation is to reduce the disaster's impact on the economy and on the economic well-being of the disaster victims. This is done by strengthening those sectors of the economy that are particularly vulnerable to disasters, by diversifying the economy, by introducing or expanding "disaster-resistant" economic activities, and by spreading or relocating economic activities to less vulnerable areas so that not all the principal enterprises would be affected at the same time. Insurance or other economic risk-spreading activities are also possible.

Economic mitigation uses the same general methodology employed to reduce physical losses. Once hazard mapping has been completed, planners identify those sectors of the economy that are vulnerable to disasters. This is done by relating risk to economic activities or means of production. First, the key elements of the economy and those that are not particularly vulnerable to disaster are identified. Often this is not difficult, especially for countries that have one-crop economies or only a few industries that earn foreign currency. Every economic activity is examined to determine if a hazard could affect a significant portion of that activity. This analysis is conducted on both the macro and micro levels. In other words, even though a flood may not have a significant economic impact on a country as a whole, it may have a major impact on a community or region.

Economic vulnerability determinations should consider other critical activities and installations. Energy facilities and systems are of prime concern, as are transportation networks, fuel distribution facilities, road systems, and financial institutions. Even though the means of production may not be affected by a disaster, the disruption of transportation networks can make difficult the marketing or distribution of goods.

Economic diversification and insurance are the two primary economic mitigation measures. Diversification spreads the risk so that if a disaster occurs, the total losses in any one area or sector are acceptable. For many countries diversification can be a difficult choice. Small nations that are dependent upon one or two crops for their livelihood may find it politically and economically difficult to justify diversification simply on grounds of disaster mitigation. In this case, long-term development choices come into play. The decision may ultimately rest more on political or economical factors than on disaster mitigation strategies.

Insurance can play a major role in mitigating disaster losses. Unfortunately, there are too few programmes currently available for low-income persons in the developing countries, although new programmes and alternative insurance schemes are being developed.

In some cases, governments and large economic institutions have found alternative ways of providing insurance to low-income people. For example, cooperatives can often be insured even though individual farmers who are members of the cooperative cannot. If a disaster occurs, the insurance pays the cooperative, which in turn divides the proceeds of the insurance among its members.

The indirect effect of insurance is also important to consider. Disaster claims paid for large institutions, facilities, installations, or structures can infuse much needed cash into the local economy. This can have a spin-off effect reflected in increased jobs, increased purchases and orders for local suppliers, and other economic boosts to the area affected by a disaster. Thus, even if it is not possible to insure low-income families and their houses, farms or business, the objective of disaster management should be to insure the maximum number of larger economic activities.

Adjusting On-Going Development Activities

Adjustment to on-going development programmes is a major way to address disaster mitigation. Many development projects have the potential to reduce either physical or economic vulnerabilty of families and communities. For example, housing programmes can incorporate, often at little or no additional cost, a variety of disaster-resistant construction and planning techniques; unfortunately these measures are frequently overlooked because the development programme planners are not aware of disaster mitigation opportunities. Thus, an important function of disaster management is to review and adjust normal development programmes so that they help mitigate or prevent future disasters. Areas of particular interest are:

- Housing and urban development programmes (siting and construction)
- Establishment of new settlements
- Forestry projects
- Agricultural development projects land reclamation
- Rangeland management
- Diversification and expansion of the social support network

The level of disorganization that results from a disaster is an inverse function of the level of social organization of the community. Societies with an overlapping complex of social organizations, both formal and informal, can more easily absorb a disaster and more quickly respond. In Third World poor communities, the network of social organizations is usually minimal; as a consequence, a disaster can have a far greater impact on the poor community.

Diversification of a community's social structure is an important mitigation measure. For the most part this can best be accomplished through extending normal development work in one of three ways. The first is institution building. Local organizations that serve as a means of coping with disasters or providing support to disaster victims should be identified and strengthened. A conscious effort to increase the organizations, capacities and skills can enhance their abilities to deal with crises.

The second activity is to increase the number of coping mechanisms within the community. By developing formal institutions and linking these groups to outside resources, communities can establish vehicles for intervention and assistance.

The third activity is to broaden the scope of service of local groups and to encourage activities that promote cooperation among different elements or groups within the society. Such cooperation can reduce the social impact of a disaster.

By increasing self-sufficiency and reliance on internal resources, agencies improve the ability of local people to cope with a disaster. This can be a mitigating factor and can help to speed recovery.

Measures for Mitigating an Impending Refugee Crisis

Unfortunately, measures for mitigating refugee situations as they begin to occur are poorly developed and documented, and rather unsuccessful. The few measures that the international community has at its disposal are not well defined, and governments are often reluctant to exercise the ones that they do have. In the early 1980s, many humanitarian agencies began to talk of "early warning activities" and the development of political and humanitarian interventions that could possibly prevent or mitigate a crisis from escalating into a massive refugee situation. These discussions have thus far proven unfruitful, except to further emphasize the links between certain natural disasters and the political consequences that often follow-along with conflicts that lead to refugee migrations.

For refugee mitigation measures to be successful, a system of early warning must be in place to alert governments and humanitarian agencies of an impending crisis. The early warning would be based on indicators that a political situation could lead to armed conflict resulting in displaced persons and possibly in refugees seeking asylum in another country. Recent research has shown that a number of indicators can point to an impending crisis. Unfortunately, there is tremendous debate as to which interventions are then possible. The four most commonly discussed outside interventions are:

- **Political intervention by outside governments or intergovernmental organizations such as the United Nations.** Political interventions can range from military intervention to political or economic sanctions being taken against the country. Interventions are most often limited to expressions of concern by friendly nations.
- **Public opinion and moral persuasion.** Widespread public outcries against humanitarian abuses are considered to be the most effective tool for mitigating these abuses, although totalitarian governments have

shown a remarkable ability to ignore world-wide opinion in many cases. However, a major public outcry against a particular situation may influence outside governments to take political or economic sanctions that could lead to resolution or mitigation of the situation.

- **Linking aid to human rights policies.** One measure sometimes used by western democracies is that of making economic or development assistance dependent upon the observance of human rights standards. This policy, first introduced by the Carter administration in the late 1970s, had mixed results. Most observers attribute this to an unequal application of the policy due to geopolitical considerations. It is likely, however, that this approach will continue to be advocated as an alternative to direct political intervention.
- **Internal interventions.** Thus far, most mitigation measures that have been discussed are those actions taken by governments or intergovernmental organizations outside the country where the situation is developing. There is often little that disaster managers can do inside the country. The measures are generally limited to moral persuasion and trying to influence public opinion. These are examples of non-governmental organizations within a country helping to reduce tensions and alleviating some of the problems. For example, church organizations can often be effective mediators between parties in conflict. Relief organizations can frequently serve as a bridge between those seeking reconciliation. International organizations can often help reduce human rights abuses by placing large numbers of staff members in an area where abuses are occurring. These individuals serve as de facto observers and, by their presence, reduce human rights abuses. Nongovernmental organizations can often work in a partnership with the press to create a climate of accommodation and/or to help stem a growing crisis.

We must acknowledge, however, our minimal understanding of effective means for reducing a crisis that would create displaced persons or refugees. Agencies must understand that attempting to exercise these measures in a crisis may endanger their personnel.

Preparedness Tools

The most important preparedness tool is the disaster plan and its various components. Every organization that responds to a disaster should develop a plan that:

- Organizes the response
- Establishes an organizational structure for each phase of the disaster
- Establishes objectives, priorities, and goals for the organization
- Assesses resources

The development of the disaster plan permits disaster preparedness training, which is an equally important tool in preparedness.

Tools of Post-Disaster Management

A disaster manager uses a variety of tools to plan and manage disaster response. Most important of these are plans and procedures, policies, codes and standards, and standardized programmes or programme structures. The next four sections examine in detail these important tools.

Plans and Procedures

Plans and procedures are the most important tools of disaster management because they structure and guide emergency action. Plans are based on the premise that it is better to make your decisions long before a disaster strikes than in the aftermath of a disaster, when information is inaccurate and the situation is confusing and often unknown.

The Primary Types of Plans and Procedures are:

Disaster Plans. These include preparedness plans, such as warning and evacuation plans; sheltering plans; disaster and needs assessment plans; search-and-rescue plans; and emergency services operations plans. Disaster plans are prepared on the basis of known risks, estimated impact areas, and predicted needs.

Contingency Plans. Contingency plans are actions planned in anticipation that something unexpected might occur. For example, a government may determine that it can handle a disaster of a certain magnitude; it would then develop its plans accordingly. However, on the chance a larger magnitude disaster would outstrip its capacity to meet all the needs, a contingency plan for outside assistance might be developed.

Forward Planning. This planning term concerns the development of specific plans to meet an immediate emergency. Forward planning is usually based on an early warning of an impending threat (for example, a warning from a meteorological service that a cyclone is likely to strike a certain community, or information that large numbers of refugees might soon seek asylum in another country). Forward planning usually involves the pre-positioning of emergency supplies and the preparation of emergency response services and resources for action.

Standard Operating Procedures (SOPS). SOPs are developed within an organization to provide standard responses to anticipated situations. The objective of a standard procedure is to help make the response routine and to eliminate the need for a lengthy decision-making process. If certain criteria are met, the response is triggered automatically.

SOPs for specific disaster types in certain regions can often be compiled and presented in an emergency action manual. These manuals establish the tasks that must be carried out during each phase of an emergency and describe the procedure for accomplishing each in the proper sequence. They also structure the response so that everyone in the organization knows what is expected and at what point each event should happen. They also structure the response so that each succeeding activity builds upon previous actions.

Policies

In providing assistance to disaster victims, organizations often propose many differing approaches and programmes. Different approaches often result in unequitable or unequal provision of materials and services. This can cause problems for the host government and for organizations with long-term commitments to the disaster-affected area.

Uniform disaster policies are one way to avoid these problems. Such policies provide a mechanism for shaping disaster mitigation and vulnerability reduction efforts as well as emergency response and reconstruction. They also provide a basis upon which programmes can be coordinated, and in some cases, integrated.

Relief and reconstruction policies should ideally be set as part of the disaster preparedness process. However, if they do not exist at the time of a disaster, they should be established during the initial stages of emergency response.

Normally, the host government is responsible for the development and implementation of policies, but all major organizations, especially those that will be providing substantial relief aid, should participate in the process.

Policies should be straightforward and concise. Simplified, brief policies increase the chances of voluntary compliance. Policies must be flexible, permitting relief agencies to adapt their programmes to the specific requirements of the communities in which they are working. The objective of policies is to guide action, not to dictate the precise nature and approach of all agencies. It is also important to incorporate a consistent development philosophy and goals into disaster policies.

Codes and Standards

Codes and standards are a primary disaster management tool used to mitigate losses and control reconstruction activities in certain sectors. In the housing sector, building codes or performance standards are used to set the minimum acceptable safety levels for houses and buildings. Specific codes and performance standards are also developed for hospitals, lifelines (water, sanitation, electrical and transportation systems), and critical facilities (government installations, communications installations, etc.).

Programme standards are used to establish the minimum levels of assistance and support that should be provided to disaster victims. In famine and refugee relief programmes, feeding standards are set according to nutritional requirements. For example, 1800 calories per person per day is considered the minimum average standard for food supplied to refugees or famine victims as part of a daily ration. Other standards may be applied to water supply, material assistance and services offered by relief agencies.

Standards are normally set by disaster managers in each relief agency, but there is a growing trend internationally to develop common, uniform standards for many of the social and humanitarian services offered universally.

Standardized Programmes or Programme Structures

A relief agency will commonly develop a standard approach for responding to a recurring need in a specific type of disaster. Agencies trying a particular approach in one disaster will often develop a programme model that can be used in similar disasters in the same region. Some successful examples of standardized programmes are:

- Supplementary feeding programmes
- Shelter-to-housing programmes
- Housing education programmes
- Materials distribution programmes
- Food-for-work programmes.

Some agencies feel that a standard programme will not meet all the needs of victims in different situations; yet they recognize the need for standardizing the management of the disaster response. These agencies often develop standardized programme structures, which establish the key positions in an emergency programme, develop an organization chart, and provide the preliminary resources necessary to initiate programmes. Sufficient authority is delegated to the programme staff to enable them to design and implement a programme tailored to the particular needs of the affected community. Standardized programme structures are workable only if the personnel are experienced and trained disaster managers.

Programmes

Programmes are the principal tool of relief and reconstruction. In disaster management the term "programme" describes a set of activities carried out by an organization within a specified time, to accomplish predetermined objectives. A programme may be made up of two or more sub-units of activities generally called projects. In a pre-disaster environment programmes are usually long-term and have a small, full-time, professional staff. In a post-disaster environment, programmes are usually short-term, with limited budgets and a large temporary staff formed around a small core of professionals. Some common examples of programmes are housing reconstruction programmes, food aid programmes, preventive health programmes, and food-for-work programmes.

Public Awareness

Post-disaster programmes can have an enormous impact on a community. It is essential that they are planned to be effective and appropriate for the community, that they meet only the needs the community cannot meet for itself, and that the programme contribute to the development of the community. This frequently means that a programme's objectives should include the participation of the victims in the programme planning and design. The programme should have an educational component that will upgrade the level of knowledge in the community, to prevent or reduce a future disaster. The programme should also be tied to a long-range integrated development scheme.

Emergency Response

The primary purposes of public awareness activities during an emergency are to:

- Alert the public
- Instruct the public about the nature of the danger

(repeating information from the preparedness stage)

- Describe actions the public can take to protect their property and personal health, and warn people about what not to do
- Explain what to do for food, shelter, medicine, or how to obtain assistance in locating missing persons.

The duration of the emergency period and its time of occurrence are functions of the type of disaster. The emergency period for an earthquake is usually the first week after the event. The period for high wind storms begins 48 hours before the storm strikes and lasts for approximately a week to 10 days afterward, depending on flooding. Slow-onset disasters such as droughts have an emergency period that continues until lives are no longer in danger. The timeframe for the emergency period is typically very compressed, and public awareness messages are usually coordinated with the civil defense or national emergency organization. The most common media are the radio, newspapers, special printed bulletins, and posters.

Emergency public awareness programmes emphasize getting people to react. To do this, a well-planned and thoroughly developed system of getting timely messages out needs to be in place before the emergency occurs.

Awareness Activities for Recovery and Reconstruction

The general objective of public awareness during this period is to inform the victims how they, individually or collectively, can begin the process of recovery. Planning for these information activities should begin as soon as possible after the disaster.

The information needed includes advice about reconstruction of housing, sources of employment, or recovery in the agricultural sector. Recovery and reconstruction can and should begin immediately after the emergency has passed. Unfortunately this period is commonly characterized as one of false starts, mistakes, and waste. Accurate and timely information can help reduce delays.

As mentioned previously, the reconstruction period is often a long one, lasting several years for severe disasters. The public awareness programme needs to have a similarly long perspective, and reconstruction information needs to be kept in the forefront of the public's attention. It is also important to remember that reconstruction and recovery programmes should encourage mitigation of future disasters.

The information or educational materials used for the post-disaster reconstruction period will probably be developed specifically for the reconstruction project. The public awareness programme should be in support of and coordinated with reconstruction programmes and government policies.

Enabling Legislation

An important tool for governmental disaster agencies is legislation to give the agency the extra-ordinary authority and resources it needs to operate both before and after a disaster. Without this legislation many agencies find themselves unable to direct or coordinate vital activities. When lines of responsibility are unclear, needless duplication of assistance may occur in some areas while other areas receive little aid.

Letters or Memoranda of Agreement

Coordination between intergovernmental agencies and among some VOLAGS is often facilitated by formal letters or memoranda of agreement (or understanding). These define each agency's role in relation to the other and set out spheres of joint activity as well as areas of sole responsibility.

CHAPTER 10

Technologies of Disaster Management

Disaster managers should be familiar with certain technologies or sets of information used in disaster management. Among the more important are mapping, interpretation of aerial photography, communications, information management, logistics and computer applications, epidemiology and preventive medicine.

Mapping

Disaster management relies heavily on the use of maps and mapping techniques for control of disasters and for managing response. At a minimum, disaster managers must be familiar with a variety of different types of maps including topographic maps, land-use maps, hazard maps, geologic maps, vegetation maps, population distribution maps, seismic maps, and hurricane tracking maps. Disaster managers must know how to read maps. They must also know how to plot information accurately on the maps and how to interpret trends through map reading.

The introduction of microcomputers to disaster management will increase the use of computer-generated maps. Schematic maps generated through computer graphics are being used to provide updated information about disaster situations as they develop. For example, these maps can be used to monitor flooding and guide a disaster manager who must decide when to evacuate certain areas. By monitoring the stream flow and water level at an upstream location, a disaster manager can map the expected flood zone and predict threatened areas, the extent of the flooding, and areas that should be evacuated on a priority basis. The manager can likewise determine where to focus flood control activities.

Computer-generated maps are used in risk analysis, vulnerability analysis, evacuation planning, flood monitoring, damage assessment, and reconstruction planning.

Aerial Photography and Remote Sensing

Aerial photography used wisely is a valuable tool for disaster managers. It can be an expensive tool if misused. Disaster managers must know how to interpret aerial photography and how to apply it to both pre-disaster planning and post-disaster response activities. Possible uses of aerial photography include hazard analysis and mapping, vulnerability analysis and mapping, disaster assessment, reconstruction planning and management.

Remote sensing is the acquisition of information about a subject that is at a distance from the information-gathering device. Weather radar, weather satellite, seismographs, sono buoys, and videotape are examples of remote sensing systems. Aerial photography is a form of remote sensing, but in disaster management the term generally refers to the use of satellites with imaging systems that produce a computer-generated image resembling a photograph and with other electronic monitoring devices. For example, meteorological satellites track hurricanes by remote sensing. The "picture" of the hurricane is a computer-generated image made by the satellite's sensors.

The use of remote sensing in disaster management is increasing. Pre-disaster uses include risk analysis and mapping; disaster warning, especially cyclone tracking, drought monitoring, volcanoes, large-scale fires and agricultural production; and disaster assessment, especially flood monitoring and assessment, estimation of crop and forestry damages, and monitoring of land-use changes in the aftermath of a disaster. Meteorological satellites monitor weather patterns, detect and track storm systems, and monitor frosts and floods.

Communications

Electronic communications are an important technology of disaster management. Electronic communications are used for coordination and control, assessment, reporting, monitoring and scheduling logistics, and reunification and tracing separated families. A disaster manager must be familiar with communications equipment and their limitations. He or she must understand the effective use of communications networks both prior to and in the aftermath of a disaster.

A disaster manager must above all know how to communicate, what to communicate, and with whom to communicate, using the different technologies available. Electronic communications too often give disaster managers the impression that they can control a situation simply by communicating. The information that comes in through electronic communications can often overwhelm and/or misinform a manager. Thus the manager must be knowledgeable about the systems, but he or she must also know how to structure the communications systems. Structuring will allow rapid communication of vital information and accurate assessment of a developing situation.

Information Management

Disaster management is highly dependent on accurate information collection and interpretation. Disaster managers must therefore be familiar with how to collect, structure, and evaluate information in emergency situations. This is usually done by establishing an information management system. In recent years microcomputers have provided disaster managers with a new tool for structuring information and data and analyzing information patterns and trends. Microcomputers are now routinely used for programme planning, project scheduling and monitoring, management of logistics, damage assessment, casualty management, communications, and cost accounting management.

Logistics

Every disaster manager eventually becomes involved in logistics. Therefore, he or she must be familiar with basic logistics planning, inventory management, warehousing and stock control procedures, materials distribution methods, and accounting procedures. Logistics planning can include, for example, evaluating the capability and capacity to move supplies through the relief system identifying bottlenecks and developing alternate solutions. Logistics planning in a country struck by a disaster might include the estimation of the capacity to receive supplies at air and sea ports and to unload the supplies and reload into trucks. It might include determining the sufficiency of trucks of the right size and type, and the availability of parts and fuel for the trucks. Other considerations might be adequate roads to the site of relief, adequate warehouses at collection points, and a distribution system with the administrative capability and the methods to deliver the goods to the final point of utilization.

Epidemiology

Epidemiology is the branch of medicine that investigates the causes and control of epidemics. In relation to disasters epidemiology has come to mean the evaluation of all the causes of the occurrence or nonoccurrence of a disease (and more broadly of the death and injuries) resulting from a disaster. Epidemiologic surveillance after disasters and refugee crises includes identification of diseases to include in the surveillance; the collection, interpretation and utilization of data; laboratory diagnosis of samples; development of policies and plans for a public health programme; and establishment of a programme for the control of communicable disease. The last two points coincide with programmes in environmental health management and preventive medicine.

Additional Technologies of Disaster Management

Many disaster managers become involved with disasters through their specialized job skills or through their work in a specific sector of the government or economy. For example, an engineer in a department of public works may need to know the technologies of road repair after flooding or landslides and of bridge repair after an earthquake. The following are other examples of skills or technologies for which special training may enhance the individual's disaster management capabilities.

Agriculture, production, and food systems and technologies that relate to disasters identify disaster-resistant crops, methods of restoring crops damaged by disaster, restoration practices for soils damaged by a disaster, and alternative crops to replace quickly the losses from disasters. The last action will minimize dependence on outside food and economic aid.

Disaster assessment is the technique of evaluating the damage and the needs created by a disaster. Useful disaster management assessment identifies procedures for data collection and information dissemination; it also identifies priorities for relief assistance.

Refugee camp planning is essentially the discipline of town planning but with the added requirements of developing a human community environment under the crisis of emergency conditions. Such planning must take into account a volatile political reality and an uncertain future for the camp's residents. Additional aspects of refugee camp planning include the technologies of sanitation, security, circulation and transportation, water and food supply.

Meteorology is of use to disaster managers involved with warning, communication, search and rescue in areas subject to high winds, flooding, and even drought.

The following are additional specialized technologies that will further enhance a disaster manager's skills:

- personnel administration
- cost accounting
- government and nonprofit accounting
- critical path techniques
- general geology

Such a list could be much longer, but the purpose of this section is to bring to the attention of the reader the existence and the importance of these technologies. As stated at the outset of this course, a better trained and more knowledgeable disaster manager can contribute to more effective disaster services; he or she can ultimately reduce the disruption to society caused by natural and man-made disasters.

CHAPTER 11

Initial Emergency Operations

Warning and Evacuation

Public Warnings and Information

Although timely and accurate warnings coupled with an effective and efficient state of disaster preparedness make it possible to reduce the severity of the consequences of an event, no warning will be of any value unless it is acted upon. It is assumed that the emergency manager will take the necessary steps to disseminate the warning to the public, as well as setting into action other arrangements suitable to the nature of the individual case.

From the point of view of the public, the warning will be most effective if it is:

- issued by a person or organization in whom the public places confidence
- as specific as practicable in its information concerning the magnitude of the event, the place at which it is expected, and the time when it will occur susceptible to independent confirmation.

In emergencies which call for a response by the public, the degree of reliability which is accorded to the source of information and instruction is known to be a major factor in determining the quality and speed of the public's response. This is especially true in emergencies in which individuals cannot perceive the danger through their own senses. For example, impending industrial, or even radiation, accidents can be foreseen by the competent authorities, but to the layman's eye everything in the vicinity of the plants appears absolutely normal. The credibility of the source of public warnings about emergencies must be protected if mutual understanding and confidence are to be achieved: not only through positive action but also through avoidance of inappropriate actions, such as the issuance of inaccurate information, or tardy dissemination of accurate information.

Warnings should:

- Be *specific,* i.e. they should give specific local information about the threat which listeners can conveniently remember. Sirens, or the sound of church bells, for example, are non-specific and are easily imagined to be something else, or not very important, unless an adequate information and education campaign has already been effectively conducted;
- Be *urgent* (they should get people moving and not allow time for rationalizing the warning away); spell out the *consequences* of ignoring the warning (probably in explicit detail) so that people cannot casually dismiss them;
- Be absolutely clear about the *probability of occurrence,* since people tend to pay little attention to something labeled "a probability." One warning is usually not enough; they should be *continuous,* because people also need to be kept up-to-date about what is happening and to be given instructions appropriate to the development of the situation.

Different sectors of the endangered population may have to be given different messages. For example island or coastal territories subject to storms will have to take special precautions for the benefit of inshore and coastal boat traffic. Special consideration will be needed by the disabled, who may not be able to see or hear warnings, or act upon them if they do.

Planners must guard against the community's tendency not to want to believe that conditions will change for the worse. Some people may go further, and actively seek justification for ignoring warnings. When the "warning" cannot be truly specific, as in the case of a prediction of an earthquake, the issue of credibility becomes of even greater importance, particularly when there is no agreement between scientists about the accuracy of the prediction.

Community Warning Broadcast (Australia)

The following preplanned messages (Exhibits 11.1, 11.2, 11.3) are to be broadcast by radio/TV when a specific cyclone threatens. The frequency and timing of the broadcasts are decided at the time. Suggested texts are given which may require changes depending on specific circumstances.

Evacuation

How to Develop a Workable Evacuation Plan.

Introduction

Only in the last few years has the ability to warn populations of impending disasters become a reality. In the case of cyclone storms, advanced meteorology has provided the ability to track and forecast severe storms. Various monitoring devices have been developed which closely estimate the flood potential of a particular storm.

The ability to track and warn, however, must be complemented with the capability of effecting a timely evacuation of potentially threatened areas. By and large, this problem has been met in the industrialized countries. In those underdeveloped countries where communication links to remote settlements are still sporadic, evacuation is more difficult. Two problems exist. The first is the ability to adequately disseminate a warning of an impending disaster. The second is the problem of producing an evacuation once the warning has been received.

Problems in Evacuation

Five major problems, identified from past experience, must be overcome in order to effect a successful evacuation. These are:

- the psychological hesitancy of the potential victims to leave their homes and lands
- evacuees' fear of theft and confiscation if they leave their homes

- perception on the part of the potential victims that destinations for evacuation are unsafe
- the lack of adequate transport systems to move large numbers of people out of threatened areas
- organization of the evacuation in such a way as to reduce confusion and to prohibit "log jams" during the evacuation process.

Overcoming the Problems

The major methods currently seen as means of overcoming the problems listed above are:

- the development of a timely and accurate warning system
- identification of escape routes and dissemination of information to the potential victims as to where escape routes are
- establishment of a policy wherein everyone within a threatened area is required to evacuate when an evacuation order is given
- establishment of a policy wherein all traffic moves out of the area with no traffic or vehicles moving into the area to effect rescue (a one-way system)
- establishment, wherein possible, of a policy which requires evacuees to walk out of the endangered area.

Other approaches which have been suggested for helping overcome the problems include: the establishment of adequate support facilities in the peripheral areas and the development of a series of incentives to encourage compliance with the evacuation order. These incentives are described in the following section.

Information Needs In Order to Establish an Evacuation Plan
Establish the preconditions for evacuation.
Establish the preconditions for successful warning.
Establish the best point within the existing community structures (such as social support agencies) to have an impact.

Establish the differences between urban and rural households and their information and support needs.

Identify the types of organizations that should be most *effective* at distributing warning information.

Exhibit 11.1: Community Warning Broadcast— Message 1

COMMUNITY WARNING BROADCAST - MESSAGE 1

Message No. 1.

When broadcast: On "Cyclone Watch."

Frequency: At least six-hourly with every "Cyclone Watch" issue.

Suggested text: To be broadcast following the actual "Cyclone Watch" message.

This is a message from the Port Hedland Counter-Disaster Committee. Although the cyclone is not a direct threat to the community, certain precautionary measures should be taken at this time. These are:

Ensure your transistor radio and torch light are working. Keep spare fresh batteries.

Check your house roof is sound.

Clear property of loose items which could cause damage by being blown around in a high wind.

Collect tinned food, water containers, first-aid kit and medicines.

If a cyclone shelter is located on your property, ensure its readiness.

Fuel car.

Listen to your radio and television for further warnings.

It would be a kind gesture if you just checked with your immediate neighbours that they are aware of the situation.

Should you be new or a visitor in the area, ask around what you should do, or ring or for further information."

Exhibit 11.2: Community Warning Broadcast—Messages 2 and 3

COMMUNITY WARNING BROADCAST - MESSAGE 2

Message No. 2.

When broadcast: On "Cyclone Warning."

Frequency: At least three-hourly with every "Cyclone Warning" issue.

Suggested text: To be broadcast immediately following the actual "Cyclone Warning" broadcast.

This is a message from the Port Hediand Counter-Disaster Committee. Latest reports indicate that gale force winds caused by the cyclone off-shore are expected to hit Port Hediand within the next twenty-four hours. The cyclone could still change course, but just in case it does not, the following additional precautions should be taken:

Board or tape windows.

Store loose articles inside the house.

Lock up pets.

Fill water containers.

Store essential items (food, water, first-aid kit, etc.) in strongest part of house where you will ultimately locate yourself and family. This could be the cyclone shelter if you have one.

Do not wander out of the house, if posstole.

Listen to your radio/television for further warnings."

COMMUNITY WARNING BROADCAST - MESSAGE 3

Message No. 3.

When broadcast: On "Cyclone Warning" when it is imminent, the cyclone is going to strike

Port Hediand or parts thereof.

Frequency: At least hourly.

Suggested text: To be broadcast immediately following the hourly "Cyclone Warning"

broadcast.

This is a message from the Port Hediand Counter-Disaster Committee. The cyclone is going to hit us directly (or partially—whichever is applicable).

We advise that:

You stay indoors.

Shelter in the strongest part of the house, or your cyclone shelter if you have one.

Protect yourself with mattresses, blankets. Anchor yourself to a strong fixture (such as water pipes) or get under a strong table.

Beware the "calm eye." Remain indoors until you are advised that the cyclone has passed.

Listen in to your transistor radio for further information."

Exhibit 11..3: Community Warning Broadcast— Messages 4 and 5

COMMUNITY WARNING BROADCAST - MESSAGE 4

Message No. 4

When broadcast: On "Cyclone Watch/Waming" after impact and when cyclone is abating

with winds less than 70 kmph.

Frequency: Hourly.

Suggested text: To be broadcast immediately following the "Cyclone Watch/Warning" message.

This is a message from the Port Hedland Counter-Disaster Committee. The cyclone has passed over Port Hedland; however, the threat is not yet over. Survey and reconnaissance teams will be touring the area to assess damage and assistance required. You are advised to:

Remain indoors.

Listen in to your transistor radio for information and instructions.

Do not jam the telephone exchange with information calls.

If you are in need of emergency assistance (life and death matter), then ring or contact the survey and reconnaissance teams moving in your area.

Your local counter-disaster organization is doing everything possible to assist you."

COMMUNITY WARNING BROADCAST - MESSAGE 5

Message No. 5.

When broadcast: On "All Clear."

Frequency: To be decided at the time.

Suggested text:

This is a message from the Port Hedland Counter-Disaster Committee. This is the 'All Clear' signal. The cyclone has passed and is no more an immediate threat to Port Hedland. Should you require any assistance, you should report to the welfare centres located at:

(a) Cooke Point Youth Club.
Cooke Point, Port Hedland.

(b) Salvation Army Community Centre
Kennedy Street, South Hedland.

(c) Hedland High School Gymnasium,
South Hedland."

List of "To Do" Things in Case for Warning Message

- Establish the types of organizations that are viewed by the potential victims as the most *credible* for issuing a warning.
- Establish the point in the information distribution system at which further warning efforts will have little effect (the point of diminishing return).
- Establish the point at which the majority of people begin to take action and evacuate (in relation to the warning).
- Determine whether it is necessary for potential victims to receive more than one warning (from different sources).
- Establish what factors or constraints bear on a household making a decision to evacuate.
- Establish alternative evacuation plans necessitated by different types of disasters.
- Establish the target number necessary to reach in order to begin an evacuation movement (target numbers

should include separate target numbers for organizations and for numbers of families contacted).

- ❐ Determine if there are significant differences between information needs for land owners and tenants.
- ❐ Determine if practice or drill will play a successful part in achieving a successful evacuation.
- ❐ Determine what counter-instructions must be announced to the warning system if a warning is issued and a disaster *does not* occur.
- ❐ Determine the level of public comprehension and public education that is necessary to effect a successful evacuation.
- ❐ Determine how the perception of vulnerability will affect a family's response to a warning.
  - Develop generic family profiles that include the following information:
  - to what extent the family is separated at different times during the day
  - the relative travel time from home to school and work
  - where people say they would go if they were separated from other members of their family.

Major Lessons from Evacuation Studies

Evacuation plans must be based on family evacuation, not individual evacuation.

In warning systems, the more the contact between organizations during non-danger periods, the higher the likelihood the necessary warning can be communicated.

It has been found that warning data is best transmitted within the community through personal contact.

Evacuation Compliance

In an article on evacuation compliance, Perry, et al. suggest several additional incentives to increase the probability that threatened citizens will comply with a warning to evacuate. The concern here is with evacuations which are instituted prior to disaster impact, and involve a short-term absence of individuals from the threatened area. From this perspective, incentives to evacuate must be devised in advance—they represent the results of careful planning and *not* simply a response to some immediate threat to the community.

In approaching the problem of isolating evacuation incentives, we have chosen four issues from the warning response literature. The following merit careful consideration: temporary shelter, transportation, the role of the family, and security and property protection. Each of these issue areas will be examined in turn, reviewing the empirical basis for concern, and enumerating possible incentives that could be employed to encourage participation from potential evacuees.

Temporary Shelter

The nature of temporary shelter facilities for evacuees has been a source of considerable controversy among disaster researchers. It has been frequently reported that evacuees tend not to use public or planned shelters. However, even if many evacuees rely on other means of shelter (such as the homes of friends and relatives), there still remain at least some people who depend upon public shelters. Three general conclusions about evacuees' sheltering behavior are stated by Perry, et. al.:

When relatives are within a reasonable distance of the disaster site and some forewarning is possible, evacuees clearly prefer the homes of relatives as shelter. As the amount of forewarning decreases, people tend to seek shelter in the homes of friends. When forewarning is short and community preparedness is low, people tend to seek any known protection (such as high ground in floods) to gain enough time in which to evaluate the situation themselves.

The use of public shelter increases when community preparedness is high, when the entire community must be evacuated, and when the evacuees anticipate that the necessary period of absence will be long. Generally, though, public shelters seem to attract, even under the conditions described above, approximately one-fourth of the evacuees at a given site.

In communities where flooding is recurrent and a public consciousness is well developed, use of public shelter tends to be low, and evacuees primarily seek shelter in the homes of friends or relatives.

These points argue for the development and use of reasonably flexible shelter plans for evacuees, particularly in small communities which are part of or close to large metropolitan areas. It may be both cost effective and efficient to use temporary "shelter checkpoints" where evacuees could report to gain additional information about the evacuation effort and then *either* depart to stay with friends or relatives or be assigned to stay in a public facility. Such a plan would minimize the need for elaborate and extensive shelter facilities, permit evacuees their choice of arrangements, and allow for more careful accounting of those who do evacuate. Shelter checkpoints would aid in the operation of "family message centers" where concerned relatives or friends from outside the disaster area could quickly find data on evacuees. Note that a shelter checkpoint should be located in a "safe" area which could probably also be a public shelter. It should *not* be confused with "roadside checkpoints" which tend to snarl traffic and generally impede the flow of evacuees from the threatened area.

Another alternative to traditional public sheltering might involve distribution of information to residents of frequently threatened areas. The information would describe, in advance, safe areas and access routes to them for potential evacuees. Residents could then be instructed to make contact with friends or relatives in the safe area and arrange in advance for shelter in that home in the event of disaster impact. In this way as soon as an evacuation warning is issued, evacuees can depart for their host home.

An additional option involves the continued broadcasting of relevant information about the hazard and about evacuation procedures and destinations. The broadcast medium could be either radio or television (assuming the local availability of both) but it is important that the station be officially designated as the community's source for disaster information and that the public be aware of this designation. Establishing credibility of the warning source can be nearly as important as the information disseminated.

Transportation

When a warning message calls for evacuation, local officials are asking the public to undertake a specific adaptive action whose timing is critically important and where effective adaptation by the community depends upon a coordinated exodus. Under such circumstances the question of how best to handle the exit of citizens arises.

Numerous studies have indicated that evacuations can be more effectively accomplished if the people involved have a plan—a route of egress and safe destination. This also helps to minimize traffic coordination difficulties as well as the problem of families not evacuating or evacuating to an even more dangerous location. Thus an incentive to evacuate could center upon the establishment of safe destinations and plausible routes. Information about these could be distributed to citizens in advance as part of general community emergency preparation. Such a plan need not be elaborate and could be made available to the public in the form of a labeled map.

One alternative strategy minimizes the contingency supplies citizens must store until an evacuation is necessary. The strategy involves making detailed route and destination information available at the time of warning. In small communities, evacuation warnings could be issued on a face-to-face basis by designated emergency officials. These officials could explain the warning and hand residents a single sheet of paper with map and other appropriate instructions. This procedure would accelerate and simplify the evacuation process since details (to which the Individual could refer later) would be supplied in written form and only minimum vernal explanations would be needed. The amount of lead time and the number of personnel available for delivering warnings serve as limiting factors with this strategy.

Role of the Family

Families tend to evacuate as units; and the separation of family members often involves anxiety and attempts by evacuees to reunite families, sometimes by returning to previously evacuated areas. However, keeping families united is not necessarily as important as simply having information available regarding the whereabouts of family members. Therefore evacuation would be facilitated if some means were available through which families could communicate if separated. The establishment of "family message centers," where evacuees could obtain information on the whereabouts and condition of family members, could be included in evacuation shelter planning and may be seen as an incentive for compliance with an evacuation warning. Such a family message center—which would of course only maintain minimal records—could be structured around a shelter check-in system like those described in the previous section. It is possible that the message centers could be centralized and accessed by telephone: different shelters could call with name lists as available and people who wished to use the service but not the public shelters could report directly to the central location.

Security and Property Protection

While research has shown that looting is not a common occurrence in evacuated areas, it Is widely assumed by disaster researchers that if evacuees feel that their property will be safe from potential looters, they will be more likely to comply with an evacuation programme. Therefore, as part of an incentive programme, local communities could communicate the general nature of whatever official security measures will be undertaken lo the public. Such measures need not be elaborate; the purpose of communicating them Is to inform potential evacuees that some measures are being taken.

It may be worthwhile to incorporate community members into the protection process. This would involve assigning a few selected Individuals security duties within their own neighborhoods. These people would coordinate with local police departments and act much like auxiliary police personnel. Such a programme would appear to be particularly useful since it would free some police personnel for other work, reduce slightly the number of residents who would have to be evacuated simultaneously, and provide the "peace of mind" necessary. This would also help to convince the evacuees that they are a part of their own community protection plan—which enhances citizen participation in community preparedness plans.

Summary

This review of incentives to evacuate is meaningful largely in the context of planning for and managing the consequences of the impact of riverine floods. Many of these ideas should also apply to cyclone evacuations. Of course, incentives do not constitute an emergency plan. At best, they should be seen as suggestions for structuring some elements of a plan. Furthermore, the enumeration of Incentives presented here is meant to be suggestive rather than exhaustive. A primary objective of this section has been to underscore the importance of advance planning in coping with hazards.

The incentives described here are drawn from empirical research on (he public's performance under flood disaster conditions. It reflects the view that it Is important to build emergency planning around people's known reaction patterns. Too often emergency plans which are devised by administrators turn out to be based upon misconceptions of how people react and, therefore, create more difficulties than they solve. One must be caulioned, however, that although the data indicates that people say they would support the idea of various evacuation incentives examined here, the real test of evacuation Incentives lies in their implementation and in evaluating pilot programmes. In the final analysis, it is wise to develop emergency plans which guide and channel Citizen actions into complementary and productive protection behavior patterns.

Public Information in the Post disaster Phase

A disaster manager would be well advised to appoint, or to have seconded to the staff, an experienced public information/ press relations officer who can act as chief spokesperson during the relief operation. This person's duties will be directed to two different types of audience: members of the public who have to be addressed as a group, either generally or as subgroups (e.g., all teachers; all who live in a certain area; all business owners) media representatives.

This officer must be fully briefed not only on the progress of the operation itself but also on the implications of the events associated with it. If a state of emergency has been declared officially, then not only the fact but also its main effects must be described. The disaster may have disrupted certain facilities which people had earlier been advised to use: new instructions will be needed. If casualties have been heavy, people must be told to whom and where enquiries should be addressed.

The media representatives can of course be used to convey messages to the public, but they will also tend to be more demanding in their search for information which they can use to prepare their descriptive reports. Accuracy and frankness in the spokesperson's response to these queries will help to instill confidence in the emergency organization and at the same time help to counteract the rumors which usually abound at such times.

Requests for information which are received from individual members of the general public may be handled by the chief spokesperson's staff—who must naturally have been given a full briefing also - or referred to services more competent to deal with the *minutiae* of personal affairs. If services like the Red Cross Tracing Service, Citizens' Advice Bureau, legal aid centers, and local government offices are still operational, they will be of great assistance. For example, the question of casualties brings to the tore one point of information which always attracts attention: the number of dead. From the point of view of the disaster manager, the size of the death toll is almost irrelevant, for the chief concern is for the survivors. The numbers of dead are a social problem but create a minimal danger to public health. The spokesperson for the disaster manager must be able to say what arrangements are being made for recovery, identification, and disposal of the dead, and especially to reassure and advise those who may require proof of death for legal or other purposes. This last is a matter which will require particular attention in countries which depend on foreign tourists. If it is possible to do so, a casualty information bureau, linked to but separate from the emergency operations center, should be set up with its own communications which enquirers can use without interfering with emergency operations.

In order to avoid the usually disruptive presence of media representatives in an emergency operations center, it is desirable that an information center should be set up. This may be adjacent to the operations center itself, if the latter is located in a capital or other large city, with reasonable communications out to newsrooms, etc., or at some distance away—provided that there are also good communications between the operations and information centers.

Disaster managers must, then, be aware of what action they will need to take in the area of public information after a disaster-If the manager is to establish and maintain mutual understanding between his/her organization and the public, the public must receive accurate and authoritative information either from a single spokesperson or. at the very least (if different sources have to be tapped), from spokespersons whose several announcements are not only accurate and authoritative but also consistent and compatible.

Search and Rescue

This section, as with the preceding, refers to rapid-onset disasters and has little application to slow-onset disasters. The following section summarizes key information required to implement a search-and-rescue operation.

Search-and-Rescue Requirements in Disaster Situations

Search and rescue, often known by the acronym SAR, is the process of identifying the location of disaster victims that may be trapped or isolated and bringing them to safety and medical attention.

> In the aftermath of cyclones and floods, SAR usually includes locating stranded flood victims, who may be threatened by rising water, and either bringing them to safety or providing them with food and first aid until they can be evacuated or returned to their homes.
>
> In the aftermath of earthquakes, SAR normally focuses on locating people who are trapped and injured in collapsed buildings.

In recent years, searchers have been greatly aided by new technologies. These advances range from dogs that have been specially trained to find victims trapped beneath collapsed buildings to sophisticated radars and listening devices that can penetrate rubble to locate those who are trapped. (One device is so sensitive that it can detect heartbeats of victims who are partially buried.)

Rescuers have also received new tools for their work. Pneumatic tubes that can be inserted under the rubble, then inflated to lift debris so that rescuers can tunnel through to the victims, speed fescue of those trapped in large buildings. Heavy-lift, mobile cranes can be used to move heavy partitions and other materials that have collapsed. And for flood victims, helicopter rescue techniques are now highly advanced.

The SAR Process

Experience has shown that most search-and-rescue operations are conducted by *survivors* immediately after the threat is passed, and there is little that disaster management authorities can do to aid this process except in the preparedness phase when first aid and some rescue techniques can be demonstrated. Neighbors, working together, can usually locate and rescue survivors pinned in the rubble of low-rise structures such as houses and small shops. Pre-positioning of lightweight, hand-operated rescue equipment such as block-and-tackle, crow-bars, sledgehammers, etc., with neighborhood groups like the local Red Cross/Red Crescent chapters, police and fire brigades, can greatly aid the immediate rescue process.

After the victims that can be located quickly have been rescued, SAB turns to the more complicated and delicate task of locating survivors trapped in isolated locations or in more complex (and usually heavier) buildings. This type of rescue requires trained professional supervision (although the workers may be volunteers), the use of heavy equipment, and often the use of special detection equipment for locating people trapped under the debris. At this stage of the emergency, systematic search-and-rescue efforts are carried out, led by specially trained and equipped groups operating in close coordination with medical personnel. Organizations that typically have responsibility for SAR include fire brigades, civil defense SAR teams, the police and the military. In many countries, especially in Latin America, volunteer rescue brigades (often highly trained and well equipped) play a major role. In addition, government ministries with access to heavy equipment, especially Public Works, are often assigned major SAR responsibilities.

The SAR Sequence

The sequence of action that takes place in all search-and-rescue operations is called the "Five Fs." They can be summarized as: FIND them, FIX their location, FREE them, FEED them, FIRST AID.

"Find them" refers to the obvious first step of locating the survivors. This requires a systematic search process, making sure that, before searchers leave an area or a building, every possible location has been thoroughly checked and re-checked to ensure that there is no one left who needs assistance. It is especially important to search buildings where small children, especially infants, may have been because they often will not respond to calls. Buildings where the elderly reside should also be checked thoroughly because they often weaken more quickly than others and may not be able to signal or call out to searchers.

"Fix their location" refers to the practice of marking or recording the exact location of survivors. In the search process, there are usually victims that require more urgent attention than others, and some people may have to be temporarily left where they are until others have been reached or until the necessary equipment arrives to complete their rescue. In these cases, it is important that searchers clearly identify the locations of those who are awaiting rescue so that they will not be forgotten. Where people are trapped in buildings or under debris, someone should always be assigned to stay with them; people left alone after initial contact has been made often worry that they have been or will be forgotten, and may panic, in the case of isolated flood victims, searchers should make detailed notes on the survivors' locations and mark the spots on maps, If the search Is being conducted by aircraft, photos showing the location should be taken to aid the rescuers.

"Free them" refers to the most important step-freeing the survivors as soon as possible. In the case of victims trapped in structures, care must be taken not to injure them during the rescue process. If they are suspected of having sustained back injuries, trained first aid workers should be brought in to lift them from their position.

'Feed them' if people have been, or are going to be, trapped for a long period of time, they may need to be fed promptly. Fear, cool weather, rain and other factors can cause people to lose body heat, and lack of food and water will weaken even those with minor injuries. Once survivors have been located, they should be given food according to the following principles:

- Provide as much fluid as the victim is willing to drink
- Furnish electrolytes in a form (such as soups or oral rehydration solution-ORS) as close to a normal diet as possible provide foods that are high in caloric content, such as carbohydrates avoid giving alcohol as it will Increase the rate loss of body heat as much as possible, provide hot foods to help maintain body heal;
- There are a few exceptions. If a survivor has been injured in the abdomen, neck or head, or if injuries are likely to require major surgery that would necessitate general anesthesia, food should only be given on the advice of medical personnel.
- When feeding a trapped victim, the time nourishment is given should be recorded and given to medical authorities once the person is free.
- "First aid' is the immediate medical attention that is given to survivors throughout the rescue process and especially after they have been treed or rescued.

SAR Planning

Experience has shown that the most effective SAR actions are those that have been carried out on the basis of plans drawn up as part of an overall preparedness plan before the disaster strikes. Both pre- and post-disaster SAR plans follow certain basic patterns.

Search activities are divided into two phases, the identification phase and the search phase. During identification, SAR coordinators evaluate preliminary reports and identify areas or zones where the largest concentrations of people need help, then subdivide the search area into small areas that can be rapidly, but thoroughly, checked by search teams. (This is often done by dividing a map of the area into a grid of small squares. This is called a "search grid.")

During the search phase, search teams methodically move through the disaster area, checking each sub-area in sequence to identify the locations of survivors. If the survivors can be rescued quickly, search teams perform this task on the spot. If more sophisticated equipment is required, the needs are communicated back to the SAR coordinator. All buildings or areas must be double-checked during the search phase. As soon as each square has been double-checked and all survivors rescued, the grid is "dosed" and searchers move on to the next.

Rescue operations should be decentralized as much as possible. Local authorities should be given responsibility (and should be trained as part of overall disaster preparedness activities) to coordinate rescue efforts in their communities. Larger municipalities normally have sufficient equipment to initiate more complex rescues and must be relied upon as the first to respond.

Rescue operations after large-scale disasters must usually rely on volunteers tor a large part of the rescue team. Bearing this in mind, it is important to utilize the professional and trained rescue workers as team leaders to the greatest extent possible. Specialized rescue teams, such as those that use rescue dogs to locate buried victims, should be controlled by the central SAR coordinator.

Principles of SAR Planning

The following principles should be observed in planning a SAR operation:

- Search activities must be systematic and methodical.
- Searches should be redundant, i.e., double-check!!
- Responsibility for searches should be decentralized but coordinated.
- Responsibility for search-and-rescue coordination should be placed in departments of government that have access to heavy equipment, rescue apparatus, and their own internal communications (radio).
- Responsibility tor control of specialized rescue teams should be assigned to the central SAR coordinator in each municipality.
- As a general rule, police departments should not be assigned the role of coordinating SAR since they will

be needed for civil protection duties.

When a potential disaster can be forecast (e.g., flooding, cyclones) departments with equipment that may be needed for SAR should be instructed to position their equipment in or near suspected vulnerable areas if protected from damage.

Local groups, such as Red Cross/Red Crescent, can play a vital role in SAR. Rapid identification of the groups and a thorough briefing on sectors to search, identification ot techniques, etc., is mandatory before they are sent to the field. (Knowing their capabilities before a disaster will greatly enhance SAR planning and response.)

Planners should remember that there is no substitute for good footwork. While the newest technologies are extremely helpful, the vast majority of survivors are still found by rescuers responding to cries for help.

Content of Search Teams

There is no standard or model search team, but experience has shown that it is helpful to include certain people if they are available. Each team should include a person trained in first aid as *the* top priority. Next, a person should be assigned to keep a tog of the areas and buildings searched. Several members of the team should be assigned responsibility for remaining with victims that are traced in debris until more help arrives, and several persons should be assigned to act as messengers.

Summary

Even with the best planning, search and rescue is *never* perfect and is often very much an ad hoc process. The most important factor is for the search pattern to be methodical and systematic. The more planning, training and preparation that can be done before the disaster, the easier and less problematic SAR will be after the disaster.

See also Appendix B, "Emergency Rescue Training," a manual on search and rescue.

Disaster Assessment

Introduction: The Assessment of Survivors' Needs

Principle

The accurate assessment of survivors' needs is in the short term more important than a detailed assessment of damage to houses and property. Partial or inaccurate assessments of the human needs by assisting groups have been a frequent cause of past failure of relief efforts.

Common Failures of Assessment

One of the first responses to natural disaster is to estimate the extent of the damage. Assumptions are then made about the kind and scale of the survivors" needs. Specific failures in assessment occur in three categories:

Lack of familiarity of assessors with the local situation. A lack of knowledge of physical and economic conditions prior to the disaster often makes it difficult, if not impossible, to distinguish between disaster-related needs and pre-existing problems. Consequently, post disaster requirements may be overstated, attributing residual deficiencies to the disaster. Lack of familiarity with the local situation can also result in overlooking local resources, which may be extensive: social "coping mechanisms" which can assist in providing emergency shelter; material goods, including existing supplies of building products and tools stocked—in the normal course of events—within any large community; local skills and manpower which can be used for both emergency shelter and reconstruction; local agencies or institutions (e.g. cooperatives) capable of managing emergency response and reconstruction programmes.

Lack of understanding of appropriate techniques for damage and needs assessment. Conventional methods of data collection do not work in the chaotic conditions of the immediate postdisaster phase, and assessment techniques to measure survivors' needs have to draw the subtle, but vital, distinction between "needs" and "wants." However, information-gathering technology may not be appropriate to the technical level of the country being surveyed (data requiring computer analysis, for instance, is useless if a computer is not readily available either in time or locally).

Weak management of the assessment. Inappropriate assessments can be characterized by:

- The overestimation of needs by local or national officials in order to receive maximum assistance
- A higher priority placed on damage information than on estimates of basic human needs
- A tack of active participation by the surviving community (or even the surviving local administration) in the assessment of needs
- Confusion as to who has the responsibility for making the assessment problems of communicating the assessments of assisting groups lack of definition of the objectives of the assessment (for example, is the assessment of needs aimed at regenerating the self-help process in housing reconstruction, or is it aimed at providing emergency shelters before all other considerations?).

Defining Who Should Make the Assessment. The Problem of Authority and Information Needs

It is characteristic of all major disasters that too many regard it as their role to assess survivors' needs. There may be confusion within government departments about where this responsibility lies. Health, housing and emergency planning officials have all often regarded it as their particular task. In addition, groups such as the military frequently make their own assessments, as do voluntary organizations, representatives of International agencies, etc. They often do so either to suit their own views and operational policies, or as verification of official assessments which they may be inclined to distrust, or which may not be sufficiently detailed for their purposes.

Given this situation, if the government is to maintain full control it will be necessary tor assisting groups to accept ultimate governmental authority in the assessment of needs, as in all other relief matters. On the other hand, the government must recognize the value of assisting groups' advice on assessment, since many of these groups will probably have more experience of disaster impact than the government itself. Further, the government must be prepared to accept—where the assessment ot needs and damage is a task beyond its resources—to enter into a close working relationship with all assisting groups, and, from the information so collected, to act as the information clearinghouse.

Policy Guidelines Policies to AvoW

Encouraging a proliferation of independent assessments, without coordination or agreement on the sharing of information.

Requesting the assessment of needs from those without pre disaster knowledge of the locality.

Awaiting the results of damage surveys and subsequent vulnerability analyses before starting any reconstruction activities. Although damage surveys reveal the need for detailed vulnerability and risk analyses of various building types and sites, the evidence indicates that if such studies do not already exist, it is not advisable to wait for their completion before starting the reconstruction process—both should proceed in parallel, tor delays dissipate commitment and resources.

Isolating damage or structural surveys from the assessment of social, cultural, and economic needs.

Assuming that the assessment of needs and damage surveys can be undertaken after a disaster without first establishing a methodology for it.

Over-reliance on sophisticated technology, such as remote sensing or high altitude photographs, for damage surveys.

Policies to Adopt

The governmental body in charge of relief must allocate all roles as a matter of priority to those individuals or organizations best equipped to make the assessment. It is advisable for the assessment of needs to be undertaken by a mufti-disciplinary governmental team, covering public works, housing, sanitation, community development, relief, etc. The composition of the team will vary according to the type of disaster and local conditions. Although there may be extensive damage to housing, damage to the infrastructure and other sectors of the economy may be of equal, or greater, concern to the survivors.

Some members of the team should be familiar with the normal pattern of life in the affected area, so as not to confuse immediate emergency needs with the norm for the area. This is not an easy task in marginal or squatter settlements, where, for the most part, people subsist in a state of chronic shortages and need.

The assessment must be verifiable. Many assisting groups will be well experienced in disaster management, and will be quick to detect overestimations. Once assisting groups recognize the accuracy of the assessment, they will be less likely to insist on their own independent assessments. It is essential to capitalize on relief assistance for the medium to longer terms. There is an urgent need to transcend exclusive preoccupation with immediate relief needs, and to give more thought to reconstruction needs at the outset.

The First Step in Disaster Assessment

The first step in disaster assessment is the *situation assessment* {also known as *initial reconnaissance).* When an immediate estimate of the impact of a disaster is made, a situation assessment is normally earned out immediately to determine:

- The extent and nature of the disaster's principal effects
- Locations of critical need and number of people affected
- Directions for search and rescue
- The operating status of lifelines and critical facilities

The importance of an accurate disaster assessment cannot be overstated. A swift, accurate and credible assessment will enable programme planners to proceed expeditiously with programme plans. An assessment that is incomplete or inaccurate does not address major needs; it can provide misleading data and may lead to inappropriate relief efforts and costly delays.

Dissemination and Sharing of Assessment Information

The dissemination of assessment information to all interested parties must be assured. A possible means of information sharing might be the creation of a council of assisting groups working in the disaster area. The council could be structured with one agency responsible for liaison and acting as the information clearing-house. Whatever the means, it is essential that the information reaches the head of each force and is placed in the hands of staff capable of effectively interpreting it.

This is followed by a new assessment that classifies victims' needs as *immediate,* which usually concern health, life support, and safety, and *long-term,* which refer to housing and economic needs."

Damage Surveys" Survey Methods

The process of collecting the necessary information obviously cannot be a systematic family by family survey. Therefore some type of survey is essential to obtain usable data. However, natural disasters often reduce access to the stricken area by cutting lines of communication (rail, roads, bridges). The most useful survey method may include low-level reconnaissance flights. A trained observer can determine the geographic extent of the disaster area, the relative degree of damage at each location, the patterns of damage, and perhaps the patterns of the survivors' emergency response. The aerial survey can also be used to identify areas that are accessible by land for limited though more accurate ground assessments, and to identify those areas on which to concentrate relief efforts.

But it should be noted that although such a survey can help calculate Information such as the number of buildings damaged, it cannot, of course, provide information on damage invisible from the air (e.g. cracked adobe walls, weakened foundations, roofs nearing collapse, broken gas lines, etc.). For this reason, the data assembled must be assessed in conjunction with that collected by sample field surveys. Interviews with reliable eyewitnesses may also provide additional information of value.

Field Surveys

The field survey must be regarded as the most useful method of information collection, as opposed to aerial survey or sample interviews. Field surveys may be limited by the following factors:

Depending on local conditions and survey objectives, the cost can be high in money, time, and expertise.

The affected areas may be difficult to reach.

Cultural heterogeneity in the area to be studied may make it difficult to obtain useful data from sampling.

Interviews may distort the information, depending on the interviewer/interviewee relationship.

Field surveys require considerable local knowledge to distinguish damage from poor building techniques,

Cultural differences between the affected population and foreign or national experts may produce differences of understanding and therefore difficulties in designing appropriate reconstruction programmes.

Nevertheless, field surveys have some important advantages:

- They permit consultation with and observation of victims.
- They generally cost less than more sophisticated assessment methods, such as remote sensing.
- They use less sophisticated, and therefore more accessible, technologies and equipment than in aerial observation and remote sensing.
- They yield high volumes of information. In sudden disasters, data collection includes estimates of the number of injured people, types of Injury, number of deaths, availability of health facilities, medical and paramedical resources, locally available medical supplies, damage to water supply and waste-disposal systems, risk of communicable diseases, damage to lifeline systems and to physical structures. Field surveys are also particularly valuable for inventorying useful resources, such as building materials for temporary and permanent shelter, reusable debris, labor, building contractors, etc.
- They make it possible to generalize from relatively small samples, if adequate techniques are used.
- They permit the participation of local personnel who, after a short period of training, can conduct interviews and assist in other field survey tasks. Skilled personnel are needed, however, to plan, supervise, and analyze the collected data.

Assessment Information

Disaster assessment information that is gathered must be geared to the specific needs of the relief organization.

Identification of Users

Disaster assessment should be designed to collect information for specific users. In planning an assessment, the users can be identified (usually by sector or region) and they can help specify their information requirements. For example, health and medical organizations need certain types of information, whereas housing agencies have very different information needs. Each agency has specific information needs and general information is usually of little value.

Specifics of Situation Assessment

Role of Survivors in the Assessment of Needs

As has been stated, survivors must have a full and effective role in determining their emergency needs, especially shelter. This principle must be applied to the process of damage and needs assessment. In the event of a slowly developing disaster, such as drought, there is usually ample time to involve the affected population. In the immediate aftermath of a sudden disaster, when there is considerable damage and chaos, the immediate involvement of survivors in assessment may be inappropriate, at least until the initial rescue and relief operations have been organized.

Beyond the emergency period, however, survivors should begin to take an active role in the assessment of needs. The interview of key individuals within the community Is often considered the appropriate course of action. Forthistobe successful, the individuals interviewed must be well informed about the extent of damage and needs, but also willing and capable of providing information and fully representative of their community. Obviously, the more familiar the authorities and assisting groups are with the community, the more secure they will be in obtaining reliable information.

(For a complete discussion of disaster assessment objectives, techniques, uses, and options, see the University of Wisconsin-Madison Disaster Management Center textbook, Disaster Assessment)

CHAPTER 12

What is Effective Disaster Communication?

Objectives

Identifying media players and assigning them the right place in media management chart is the key to communicate effectively during a disaster. The chapter enables reader the to picture a typical corporate communications and pubic relations set-up which is geared for disaster communication.

It is almost universal experience that even the best of the public relations outfits in well-known and highly experienced companies have failed to mesure up to media expectations when disaster strikes. The Union Carbide, when confronted with the worst ever industrial accident at Bhopal over a decade ago, became almost paralysed to handle the media blast after the incident. The Exxon Valdez become an international scandal in hours without the company's corporate communication people having made a single move to stem public opinion. It is equally well-known that earnestness for honesty and helpfulness of a company facing a disaster often finds the right note of approval from the media, which many companies in the energy industry facing potential environmentally disastrous situations have experienced.

To react well and with force, the company should be fully trained in disaster communication management and it should understand the nuances of handling media during a disaster, which are vastly different from that in normal times.

The organisation should have a proper communications structure, trained personnel, infrastructure and a clear-cut management approved plan for handling media during a disaster. When disaster strikes, no one has the time to go back to books or call up their superiors. They have to act with their wits about and based on rigorous training hours they must have spent in the past.

The Organizational Structure

The corporate communication or public relations department of a company should have personnel trained in handling information and communication. At least one or more person, other than the head of the department, should have specialised media management capability. Media management involves complex and highly sensitive handling which only a trained person is capable of executing. The head of the department should also have media handling skills and should be capable of using this ability to conduct the affairs of the entire department.

Media skills by the required Department

Interacting with the media at all levels. This would involve the following:

- A continuously updated database of media organisations and individual media personnel with a focus on the area in which the company is involved, in this case energy sector.
- Special information and background profiling of each of the top publications and the specialised publications in the area of energy, oil exploration, etc.
- Special information and background profiling of the top personalities including the publishers, the owners, the editors and the chiefs of bureaus of the top news publications, television channels, etc.
- Highly developed infrastructure to help the media with all its needs.
- Capability of constantly updating and keeping in touch with all types of media.

Capability to conduct press conferences. This would involve the following:

- Ability to write clear and legible press releases.
- Ability to put together relevant information kits for the press conference.
- Ability to organise press conference at the appropriate venue to suit the occasion.
- Ability to manage the press of diverse background.
- Ability to facilitate press at the press conference.
- Follow-up with the newspapers, television channels, radio, etc.

Capability to produce or commission television news, documentaries and such other media. Functional research in the area of the company's business. This would involve the following:

- The research should be generic in nature and useful to the media at all levels.
- Research material that is easily retrievable.
- Collection of archival materials of relevance including text documents, photographs, graphic footages, multimedia backgrounders

Ability to conduct press tours

- Invite the right type of media for factory, plant or field visit.
- Ability to brief the press on the technical aspects of the industry.
- Ability to provide comforts during the entire tour.
- Follow-up.

The Organisational Chart

Public Relations Officer/Corporate communication head Media relations officers Photographers Multimedia specialists

Infrastructure

Disaster communication information could include the following:

1. Media Centre

(i) The centre should have a well equipped communication infrastructure including, telephones, computers with internet facility and provision for water and snacks.

(ii) A well stocked magazine/newspapers library for references.

2. Computers with internet for regular interaction with the press/media

3. Research support

While there is no specialised infrastructure needed for disaster management the entire media centre and other infrastructure of the organisation would be stretched to its limits during a disaster.

It pays to have company's internal guidelines for the media which may or may not be communicated to the media as such. These set of guidelines would act as a benchmark or touchstone to plan media management strategy. These set of guidelines could be circulated to all the members of the public relations department staff and also top management

General Guidelines for Press People

1. Call the company top management person or any other person connected with the company, whenever you come across any information relating to the company/ industry
2. Be precise as to what sort of information you want so that the company can provide you with an appropriate information source.
3. Be in touch with the corporate communications department for routine information.
4. Visit the company on occasions and make it a point to attend the annual press meets.
5. In case of any disaster involving the company make sure to contact the company first.
6. Even if you have precise information, it would pay to

get in touch with the corporate communications or PR department for backgrounders, faster contact options and additional experts to give further fillip to your story.

7. Always contact the following key media reponse personnel

(a) Television Crew Guidelines

In all cases, camera crews must first receive permission from the public relations or corporate communications office before taping or broadcasting on the company's property. Representatives from the office can help guide a video crew, including lighting and sound technicians, through the process of setting up a video shoot. They can help to determine where to set up and make the necessary arrangements involving the security officers. With prior notice, it can also be arranged for a camera crew to attend a medical procedure, tape a live event or conduct interviews. The more notice they receive, the better access they can provide.

(b) Radio Guidelines

The company can permit any of its officials to give radio interviews and other programmes. The radio stations, however, should verify with the company before broadcasting the work of any of the company personnel. The personnel, in turn, should always inform the company since the information may be sensitive in nature. The corporate communications department would assist in all manner to get interviews and other programmes recorded by the radio stations.

(c) Photography Guidelines

The public relations office would be happy to assist photographers in getting original shots of the company, its field level equipment, process, etc., whenever needed. The photographers, however, should first call and fix up a date and time for carrying out such shoots. One or more personnel of the PR department should be present compulsorily when such photoshoots are carried out. The company would, however, reserve the right to limit access to the photographers to any of the areas of the factory or premises which the company management may deem fit. The company should also stock photographs and provide the same to the media personnel, researchers and others needing such photographic material.

Disaster Communication Plan

The disaster communication plan would have a general basis and background for all organisations. However, for each, the response would be different and would be specific to the industry and as such the disaster response teams would also be different. The hierarchies, the structures, the decision making methods, the response time, the budgets, etc., would vary from company to company. Usually any disaster, if not handled properly means some sort of negative fallout on the company. Media response can be quick and decisive based on the extent of disaster, whether natural, manmade or otherwise.

One crucial point to remember in a disaster is to tell it all, tell it fast and tell the truth. If you do this you have done all you can to minimize the disaster.

When a situation arises that may possibly be a disaster the first thing you should do is contact your CEO and the chief of your public relations department. The sooner you get those two organizations involved the sooner you can implement this plan.

Disaster Communication Team

A disaster communication team should be put together. This team is essential to identify the actions that need to be taken. The team should be comprised of individuals who are key to the situation. It should include the CEO, the chief of public relations, the vice president, the senior manager from the division in charge of the area that was involved in the situation that led to the disaster, the safety and/or security officer, the organisation lawyer, and anyone else who might be able to shed some light on the situation such as eye witnesses.

The job of this team is to come up with a plan of action and decide who the spokesperson should be.

A copy of the management recall roster should be attached and should include cell phone numbers and contact details. As you will find out, a disaster is not always at the most convenient time and place. A complete management list is recommended as you never can tell who may be needed.

Once the disaster communication team is selected a list should be made of the people on the team and what each team member is responsible for.

The following points should be kept in mind while constituting a communication team:

- Only one individual should be designated as the primary spokesperson to represent the company, make official statements and answer media questions throughout the disaster.
- A back-up to the designated spokesperson should also be identified to fill the position in the event that the primary spokesperson is unavailable.
- In addition to the primary spokesperson and the back-up spokesperson, individuals who will serve as technical experts or advisors should be designated. These resources might include a financial expert, an engineer, a leader in the community or anyone whom the company deems necessary during a specific kind of disaster. This will require some brainstorming by the disaster communication team since what is needed may not always be apparent. There should be an authority or technical expert in every field who should be available to supplement the knowledge of the spokesperson.

In addition to the disaster communication team, the public relations or communications department should be supplemented with competent people who can answer phones and if required escort media. Having calls from the media answered promptly is essential. As soon as possible a prepared statement should be given to this staff. This statement should be something such as "Facts are still being gathered but there will be a press conference before 4:00; give me your name and number and I will call you back to let you know when."

One of the first responsibilities of the disaster communication team should be to determine the appropriate positioning or message to address the emergency.

This is where "Tell it all, tell it fast and tell the truth" begins.

It is always best to admit when a mistake has been made, and begin doing whatever is possible to re-establish credibility and confidence with internal and external audiences. This may be difficult for senior management to do, especially if the lawyers are involved since it is their job to minimize the eventual legal cost to the company. However, if you do some homework you will find that following the advice in the plan will minimize the legal costs. Many Public Relations case studies are made of issues where the lawyers had too much say in what was done and upper management didn't get involved from the beginning.

PR Agenda

The first and foremost goal is protecting the integrity and reputation of the company.

- Never try to lie, deny or hide your involvement.
- If you ignore the situation it will only get worse.
- Don't go beyond the brief given by your management.
- Don't prolong the press briefing.
- Provide information, photographs, quotes and sound bites adequately to the media, it is usually less information that makes media come back and dig for more.
- Don't let the lawyers make the decisions. While they are good intentioned it may cause the disaster to escalate.
- Don't mix official briefing of the stakeholders or even shareholders or government officials with that of media.
- Ditto for press visits. Take care to see that no unconnected government or other official teams are on the scene when the media team is visiting.
- Trust begets trust. Learn to trust the media and you would never regret.
- "Planting a story" or briefing media informally about the line you would accept them to take during any disaster can be disastrous.

Criteria for the Spokesperson, Back-up Spokesperson and Disaster Communication Expert

These persons should posses the following attributes:

Comfortable in front of a TV camera and with reporters.

Preferably: skilled in handling media; skilled in directing responses to another topic; skilled in identifying key points; able to speak without using jargon; respectful of the role of the reporter; knowledgeable about the organisation and the disaster at hand; able to establish credibility with the media; able to project confidence to the audience; suitable in regard to diction, appearance and charisma; sincere, straightforward and believable; accessible to the media and to internal communications personnel who will facilitate media interviews; able to remain calm in stressful situations.

In addition to the designated spokesperson and back¬up, it can be anticipated that other parties involved in the disaster—police, fire department, health officials, etc.—will also have a spokesperson. It is important to obtain the identity of that individual as early as possible so all statements and contacts with the media can be coordinated between the two individuals and their organisations/interests whenever possible.

Media Briefing

Select a place to be used as a media centre. It should be at some distance from offices of the disaster communication team, spokesperson and emergency operations centre to ensure that media is not in the middle of the action if it happens to take a wrong turn or has to pass by those offices or areas on the way to the restrooms. If there is a visual (a fire or rescue operation) don't make the media centre in such a remote site that mediapersons can't see what is going on because they may not show up and if they do you will lose their confidence and it may appear that something is suspicious.

Locations for interviews and press briefings should be decided by the disaster communications team.

Don't change the rules that have already been established for the media. If the media is currently required to be escorted then during a disaster also it should be escorted. These things should be considered and preparations made before – hand to find people who can escort media during a disaster. If there are special circumstances such as a safety hazard, that would require the media to be escorted it should be advised about it straight forward. Any change in the way the media is dealt with during a disaster may change the views of the reporters. It is important that they feel that you aren't trying to hide anything.

Reporters may want to speak to staff or at a school, to faculty or students who have been involved with or have been affected by the disaster. It is best to restrict all interviews to the primary spokesperson, back-up spokesperson or technical expert. Controlling the interview process is the key to managing a disaster.

However, remember that reporters have the right to interview anyone they want to and if they don't get the answers they want from you they will get them from their other sources. They are all after a scoop. They all want a different angle than the reporter standing next to them. They will try for that scoop from you. If there is a possibility to provide them with what they want, consider it very carefully. All media should be treated equally. What is given to one (such as access to an area effected by the disaster) should be available to all.

A disaster situation is always difficult when dealing with the media. Therefore, rehearsals are necessary to help the spokesperson prepare.

It is important, that the spokesperson, backup spokesperson and advisors, at the onset of the disaster, spend some time rehearsing prepared statements and answers to possible "tough" questions that may be asked by reporters. If possible, similar rehearsals should be conducted prior to each media interview, briefing or news conference. It is also important to anticipate and practice new questions as the story evolves.

It is better to over-prepare than to be surprised by the depth of questioning by the media. Be tough and be prepared.

The communications/public relations staff should prepare questions and answers for the practice sessions. These questions and answers should be for internal use only and not for distribution outside the organization.

Don't volunteer information regarding a question that hasn't been asked unless it is a point that the company wants to make.

Don't talk off the record.

Press Releases

If you don't communicate immediately, you lose your greatest opportunity to control events. Given is a sample news release that can be used with little or no preparation as your first news release).

Your first news release should include a minimum "the who, what, when and where of the situation".

You must give the facts that have been gathered from reliable sources and have been confirmed. Don't overreach and don't speculate. There is a limit to your role. To exceed that limit is a mistake. If you do nothing more than show concern for the public and for your employees in your first press interaction, you are already on the right track.

You must have a prepared statement on hand that can be used to make an initial general response to the media when knowledge about the disaster first becomes known on a widespread basis or by reporters.

As the disaster progresses and new information and facts become available, it is advisable to develop prepared statements to be made by the spokesperson at the onset of any media interview, briefing or news conference.

These prepared statements also can be read over the telephone to reporters who are not represented at news conferences or briefings but call to request information. The statement can also be sent by FAX or e-mail upon request.

Sample News Release

A (what happened) at (location) involving (who) occurred today at (time). The incident is under investigation and more information is forthcoming.

For instance:

An explosion at Terminal 24, Backbay Reclamation Gate of the Bombay Harbour occurred today at 7 a.m. The cause of the explosion and the extent of damage is still under assessment.

The media is being requested to assemble at the Harbour main conference room at 11.30 a.m. when some details of the explosion would be made available.

You could also add information, if it is available, such as the number of casualties known, up to a particular point of time or any other pertinent information available. Once again, this information should be definitive and not speculative, verify everything you say. This will help your credibility in the long run.

Press Kits

The press kit that is to be distributed at the press conference venue should be highly informative leaving little or no room for ambiguity. Whatever details that can be provided about the disaster along with pictures if any should be printed in the press release that is to be distributed at the news conference.

Information brochures or fact sheets about the company or the area in which the disaster has occurred are helpful in informing the reporters or anyone else seeking information about the company.

In some cases it might be necessary to create materials that explain technical systems or in-house procedures. If we explain how a technical system or in-house procedure works and point out where a breakdown occurred, there is less chance of a reporter interpreting the situation erroneously.

If one is not already in place a generic fact sheet about the company should be created and made available.

Always do whatever possible to make a complicated issue simple for reporters. If the disaster was caused by a piece of equipment consider bringing in a similar piece of equipment to show reporters. At the very least, provide a schematic or drawing. If you provide them with a visual, it may keep them from seeking one themselves. Try not to use the actual piece of equipment that failed since that is morbid and allows an opportunity to an over zealous reporter to do some yellow journalism. It may also be traumatic to the relatives of victims.

Checklist for Press Briefs:

- When preparing to give a speech.
- Use a full script with large type for easy reading. Leave wide margin for notes.
- Leave pages unstapled for easier handling at podium. Highlight and mark your script to guide delivery.
- Time the presentation to fit the programme schedule of the group to be addressed.
- Practice: Read it aloud using a mirror and tape recorder until it sounds like you are talking, not reading.
- Be sure you have the facts about your audience-size, contact person's name, facility, etc.
- Based on the audience and the presentation, determine what, equipments to use if any. If you are not familiar with the equipment, contact the communications department to arrange a briefing on how to use slide projectors, video players, or overhead equipment.
- When you arrive at your engagement,
- Be at least 15 minutes early.
- Check equipment in advance if possible.

Ensure:

- Slides are in correct order and clearly focused.
- Slide advance mechanism is convenient to use while speaking, or arrange for someone else to advance the slides.
- The lighting in the room is sufficient for the slides to be visible to the audience.
- The working condition of the microphone (whether it is free standing or lavaliere) before beginning.
- The lighting of the podium is sufficient for reading.
- The appropriateness of the type of room and size of crowd for the use of overhead equipment.
- The words/graphics are large enough for people to read.
- The planings of the overhead projector, screen, microphone and audience in the room should be ensured

While Speaking:

- Stand erect and facing the audience directly. Speak loudly, slowly and distinctly.
- Establish eye contact (or appear to do so) with audience from time to time.
- Stay within the allotted presentation time. When answering questions,
- Remain friendly, cool-headed and confident.
- Answer only the questions asked and do so as succinctly and clearly as possible.
- Remember that you do not always have to know everything. You can always say, "I will have to check that out for you, please see me after the meeting."
- Avoid allowing one person to dominate the questions by moving on: "Thank you for your interest. I'll be glad to talk to you about your concerns after the meeting. Right now let's see if anyone else has questions for the group."

When Finished with the Presentation:

Remain long enough to give individuals an opportunity to clear any doubts or make plans to visit the disaster site, arrange for interviews with any of your officials or simply say hello.

Effective follow-up along with availability on phone or on the main throughout the disaster is essential for better media response to the disaster.

CHAPTER 13

Methodology for Disaster Communication

Objectives

This chapter provides information about the different communication methods. It also familiarizes the readers with how much to inform the media and at what stage.

What and How Much to Inform

While different communication models are considered issues such as how much to inform, when should it be done, who should do it what is the accountability afterwards, who should be the audience what sort of impact assessment has to be made in order to make course correction etc. are to be considered. In this context one of the most crucial aspects of communication is to determine what exactly one should communicate depending upon the circumstances. This is on the basis that more information than necessary being provided during a disaster often would work against the very purpose of information dissemination leading the media to do negative reporting. For instance, during the entire period of Prestige disaster it was the Spanish government authorities rather, than the company which owned the vessel, who were reporting to the media owing to the complexity of ownership of the vessel and other associated problems. As a result, the media could get only the negative part of the story with no chance being offered to the company to defend itself unlike Exxon in the case of Valdez, the Ceylon refinery, Mobil, etc., who had had their say when they were caught in the web of a disaster.

Conversely, the companies themselves might decide in the interest of their own commercial and governance reasons to allow only that much and no more information relating to the disaster in which case the communication strategy should be so planned to avoid any reference to information that is needed to be withheld . In such a situation, the company would run the risk of a stray press reporter or two chancing upon the information withheld, in which case the stink that it would create would be far worse than the information being provided universally in the first place. The company and its communication team are the ultimate judges of the scope of information that should be provided.

LID (Limited Information Dissemination) Strategy

Information dissemination is characterised by one-way communication from the source to the audience, with limited contact between the two. It is a way to provide awareness and knowledge of say, the nature and extent of alcohol, tobacco and drug use, abuse and addiction and their effects on individuals, families and communities. Information dissemination also involves making others aware of available prevention programmes and services. Examples of activities conducted and methods used for this prevention strategy include (but are not limited to):

- Clearing house/information resource centres
- Resource directories
- Media campaigns
- Brochures
- Radio/television public service announcements
- Speaking engagements
- Health fairs
- Information lines/hotlines

Education involves two-way communication and is distinguished from the information dissemination strategy by interaction between an educator/facilitator and participants. Activities under this strategy aim to affect critical life and social skills, including decision-making, refusal skills, critical analysis (e.g., of media messages), and systematic judgment abilities. Examples of activities conducted and methods used for this prevention strategy include (but are not limited to):

- Classroom and/or small group sessions
- Parenting and family management classes
- Peer leader/helper programmes
- Education programmes for youth groups
- Mentoring programmes

The Main Communication Methods

Is there a clearly defined method of communication? For instance, is the speech the only way of communicating with other person(s)? It may not be, even the deaf and dumb have their own language besides.

Broadly, speech, signs, written communication, touch are the ways individuals communicate while the larger groups use all means except touch to communicate their views. The tools chosen to communicate would depend upon the kind of information being conveyed and it is purely contextual. For instance, an advertising agency may use a giant sized billboard to write three or four lines of ad copy which could easily have been written on a small sheet of paper and given to anyone.

Communication by media, takes the form of newspaper, electronic medium such as television, internet or radio among other things. Communicating with media is a different ball game. Apart from the human aspect of developing contact media men to communicate effectively, the corporate communication expert will have to employ all forms of communication to get his point across. From press releases, e-mail messages, ordinary letters to occasional chance meetings, press briefings, press conferences, interviews, plant visits and so on. The companies can use all forms of business communication methods to get their message to their audience be it media men or the shareholders. Radio, television, printed newspaper, magazines, CDs, websites, e-mails, intranet, are all communication media and methods to reach out to the target group.

Let us now look at the applicability of each method by identifying where it sits against each of the four dimensions and the media elements it is capable of employing.

Mass Media Effects

What are the mass media effects that a communication team should look for? Obvious first effect is impact that too a positive one. The greater the positive impact of communication the more satisfied the team is that their message has reached home. But to achieve that the group has to cross a number of cognitive and psychological barriers to communication using systematic scientific approach.

The mass communication research points that the message unless codified in the manner it would be understood would never have the kind of effect the propagator of the message intended.

Codification means packaging the message by assigning it different impact levels, sequencing its delivery and making sure that it reaches the right type of audience. The mass communication researchers, by analysing propaganda and information as two distinct forms of communication have arrived at the conclusion that while the same information—say the mass failure of crops owing to drought conditions—is provided in two different contexts, when used for propaganda it is better codified. The propagandist would take out information selectively, distil it and use it carefully to derive the preconceived results depending upon which side of the fence he sits, the ruling party or opposition. Otherwise, it is just information and information has no context, no full stops and no rules.

The social scientists would look at the same context from the consistency of cognition embedded in the information being conveyed. In simpler term, this means the information being provided should continue to carry the same meaning and not subject to interpretation which may lead to an opposite effect, like the propaganda example cited earlier.

The mass media theories are also concerned with how groups could be persuaded to carry the same opinion and how groups could be manipulated to take the same view. They are also concerned with the manner in which interpersonal communication could impact the group perception and understanding of a context. For instance, in the same instance cited earlier, the information about drought being conveyed to a group of newsmen by the government spokesman may have a different connotation in case the spokesman adopts the group interaction approach, and take questions from the newsmen. The intended effect of conveying the government view along with the information about the drought would then have been achieved.

Handling Mass Media

For effective mass media handling it is necessary to set

I. An agenda
II. Analyse the knowledge gaps
III. Draw up a media profile
IV. Fill out the knowledge gaps based on the media profile using appropriate communication tools

In the above, drawing up the media profile is the most tricky aspect which should be done based on the nature of the industry you are in and your perception of what media can do to your company and industry in case of any developments negative or otherwise.

The best way to prepare a media profile is to systematically track the newspapers and magazines you deal with, make a profile of the people who report your industry or company from these newspapers, keep a response sheet in each publication's context on the way it reacted to different contact attempts from the company and such other aspects. Also there is aneed to know the sort of information each newspaper is would be looking for and its knowledge levels based on your perception. If you are able to fill out such knowledge gaps you would have hit the jackpot.

CHAPTER 14
How Does Media Look at a Disaster?

This chapter deals with ways to get the best out of media and also to feel satisfied that media has reported fairly during a disaster. In the process, it explains what media really means, who drives it, what is its ethos, and how does it view any disaster

Character of Media

Before trying to understand the manner in which media looks at a disaster, it is important to understand what is the character of media, what influences its thinking, who calls the shots and why the media works the way it does.

Universally, media is independent and freedom loving, these being the factors most influential in the way media looks at an issue and reacts to it. Also media is a neutral observer rather than an active participant and as such it can be expected to remain uninfluenced by any happening. By this logic it should not come as a surprise or cause any abhorrence in the minds of anyone that the camera teams may capture the beating or even killing of people by police or a tyrannical government in the course of reporting an internal strife, a terrorist operation or a full-fledged war and not go to the rescue of the victims. In fact, such detached attachment is the reason for the mental and moral strength most reporters have to travel to the midst of a disaster at considerable personal risk and carry out news coverage. Dan Rather, the fiery managing editor of CBSL, interviewed the Iraqi leader Saddam

Hussain in the last week of February 2003 at the peak of the American led pressure for war against that country, at considerable personal risk. "My job is to present Saddam the way he is, it is for the viewer to decide how much to trust the Iraqi president or whether America is justified in pushing for a war against Iraq. If you ask me as a citizen of America I would go with the American President's views but as a journalist I have to be impartial."

Such attitude of impartiality that puts the profession above the personal views and opinions is what make a journalist think and act in a situation the way he does. Anyone dealing with the press should understand this fundamental trait of a journalist and react accordingly.

It has been emphasized again and again in this book that while dealing with media never tell a lie. Rather than telling a lie, choose which part of the truth you would like to be known and manage to keep the rest of it unspoken and disclose information only on persistent and knowledgeable questioning from the press. For instance, during a continuing disaster over an oil spill if you have conclusive evidence that the oil spill was caused by a mechanical failure which had remained not rectified despite log book entries continuously indicating the impending doom, then this fact needs to be kept away from the press until internal investigations of the reasons behind such negligence is have been carriedout. The mud-slinging that usually follows such premature disclosures often would distort truth and the real culprits behind such wanton acts of mismanagement would get away without punishment.

Media and its Ownership

Media, like most other things about it, is also peculiar the way its ownership and control are organized. Being fiercely independent, the reporters, going right up to the editor, are professionals by their own right and form a group. The editor is the one who is on the top followed by the news editor, the chief-of-news bureau or chief reporter who in turn controls a band of senior to most junior reporters. The lowest in the hierarchy is the cub reporter or reporter trainee and the highest is the editor.

The administrative and marketing setup of any media house is usually detached from that of the news sections to avoid any conflict of interest or any undue business influence over the independence of the reporters. The editor is the only point of contact between the media and the rest of the wings of the media house including that of the owners. Almost all the top newspapers of the world including the New York Times, Washington Post, The Times London, The Globe, the Indian Express, the Times of India, Hindustan Times, The Hindu, etc., are run on these lines.

When it comes to ownership of the media it often becomes a grey area. There are a number of examples of the proprietors themselves doubling up as editors and finding themselves difficult to put their media independence above their business interests.

Media and its Means

What Really is Media?

Mass media is print, broadcast, news agency, electronic and internet based. Within print, it is daily newspapers, the magazines, newsletters and specialized journals which dominate the scene.

The print medium is the most influential and crucial for disaster managers and the media men here are different from all other segments and the way they have to be handled would be quite different from the rest about which we would look at in the next section.

Print Comprises

1. Daily newspapers
2. Afternoon newspapers
3. Tabloids
4. Weekly newspapers
5. Occasional newspapers
6. Newsletters
7. Magazines (weekly, fortnightly and monthly)
8. Specialised journals

During a disaster, dailies are the most active and they send their reporters, photographers and editors to the scene depending upon the gravity of the disaster. The reporters are trained to look for news as it happens and they are expected to report the actual happenings of the day which may some time lead to the funny story reported in a section of American press. All reporters universally are trained to look for stories behind the scenes and are expected to be extremely curious and hard nosed. The hallmark of a good reporter is to ask persistent questions and clarify his doubts from all possible sources.

Dailies have different sections within the newspaper and the bigger the paper more are the sections. The dailies have sections that are national in character along with some purely local ones. Even regions within the city are these days catered to with specific sections printed and distributed in only that part of the city. These sections are also sometimes specialized dealing with industry, science, perspectives, edit page, etc. (more of this later).

The best examples of dailies in Indian context are Times of India and Hindustan Times with editions coming out of every major metropolis and a combined circulation exceeding a million each. The Hindu, Deccan Herald, Deccan Chronicle, Navbharat Times, etc., are other examples of regional dominance. A number of top ranking other language dailies led by Dainik Jagran, Punjab Kesari, Malayala Manorma, Dina Malar, Daily Thanthi among other papers influence public thinking.

Magazines are genre of their own and their style of reporting is vastly different from that of the dailies and the reporters that they employ are also different in their approach and characteristic in gathering news. The magazines, owing to the longer gestation period in tracking a story or event and reporting on it, are interested in greater details of the event or disaster, the people behind the scenes and the impact the disaster would be having on the company and the industry. Magazines are broadly divided into two categories, namely general and specialised. The general magazines report politics, social and environmental issues while the specialized magazines are usually the business magazines, education, science, the IT magazines, and other industry specific magazines. The best examples of magazines of general category in India are India Today, The Week, The Outlook and the specialised ones are mainly the business magazines, Business

India, Business Today, Business World, in the case of IT magazines, PC Quest, Dataquest, etc.

Journals are new phenomena to India though they are in small numbers. The journals are more research oriented and mostly cater to issues that may arise in the aftermath of a disaster (see unit 15). Journals, however, are highly influential in formulating long-term follow-up and policy formulation after any major disaster.

The print medium uses photographs widely and almost all the dailies and magazines have a strong photo section with highly trained photographers. Sometimes, the photographers themselves write their stories as photo journalists. An albatross making an unsuccessful attempt at flight with its wings dripping with oil told the story of the Prestige tanker accident off the Spanish coast far more eloquently than a thousand pages of written matter.

The broadcast media is mainly radio which is universal and still very strong in influencing public opinion through news and features. The dominance of radio is still strong owing to its mobility, versatility and experience. The introduction of FM channels in the urban cities has brought radio back into reckoning as a powerful entertainment and news medium on the wheels. All India Radio and its widest domestic and international short wave and medium wave broadcasting has been the longest standing example of radio broadcasting since Independence. From around six radio stations at the time of Independence, the AIR has grown to have 200 plus stations.

News agencies are perhaps the most influential but least understood component of the media. The news agencies are also the oldest form of organised news distribution in the country since the discovery of telegraph. The news agencies are fast and sharp and they usually alert most newspapers of a disaster or disaster through their "flashes" or one-line newsbreaks. The agencies, after breaking the news, continue to stick with it till the disaster peaks and gets sorted out, all the time updating the news almost on real time basis. The foremost examples of news agencies in India are the Press Trust of India and the United News of India. All other major global agencies like AP, UPI, etc. have offices in India. The international media presence in India is one of the largest in the world with practically the entire media universe being represented through their offices located in Delhi.

The electronic media comprises of television and documentaries.

Television channels are broadly be classified into two: news channels and entertainment channels.

News channels, either in English or any of the national or regional languages, are quite popular in the country. Channels like Aaj Tak, Zee News, Star News, Sun News, Punjabi News, Etv etc. are popular means of tracking and reporting news exclusively in the country.

BBC and CNN also have considerable influence on news coverage about India and are watched by a lot of people. The news channels, at times,follow a disaster "live" and report the events as they happen by sending camera crew right to the spot. Be it terrorist attack on Akshar Dham temple at Ahmedabad, more than a fortnight of ethnic strife in the same city prior to that, September 11 plane bombing of World Trade Centre in the US, continuing global standoff over the Iraqi president Saddam Hussain, the television news channels have been covering the events live as they happen.

The National Geographic and The Discovery are channels of a genre by themselves which specialise in documentary reporting of events and ongoing policy debates. Their detailed coverage of natural disasters and man-made ones like the sinking of the world's largest oil rig off Brazil coast are quite detailed and highly sensational.

The documentary medium, applicable to both the small screen and the big screen, is usually highly influential in presenting a disaster and affecting opinions. The Bhopal Gas tragedy aftermath, the Kargil war, the Enron power company collapse, the continuing opposition to the ambitious Narmada Dam project ....were issues on which powerful documentaries were taken out by influential film makers. These are being regularly screened on the small screen and also in select theatres and other focus groups forming and shaping opinion.

What Excites the Media

"News". Just one word. Media thrives on News. Though ironical it may sound, the bigger the tragedy, the better is the media interest, which sometimes makes people say that media, in fact, influences people to act far worse than they would have otherwise acted if there were no arc lights on them. While this may well be true in the case of certain diehard media savvy perpetrators of crime on mass scale, the media has almost always been able to influence opinion while reporting news as it happens.

Conversely, the bigger the scale of the tragedy, you have to be prepared for a fairly large share of media interest which also means with better preparation and anticipation you would be able to influence media to see your way while you handle your disaster communication challenge.

Taking a refinery fire as a mock case example we have made an attempt to explain what could possible excite media in such an event.

Event

A medium to high range fire broke out at 3.15 hrs at the Korelu Refineries off the Andaman coast owned by the state owned Indian Crude Petroleum Corporation. Though there are no immediate casualties, the on-duty personnel in the inner areas of the refinery are yet to be accounted for. Communication with the inner section has failed with the main operations control room being engulfed in the flames and the radio frequency transmitters going on the blink and the intercom system having failed completely. Since the fire has circled the vast inner core it is difficult to say at (5.00 hrs) how many are trapped in the area. The cause of the fire is not known.

An Analysis of the Disaster Communication Challenge

The story of the refinery fire cannot be kept away from the media or the neighouring area even for more than five minutes. Besides a call to the fire service would immediately be conveyed to the media as it invariably has "sources" within the fire service community who would alert them of the accident. The media has started converging on the scene along with the cameras.

Internally, since the people are trapped, the management is busy sorting out the issue and has no time for the PR department.

PR head lives near the refinery and therefore has not wasted a minute in arriving at the scene but there are no assistants at hand.

How the Challenge is Taken

Scenario I:

A well trained PR chief would handle the disaster without any problem as the training encompasses everyone. All players within the management and other stakeholders are already aware of the disaster communication challenges and as such they know how to react to the media. Besides, the manuals are already there, the drill is complete. In this scenario, the management would have already deputed one person to talk to the PR chief who in turn would already have a few volunteers from among the night shift workers. Rather than wait for the media to converge, the team would have already started contacting the media themselves to inform them of the accident and actually request them to come to the scene. By helping the media to assemble on a designated spot and take pictures of the raging fire, the PR head could actually buy time for the management to sort the bigger and more sensational issue of people trapped in fire.

Scenario II:

A not so well prepared PR chief with a management that is equally unaware of disaster communication challenges would let the press run all over the place trying to draw its own inferences and taking out pictures at its own will. The media would generally form a poor opinion about the way the refinery is run, a factor that would broadly influence the press coverage of disaster that may unfold as the disaster takes its course.

One can easily see why making a good impression and winning the trust of press is crucial particularly if one or more casualties are reported among the people trapped in the fire as the day wears on.

Even though the media may be excited about the event, it is responsible enough to present the facts as they are provided these are given in the best possible manner with least possible hindrance.

Who are you Dealing with in a Media Room

Typically your call to a local newspaper office or a call from it when a disaster like the refinery fire happens would come from the night duty reporter in the above example. The night duty reporter would invariably be calling up the police, the hospitals and the fire service throughout the night to find out any "interesting" newsworthy events. In all likelihood, your call to the fire office would invariably provide the local newspapers with the are ... to get at the "story".

The reporter in turn would alert his boss, the chief reporter, about the incident who in turn would begin the process of calling up specialist reporters and seniors drawing them out of their beds and asking them to reach the spot. You are likely to have three to four specialists before the day breaks from each newspaper. These people, already familiar with the oil industry, the refinery operation, similar accidents elsewhere, would start piecing together the story.

If it is electronic medium, similar procedure would follow except that along with the reporters a camera crew also would arrive on the scene.

As the drama unfolds, it would be the electronic media which would be excessively demanding especially if the event becomes live on their channel.

Given below is a rough menu you could have on your table to feed the media, not choppiest sandwiches, pastries—of which you have to have in plenty at the press room—but news.

CHAPTER 15

Benefits of Planning for Good Disaster Communication

Objectives

The obvious benefit of good disaster communication is a positive disposition of media towards your plight while you handle a sudden catastrophe. But for this there are a lot of dos and dont's and plenty of preparedness with which you will become familiar in this unit.

Good Disaster Communication Fallout

Good disaster communication certainly has its own benefits. There are dozens of examples of how bad handling of press and its needs during a disaster resulted in distorted reporting of the incident and continuing ill will of the media towards the company or institution. It is just not the press but general handling of the disaster and its aftermath would send the right or wrong signals about the professionalism and commitment of the institution to everyone including the media. For instance, when not long ago two planes, a commercial airliner belonging to Saudia with nearly 250 people on board and an incoming cargo aircraft of Kazhakastan Airways collided in mid air about 100 km from Delhi at Charki Dadri, it became an international event. But the way the agencies concerned handled the affair made the incident stay in the minds of the global airline disaster watchers as not just the worst passenger aviation disaster in history but also one of the worst disasters from the disaster handling point of view.

Following were the aspects that stood out starkly as the disaster continued and in its aftermath:

(a) Despite being merely 100 km away from the Delhi airport, there were no ambulances or paramedics even four hours after the crash.
(b) Until the next morning, no helicopter nor heavy duty trucks came to the crash site to assist in clearing the debris and collecting the bodies strewn all over nearly four square km area.
(c) There was hardly any light source save for the headlights of some local police jeeps and that of the mediamen who had assembled in strength.
(d) There were no functional methods of collecting the bodies, identifying them and preserving them for their relatives to identify. The local mortuary, some six km, had a single room in which the bodies were heaped up after they were ferried in friendly farmers' tractor trailers.
(e) The passengers' next of kin waiting at the airports on both ends at Delhi and Saudi were clueless about the number of passengers dead, nature of accident, etc.
(f) There were no spokesperson either at the disaster site or at the airport for hours after the incident.
(g) There were no arrangements to ferry the passengers/ relatives to the crash site.
(h) Those who attempted to drive to the area had no one to guide them on the way.
(i) There was no security or accountability of the belongings of the dead passengers.
(j) In the aftermath of the disaster, the bodies became putrefied owing to lack of preservation and delays in identifying them before being handed over to the relatives.
(k) There were no adequate arrangements made to encapsulate each body and transport them to their respective destinations. As a result, private couriers,

transporters, taxis had a field day fleecing the next of the kin.

(l) The media also was quite clueless as to what was happening either at the crash site where the passenger plane and the cargo plane had fallen with a few miles gap, or at the airport. There was no one to brief about the passenger manifest, the identity of the aircraft, the vintage of the aircraft, the details of the crew and such other information.

(m) There was sketchy information about the cause of the tragedy even weeks after it had happened when even the black box recovered from the scene of the accident.

(n) The media was never kept informed about the progress in investigation, the compensation being offered to the victims, the cause of the accident, the responsibility for the accident, who was bearing the expenses, who was paying the compensation if any, who paid the villagers whose lands were reduced to useless junk yards with burning aviation fuel, body parts and human remains strewn all over.

The above is one live example whose end has not yet been some five years after the accident.

The example also shows the gaps in communication and how these could be filled. Will and commitment on the part of the disaster managers, existence of a structure, hierarchy and plan of action in case of any such emergency, etc. are sine qua non for good disaster communication. Media briefing is just one part of such disaster management plan.

If you revisit the Charki Dadri air disaster you would find the following have been the hallmark for good disaster communication:

(i) Since Delhi with its vast array of army contingents, police, paramilitary, volunteer forces, Red Cross and other international agencies was just 100 km from the accident site the place should have been swarmed with these personnel within minutes of the disaster using helicopters, light planes and fast trucks to reach the spot.

(ii) A well honed disaster management plan would started working which should have placed trained personnel at the airport, look for all the relevant information, make sure that the passengers' relatives are informed as to the exact details and developments.

(iii) The plan should have also included transportation arrangements to evacuate bodies from the disaster site and ferrying of relatives to the site by organising adequate number of vehicles, personnel carriers, ambulances, etc.

(iv) Collapsible tents complete with cooling arrangements should have been flown within hours of the incident in which the bodies would have been laid out in dignity, not heaped roof high in a single room.

(v) A well honed system of media communication should have taken over to provide upto the minute update on the incident both at the crash site and also at the airport. A 24 emergency media response centre should have come up at the airport to answer all sorts of queries of the media including facilitation of media to reach the crash site.

(vi) In the aftermath of the disaster, the same emergency management plan should have made sure that the relatives of the effected have been notified, their claims verified and their compensation being provided without any delay.

(vii) The cause of the accident would have been propagated adequately leaving no ambiguity or doubts in the minds of those affected and also the general public.

Preparing for the Worst

Combined Approach

Effective preparation of the disaster response requires cooperation between heads of the organisations and their disaster management team and their staffs, and such cooperation is itself likely to be more effective if it is properly structured. Experience shows that the most effective structure starts with the establishment of a senior emergency co-ordinating group in which chief officers of the emergency services, the local representatives of the police, the hospitals, and leading mediamen are taking part.

Planning

The emergency management team would have a strong plan in place for any eventuality with the respective roles of each of the team members assigned. Periodic dry runs or mock emergency exercises have to be carried out to keep the team in high degree of alertness.

In addition to identifying and planning for specific hazards, the senior emergency coordinating group may want to give thought to particular issues which almost invariably cause difficulties during a major incident.

For Example:

(a) Organisations involved in the disaster response will need to have coordinated arrangements for dealing with the media. Plans in this area should be prepared and updated in conjunction with the network of regional COI offices and local media organisations -

(b) Communications have often proved to be inadequate in earlier disaster responses. The local authority and the emergency services will have their own chain of command and communications arrangements. There needs to be clear and effective communication between the various disciplines and identified lines of demarcation. It is important, at the planning stage, to identify the specific duties of each organisation and ensure that the organisations are able to communicate with one another.

(c) There is a need to ensure that different statutory services and authorities are not planning to use the same voluntary or commercial resources. To ensure that the voluntary sector's contribution is used to best effect, it is useful to review jointly plans for the use of the voluntary sector and to clarify with them how they fit into the contingency arrangements for responding to a disaster.

Disasters may well affect more than one local authority or police force area and the senior emergency coordinating group should include cross-boundary planning in its oversight of the combined response. Prior arrangements for mutual aid and compatibility with the plans and procedures of neighbours are essential for a truly effective response to a disaster which spans boundaries.

Plans should take account of the possible need to sustain the response at an unusually intensive level, possibly over an extended period. Arrangements involving mutual aid should be devised to enable the response to be maintained, whilst at the same time recognising the need to relieve those engaged in it. In addition, account should be taken of the extent to which business as usual has to carry on in parallel with the disaster response.

Joint Training and Exercising

Planning should be underpinned by training and exercising of both full and part-time staff, and the senior emergency coordinating group or its equivalent should oversee the multidisciplinary aspects of activities which, although interrelated, are considered in turn in the following paragraphs.

Awareness

This is a universal requirement for all who may be involved, however remotely, in the disaster response. They should be aware of the management framework within which the response is to be made. Attention should be drawn to the likely impact of disaster, to the numbers of victims which may result and to the consequences for anxious or bereaved relatives and friends and those responding, and to the potential scale and complexity of the response. For the emergency services awareness training will cover the more detailed aspects of joint operations at and around the disaster scene. For local authorities the emphasis will be on how departments can combine to support the emergency services in the initial stages of the response, to care for those affected, to maintain essential services and to prepare to recover from the disaster. Such training might also include elected members who will need to be aware of the role they may have to play in a disaster. For other services a general familiarity with the combined response will suffice.

Communications

The importance of joint planning in communications has already been mentioned. Subjects for training might include familiarisation with other organisations' documentation, terminology and call-out arrangements where these are different, and information technology and information access.

Media Relations

In addition to the training required in preparing for the media response, individual practical training in interview and news conference techniques should also be undertaken.

Exercising

The only way to ensure that plans be implemented effectively is to test them in regular exercises to assess the arrangements and then to update the plans in the light of experience. Exercises are an important management tool for informing and motivating personnel and giving confidence to those who may be required to respond in a disaster. They bring together those who may be involved with responding to an incident and they allow scrutiny of their responses under controlled conditions. Thus exercises should reflect reality as far as is practicable. They can establish and reinforce relationships between those taking part, often under stressful conditions. They bring people from different areas together to work as a team, to realise clear goals and to get to know and respect each other's strengths and weaknesses.

The clear benefits of exercising for any organisation are:

(a) Minimising the impact of disaster on people, the community and environment.

(b) Increasing significantly the likelihood of the organisation or business surviving a disaster, whatever its cause.

(c) Minimising interruption to business operation or service provision.

(d) Preserving and enhancing reputation.
(e) Minimising the social, political, legal and financial consequences of disaster.
(f) Identifying areas of an organisation's vulnerability.
(g) Training those who may be involved with responding to an emergency.

The support and commitment of senior management is crucial to the success of the exercise programme.

Exercises must not be seen in isolation but rather as part of a programme of learning and validating plans. Exercises should meet their aims and objectives in the most appropriate manner. Exercises need not necessarily be major undertakings in size, duration or involvement, but good exercises, whatever their format, can take a considerable amount of preparation and follow-up assessment.

Faith above Panic

Good disaster communication preparedness may yield results but practising psychologists tell us whether or not such exercises exist, when the disaster strikes people react and they react in unexpected but usually positive manner. In the Charki Dadri example itself, it was the unlettered villagers rather than trained emergency rescue staff who came on the scene first and without waiting for any directions started clearing and ferrying the bodies on their own tractor trailers to the nearest hospital. They also stood as vigilantes until the police came so that no belonging of the passengers should be looted or taken away by any miscreants.

By the same token group panic and irrational behaviour did not occur at the World Trade Centre on September 11, 2001. Instead the event created a sense of "we-ness" among those threatened, says Rutgers University sociology professor Lee Clarke. In his article, "Panic: Myth or Reality?", in the fall 2002 edition of Contexts magazine, he explains that 50 years of evidence on disasters and extreme situations shows that panic is rare, even when people feel "excessive fear."

Panic, according to the Oxford English Dictionary, is an "excessive feeling of alarm or fear...leading to extravagant or injudicious efforts" to secure personal safety. Panic usually refers to desperate acts of self-preservation that have the contrary effect of harming self and/or others.

People escaping from the destruction of the World Trade Centre didn't act like that; nor did they disregard the needs of others around them. Instead, they behaved civilly and cooperatively. As Clarke explains, "We now know that almost everyone ... survived if they were below the floors where the airplanes struck the buildings. That is in large measure because people did not become hysterical but instead facilitated a successful evacuation." Clarke maintains that human nature in disasters is more a function of social factors than individual self-interest; Hollywood's disaster movies show people running wildly from catastrophe, knocking over their own grandmothers to save themselves. "That's dead wrong," he says.

Clarke says that part of the panic myth is that people misinterpret their own, and others' behaviour as panic. "What they are usually reporting, though, are feelings of fear and not panic-stricken behaviour." He explains that the myth provides authorities (i.e., decision-makers, politicians, and administrators) with an easy explanation for complex events. Even when panic does happen—say at soccer matches— focusing on it usually detracts attention from more important factors such as official misconduct or police over-reaction. In addition, by using pacifying speech (e.g., "Everything is under control...") to allay public fear and hiding information from the public, spokespersons cultivate distrust at a time when nothing could be more important to public safety than trust of the information that authorities disseminate.

Citing three disasters in which panicky behaviour would be expected, Clarke shows that in dangerous situations (e.g., in a plane crash, a fire in a crowded hotel), people don't usually turn against their neighbours or forget moral commitments. People rarely lose control. The same message rises from the rubble of the World Trade Centre.

"The rules of behaviour in extreme situations," says Clarke, "are not much different from rules of ordinary life." As in normal situations, the rule is for people to help those next to them before they help themselves. Disasters are special situations but they are still social ones, and people generally follow community expectations. Furthermore, people don't usually lose their sense of community, even when every building has been destroyed. "The more consistent pattern in disasters is that people connect in the aftermath and work to rebuild their physical and cultural environments."

Clarke hopes that by dispelling the myth of hysteria or panic in cases of emergency, politicians and corporate managers will stop trying to pacify or placate the public during or after disasters. This sort of response to a mishap puts little trust in the public when there is bad news and it serves to deflect attention from more important issues. People, he says, usually respond well to bad news, if they see officials as trustworthy. Officials have to earn that trust by being straightforward about what they know and what they don't.

End Game

There is no such thing as a perfect world nor is there anything called a foolproof plan for good disaster communication. Also, it is nearly impossible to measure how a "good" plan would deliver vs a "bad" plan. There are also the human factors such as the general public disposition toward the organisation or individual responsible for the disaster happening, the political system, the scientific basis of the disaster and such other considerations that change the way we look at the end results. Even though the NASA is being upbraided for the latest in the series of the space disasters involving the aged space shuttle Columbia killing all the seven crew including an Indian American Kalpana Chawla, even the worst critic would give allowance for the possible limitations of scientific endeavours. Most would rather, than criticise NASA, look for clues for correcting the shuttle systems, test procedures, accident prevention methods rather than lament about what is obviously an irreplaceable loss.

Learning, then becomes the issue. Learning from disasters is a crucial element in the disaster communication managers' workbook.

Any disaster would teach the following home truths:

(i) However well you are prepared you cannot avoid a disaster occurring next time around!

(ii) How badly your well trained team fared!
(iii) If you did not have a trained team at least you have an excuse!
(iv) You will never be able to justify your emergency management budget!
(v) How well or badly media reacted to your disaster!
(vi) How to further fill out knowledge gaps about managing a disaster?
(vii) What sort of training would be needed based on observed inadequacies?

Planning always avoids panic and it helps manage a situation better, utilise resources to the best and generally keep everyone from getting tense. The bigger the disaster, better you are if you are reasonably well planned. The unit goes on to say how this is done, how good disaster communicaiton can be mounted and what would be the fallout of it. The preparation begins by antincipating the worst so that simpler things can be handled with elan. Also there are various ways of overcoming panic, one of which is faith on yourself, your systems, processes, soundness of your planning, etc. The end game is the way disaster is handled and communicated.

CHAPTER 16
Disaster Communication Cases

The objective of this chapter is to present real life cases where the media response of each of the institution during the disaster that they faced is indicated. Their experience is expected to provide useful lessons to the student of communication.

OIL REFINERY FIRE AT STATEN ISLAND, NEW YORK

Date: February 21 2003

Place: Staten Island, New York

Nature of disaster: Blast at Oil Refinery

Company involved: Exxon Mobil

Collateral damage: Being assessed, may run into millions of US dollars

Background

The explosion in the oil refinery area occurred when a barge containing one lakh barrels of unleaded gasoline was being offloaded at the 200 acre storage facility, which holds petroleum products including gasoline and heating oil. The blaze contained mainly in water and was confined to two barges, one that exploded and that was nearby. The barge that exploded sank almost immediately with the other barge catching fire. The fire was expected to spread to other barges and move on to the billions of litres of oil stored in the vast refinery establishment.

The explosion that could be heard for miles occurred at the edge of Port Mobil Terminal near the outer bridge crossing that links the island to New Jersey. The proximity of the twin metropolises of New Jersey and New York exposed over a million people to the hazards of oil burning smoke and other forms of pollution.

Disaster Management and Communication: The Exxon Mobil team very quickly put together a team led by its spokesperson Prema Nair to speak to the media and apprise them of the accident. The city Mayor Micheal Bloomberg also arrived on the scene and was at hand to brief the media. The normal drill of media briefing was gone through practically from the start of the disaster.

The following is the brief anthology of steps taken:

1. Quick appraisal of the nature of accident.
2. Detailed information gathering exercise undertaken within seconds after the explosion occurred.
3. The media briefing exercise began almost under the hour.
4. Temporary flight restrictions were imposed on all overflying aircraft barring them from approaching almost two miles of the explosion site.
5. Coast guard put together six boats and a helicopter to prevent anyone from approaching the island from the Arthur Kill waterway, the primary entrance for the port of Newark.
6. Damage assessment work commenced.

PRESTIGE OIL SPILL

Date: 13-11-2002
Place: Galicia, Spain
Nature of disaster: Breaking up of oil tanker Prestige
Company involved: Liberian company called Mare International
Collateral damage: 30,000 tonnes, of oil spill

Background

A Bahamas flagged oil tanker broke up off the Spanish coast of Galicia with 70,000 tonnes of oil of which half spilt almost immediately. The stricken vessel, owned by a complex group of companies and operated by dubious set of people dragged itself for miles before breaking up and going down. The oil spill hitting the beach with full import, life on the sleepy shores has become nightmarish for the Galicia fishermen. The ecosystem has been thoroughly wrecked.

Anthology of Steps Taken

The Spanish coast guards swung in to action almost immediately and isolated the beaches. They tried to put up floating bulwarks against the spilling oil, even though it was quite late for any action. The beaches had already been soaked and the rich flora and fauna totally devastated.

The captain of the ship was arrested and summons were sent out for the owners, some of whom are still to be arrested. The identity of the ship showed that there was a complex ownership of the ship and its transactions were shrouded in mystery. For the media the Prestige oil spill was a continuing story of not just a straightforward environmental disaster but a story that spoke of sleeze, bribery, maritime skull duggary and sheer opportunism of a handful of selfish ship owners.

The most obvious victims of the disaster were Europe's seabirds. They are among the first animals affected by oil, and the easiest to spot. About 3,000 dead or oil-covered birds have been found so far. Conservationists have begun releasing cleaned birds at sea south of Lisbon.

Following the sinking of Prestige, WWF called for a four-point plan of action to be put in place to help prevent future maritime disasters.

The plan focuses on regulating shipping, in particular in vulnerable marine areas. Actions include:

- Conducting analysis to identify areas believed to be particularly sensitive and vulnerable to shipping;
- Designating, through the International Maritime Organisation (IMO), those sites that qualify as Particularly Sensitive Sea Areas or PSSAs;
- Introducing and enforcing strict regulations tailored for each PSSA including banning single-hull vessels in these areas; identifying areas to be avoided or

recommended routes; requiring experienced pilots on board when ships have to pass through these areas; or requiring mandatory reporting as ships transit sensitive areas; and

- Improving maintenance and inspection globally of all vessels, but particularly those single hulled-vessels approaching their decommissioning age.

"It is high time to stop lamenting incidents like the Prestige, and start using the tools that already exist to protect fragile marine habitats," said Dr Simon Cripps, Director of WWF's Endangered Seas Programme.

WWF would also like to see more careful consideration given to the routes that ships carrying dangerous and toxic material are allowed to take. The Prestige was carrying a heavy industrial fuel oil for use in power plants, which is one of the worst possible types of oil to spill.

"Because this oil is so thick and viscous it is difficult to disperse and is likely to have a more severe long-term impact than lighter oil types. This sort of cargo should never be allowed in or near sensitive or protected marine areas," Dr Cripps added.

It is also crucial to develop a more effective global management agreement to ensure ships are rigorously inspected for seaworthiness. WWF believes that the measures that the EU is bringing into place with regard to EU controls on tanker inspections need to be applied globally — both by port states and flag states—in terms of increasing both the level and frequency of inspections.

"Three main factors affecting the risk of shipping disasters are the design of ships, the maintenance of ships and the controls on where ships can go. If you get one of these things wrong you can have a disaster on your hands. It seems that in the case of the Prestige, all three factors had a role in what went wrong," said Dr Cripps.

Exxon Valdez Oil Spill

Date: March 24, 1989

Place: Valdez Prince William Sound, off Alaska

Nature of disaster: Oil tanker breaking up

Company involved: Exxon Mobil

Collateral damage: 11 million gallons of oil spilt, 13 years down the disaster continues

Background

On March 24, 1989, an oil tanker belonging to Exxon carrying about 11 million gallons of North Slope crude oil broke up at Prince William Sound less than 30 miles from Valdez, the city after which the tanker had been named. The ship ran aground on Bligh Reef after leaving the designated tanker lanes because of earlier reports of icebergs in the area. The accident resulted in massive oil spill and one of the most visible and highly debated oil disasters ever. Ironically the Exxon oil spill has also gone down in the history of communication studies of the world as the worst public relations disaster seen from the colossal punitive damages levied on the company for its apparent lack of concern to the plight of fishermen and others in the initial days of the disaster.

The Exxon spill could have been averted by stronger prevention practices and more vigilant government oversight. Better response planning in advance could have lessened the impacts of the spill.

Birds, beaches and otters were oiled and people in the region suffered psychological and economic harm. In some cases, the ill effects of the spill linger even today.

On March 24, 1999, the following assessment of the Exxon Valdez spill emerged from the Prince William Sound Regional Citizens' Advisory Council:

"The Exxon Valdez oil spill was not simply a freak accident. While Exxon Corp. was immediately responsible, other factors were also at work. The oil industry, government agencies, elected officials and the citizens of Alaska share responsibility for the complacency that allowed the spill to occur and failed to ensure a prompt, effective cleanup.

- The oil industry failed to maintain adequate systems for preventing and responding to oil spills.
- Regulatory agencies failed to protect public resources because of ineffective or inadequate oversight.
- State and federal elected officials failed to pass laws strong enough to protect the environment and give regulatory agencies the funds they needed to protect public resources.
- Except for a few outspoken local citizens, most Alaskans simply failed to pay attention.

If anybody questions the importance of focusing on the financial consequences in disaster communications, consider what the lack of disaster communications cost Exxon in addition to the damage to its reputation as a leading oil company. The costs of the cleanup were approximately $1 billion, but Exxon was forced by the courts in Alaska to pay an additional $3 billion as compensatory and punitive damages. One can only speculate on how much less the punitive damages would have been if Exxon had expressed any empathy in the initial days after the accident to the fishermen, local citizens and millions of TV viewers who were appalled and outraged by the damage done to Prince William Sound.

Anthology of Steps Taken

Though belatedly, Exxon, one of world's largest oil refining companies, took steps to stem the damage.

It spruced up its communications team and launched a massive public contact programme which still continues.

The company set aside funds for the Exxon valdez rehabilitation trust which has become a full fledged institution helping the cause of environment.

OIL INSTALLATION FIRES AT COLOMBO, SRI LANKA

Date: 20 October 1985
Place: Sri Lanka
Nature of disaster: Oil installation fire
Company involved : Ceylon Petroleum Corporation Refinery

Background

Terrorists attacked the Ceylon Petroleum Corporation refinery and oil storage installations in Colombo in the early hours of October 20 causing several deaths and massive fires in the storage areas. Fires of this magnitude had not taken place in Sri Lanka previously and the assistance of fire fighters with experience in fighting oil fires had to be obtained from India.

The fires were accompanied by the deposition of oil which was reported by the media to have formed layers around 0.5 metres thick in some places. Some of the oil passed by way of canals and a major river in the sea. Other immediately visible impacts included those on market, gardens in nearby areas.

The Ceylon Institute of Scientific and Industrial Research (CISIR) issued a preliminary report on some aspects of the incident which may be of environmental significance. Based on information supplied by the Ceylon Petroleum Corporation (CPC), the crude and refined products presumed destroyed in a two to be day period were 39,000 tonnes of crude oil, 35,000 tonnes of diesel and 5000 tonnes of kerosene. Taking into account the sulphur contents of the oil products destroyed it was estimated that the oxides of sulphur produced during the fires could have been around 1690 tonnes (when calculated as sulphur dioxide). As regards oxides of nitrogen (calculated as nitrogen dioxide) the total produced could have been around 780 tonnes (including that resulting from the reaction of gaseous nitrogen with oxygen at high temperatures).

A significant proportion of these acidic oxides is expected to have been returned to earth with the rain which accompanied the conflagration.

This experience in Sri Lanka was followed by reports in the media a few days later of an oil fire in Indonesia due to a refinery being struck by lightning. These two incidents have caused further uneasiness among environmentalists in Sri Lanka regarding a proposal to locate a giant refinery cum power plant near Hambantota on the south coast of Sri Lanka. The project is proposed to be located not too far from extremely wildlife-rich areas including feeding grounds of flamingos and other waterfowl and beaches frequented by marine turtles for egg laying. The Yala wildlife sanctuary is also located on the south coast. Some of the coral reefs of Sri Lanka may be eventually impacted by oil.

Brief anthology of steps taken:

1. The fire was brought under control almost one week later with the help of experts from India.
2. Media was briefed immediately after the terrorist attack and the media briefings by the government continued throughout the disaster.
3. The entire area around the refinery was evacuated and sanitized.
4. Environmental impact study was made.
5. Environmental protection plan was put in place.

SYDNEY HARBOUR OIL SPILL

Date: 3rd August 1999
Place: Sydney Harbour
Nature of Disaster: Oil spill Company involved: Shell

Background

Located in Greenwich in Sydney Harbour, Australia, Shell's Gore Bay Terminal is a receiving and storage facility which provides all of the crude oil for Shell's Clyde refinery in Sydney. The terminal, which has been operated by Shell since it was opened in 1901, receives between 85 and 100 ships a year. Ships offload about four million tonnes of crude oil and other petroleum products which are transferred to Clyde by underground pipeline. The Clyde refinery supplies 50 per cent of New South Wales' (NSW) fuel market and represents about one-third of Shell's oil products business in Australia.

On the evening of Tuesday 3 August 1999, the Italian oil tanker "Laura D'Amato" was discharging its crude oil cargo at Shell's Gore Bay Terminal in Sydney. For reasons unknown at the time, 300 tonnes of oil was spilled into the harbour at 6.25pm. The spill seriously threatened Shell's reputation and business. Mishandled, the disaster could ruin stakeholder relations and encourage the government to stop commercial shipping in Sydney Harbour. A halt on shipping would directly affect Shell's Gore Bay terminal and Clyde refinery which supplies fifty per cent of New South Wales' fuel requirements.

One hour after the spill occurred, Shell Australia's External Affairs team had assembled and begun executing the disaster communication plan. Twenty four hour coverage was provided by the team for the first three days following the spill.

Media

Shell held a press conference at the site only three hours after the spill was first discovered. The first media release was widely distributed shortly afterwards. A series of six media releases followed over the next two days as the disaster developed. Background information sheets on Gore Bay Terminal and Shell's shipping operations were also sent to all media. Shell spokespeople were proactively offered for radio and television interviews, media briefings, one-to-one phone conversations and personal interviews throughout the disaster.

Government

Shell staff contacted senior advisers for the relevant ministers and government departments on the night of the spill. The next day, personal briefings by Shell senior management were instigated, including a briefing for the NSW Premier by Shell's CEO. Follow-up letters with additional background information were sent to all government officials contacted. Shell also initiated the offer to co-operate fully with a government inquiry.

Stakeholders

A personal letter from the Gore Bay Terminal manager was hand-delivered to local residents before dawn on August 4. Three follow-up letterbox drops were organised over the next week. Non-Government Organisations (NGOs) were contacted by phone to discuss the spill.

Employees

An e-mail to all Shell Australia staff was distributed at 3 a.m. on the night of the spill, so employees were updated as soon as they arrived at work the next day. Follow-up voice mail messages and e-mails were sent to all staff informing them of developments over the next week. After the oil spill cleanup, a letter of appreciation was sent to all employees and contractors involved.

General Public and Customers

Additional staff was employed at Shell's Clyde refinery to handle the increased number of switchboard calls from the general public. Shell's customer service centre was fully briefed on how to respond to oil spill queries from customers. All media releases were posted on Shell's Internet website. The media releases web page received 300 per cent more hits in August than the normal monthly average.

Shell received widespread praise on its response to the disaster. There was no discernible impact on sales during the disaster, long-term business damage was avoided and Shell's reputation with stakeholders was actually enhanced.

Support from the local community was immense. Many residents and local groups openly praised Shell's involvement and relationship with them. After the disaster, Shell recorded higher than average attendance at the community consultation committee meetings and the next Gore Bay Terminal open day.

During and after the disaster, the NSW Premier Bob Carr announced that Sydney is, and will continue to be, a working harbour that allows commercial shipping traffic. He ruled out closing Sydney Harbour either permanently or temporarily and said moving Gore Bay Terminal was not an option. Today, Gore Bay continues to operate as a receiving and storage facility for Shell.

Anthology of steps taken

1. Media briefing started almost immediately after the disaster occurred.
2. Stakeholders communication plan put in place.
3. All forms of media were used to disseminate information.
4. A special web page was created to communicate the developments.
5. The stakeholders, including the media, were addressed personally through a letter by the company.
6. Shell has put in place a permanent plan to keep the stakeholders fully informed about Gore Bay.

CHAPTER 17
Relief Work After a Disaster

This chapter deals with disaster follow-up management. Disaster may have ended but picking up the scraps, understanding how the disaster happened in the first place, sequencing the post-disaster management process, continuing to be in touch with the media to contain negative after-effects of the disaster are the hallmark of good disaster follow-up management.

Debriefing After Disaster

When a disaster happens everybody's concentration is to bring it to an early end with every conceivable resource being put into place. The Australian Bush fires are a good example of how not just the governmental machinery but even the whole towns and villages rise up to the occasion to beat out the fire, pour tonnes of water from helicopters and stationary trucks or simply take up the thick underbrush and start beating the flames. Thousands of young men, women and even school kids join the frenzy with a single aim of stopping the fire on its tracks. Similarly, when floods swept through Europe unexpectedly last monsoon, many who would never have stepped out into a puddle, leave alone help out in bunding swirling waters, were out in strength to fight the flood waters from inundating public buildings in the streets of Italy, Rome, Turkey, parts of France, Germany... Disaster brings people together as nothing else would.

However, after the disaster is over the people disperse, and hardly anyone accepts the responsibility for anything gone haywire. An effective follow-up plan is essential in order not only to continue to support the disaster management plan but also be able to fix responsibilities and also encourage those who had done commendable work when the disaster was underway.

Debriefing is essential to find out whether the disaster management plan actually worked. This is important since in the post follow-up period, the plan need to be looked at again and based on the learnings from the disaster it should be modified to suit the new conditions.

Debriefing should be detailed and thorough even though it need not actually involve each and every member of the disaster management team. It is enough if the leadership, from among the disaster management group, is able to explain the experiences.

The checklist to be used for the debriefing should include the following:

Debriefing Checklist

1. A brief description of what actually happened.
2. Was there enough help from all quarters while the disaster continued
3. Was the disaster management plan working?
4. Did every member of the team carry out his assigned roles?
5. If there were glitches name the specific area or person they related to were.
6. Was there enough material and managerial help?
7. How should have the media reacted?

The leader of the disaster management team should have his own checklist which should have the following components among other things.

Debriefing the Leader

1. Did the disaster management plan work?
2. Where were the glaring glitches?
3. Was there cooperation from the team members?
4. How did media react to the disaster?
5. What are the steps needed for disaster follow-up?
6. What should be managerial priorities?

Disaster and War

Often disaster management experts compare a sudden major disaster to a war as both happen with little advance warning and both result in major havoc in terms of material and human lives. However, there are fundamental differences any disaster, man-made or otherwise, and war as combat is always preplanned to such an extent with the help of modern technology that it is possible to predict accurately the kind of causalties and material losses that may result from any planned military strike. In the case of the American stand off against Iraq the US Generals had planned accurately the extent of destruction and planned the following restructuring of economy in finest details, including the names of companies that would be given the rehabilitation contracts.

A very large and significant disaster, such as a terror attack, flash-floods, landslide, mining accident, poisonous gas attack, bush fires, etc., has the following effects on people:

1. Everyone is benumbed.
2. Mind gets befuddled and even the most ordinary chores become highly burdensome.
3. A certain tendency of helplessness is seen.
4. Reflexes are often seen at the lowest ebb.
5. Morale is significantly down.

Interestingly, disaster management experts studying the phenomena for years are now able to distinguish the psychological and psychosomatic effects of disaster on people who are affected by it. They are now distinguishing the different sets of people involved with the disaster and are able to classify the relative degree of affectations depending upon which set or group the individual may belong to.

Normally, during a disaster the following groups of people would be involved:

1. The victims affected by the disaster
2. The bystanders who may be eyewitnesses to what is happening and who may be the first ones to rush to the aid of the victims

3. The officials of different hue and colour who would soon be part of the disaster. Within this segment there is a clear distinction between those belonging to the institution involved in the disaster and those from outside
4. The paramedics and other health officials
5. The social groups
6. The media
7. The community

The follow-up of a disaster would vary for each of the groups even though there would a lot of common factors that may cover all the sets of people. Also the disaster aftermath would be seen differently by each of the sets of people involved in the disaster. For instance, in the aftermath of the September 11 terrorist attack, the community and social groups were seen the most prominent with different pressure groups forming and regrouping to take the message of peace and not hatred to the perpetrators of violence, whereas the government officials who were involved in strength took a diametrically opposite view that the state should go after the terrorists and launched a worldwide campaign against terrorism starting with the liberation of Afghanistan from the hands of the Muslim extremists belonging to Taliban sect.

Understanding How Media Reacts

Media would invariably follow the following pattern during any major disaster. First there is an all out effort to push out as many stories, interviews, visuals, sound-bites, spot interviews, analysis as possible within the shortest possible time. The print, electronic, broadcast agency and internet journalism all of them follow the same pattern with different medium employing different types of technologies and different sets of people. After the disaster has passed, there is a sudden and significant drop in the coverage of the news relating to the disaster with the camera teams and scores of scribes shifting to the next "happening" place. There is, however, be a handful of people assigned to do a follow-up for a period depending upon the intensity of the tragedy.

The Gujarat earthquake, for instance, sustained the interest of the media some one to two weeks after the worst period which lasted for two days. The media interest, however, never vanishes until the final traces of the disaster wane like the embers under the coal dust. Media always keeping the interest in the disaster alive and it just takes a spark for the media interest to swing. For instance, the worst ever industrial accident which claimed nearly 20,000 lives in Bhopal involving Union Carbide—now Dow Chemicals, suddenly became the centre of media attention even after a full decade when the new management was slapped a hefty settlement claim by the local court. The media not only covered the development on hand but also started digging up stories of human neglect, going back to the days of the tragedy and coming up with new sets of findings of the culpability of the then management of the company.

For the official agencies like police, the fire service, the medical teams and even the voluntary agencies involved in the disaster management, the post disaster period one is of taking stock of their work and imbibing their learning so that they would be able to handle the next disaster even better than the previous. Many a times large disasters in fact give rise to the setting up of institutions that would take care not only of the post disaster follow-up but even spawn new knowledge in the chosen area of learning. For instance, the Bhopal tragedy, in its wake resulted in a number of top speciality research hospitals springing up in Bhopal, the setting up of a large number of medical and engineering colleges in and around Bhopal not only to cater to the needs of the victims but also learn from the accident and use this knowledge for applying to other situations. In the wake of the Exxon Valdez disaster, the trust created to help the victims has become one of world's significant environmental research and community support agency doing pioneering work in the Alaska region.

Use of Technology During Post Disaster Period

Disaster brings in its wake a large use of technology in the modern times. The satellite based disaster warning and prevention systems are widely used to monitor large marine, industrial and transport accidents with quick rescue operations mounted within minutes of a disaster. During a disaster, instant communication can make the difference between life and death. Information—including GIS maps—and vital data as well as voice, text and video communication has to be sent in a great hurry, which means there should be a strong reliable communication network up and running. Even in media communication this aspect is highly essential.

Table 17.1 are the technology planning priorities after the disaster has passed.

Table 17.1: Technology Mapping in Post Disaster Period

1. Verify how the communication systems worked, from availability adequacy, reliability, flexibility and accessibility point of view.
2. Check out what sort of glitches were encountered.
3. Figure out how media communication support services worked.
4. Figure out modifications needed to hardware and software.
5. Figure out sort of training that would be needed to keep the technology plan up and running.
6. The budget analyse.

Claims and Follow-up of Disasters

The September 11 accident, in its wake, sent the insurance companies scurrying for cover as one of world's worst tragedy also brought with it a whopping price tag running to billions of dollars in insurance claims. The Bhopal gas tragedy resulted in a four billion dollar settlement. The Exxon Valdez settlement has already run into several billions and the process is continuing the Air India's Kanishka tragedy, the mid-air collision near Delhi involving a Saudia passenger plane and a cargo aircraft belonging to Air Kazakastan, the Gujarat earthquake, the Divi cyclone—the list is endless.

The insurance companies, knowing the risks, fully cough up the billions in case a disaster strikes.

However, from the communication perspective, the post disaster follow-up should clearly build in an element of unambiguous settlement claims with full voluntary assistance to the victims and their families. The trauma of a disaster should not be accentuated with the post disaster follow-up. It is the responsibility of the agencies, the companies and the institutions concerned involved in a disaster to see that the systems and processes are put in place so that the victims are harassed the least and the healing process is completed earlier than planned. This is needed not only from a humanitarian perspective but even from the long term sustenance of the company it is necessary to build such trust among the stakeholders.

Legal claims and legal formalities should be the least troublesome and quite simple so that just claims could be processed fast and the victims and their kin get the benefit the earliest. Justice delayed is justice denied is more true of a disaster victim.

Research and Learning

Research and learning is definite fallout of any large disaster with a completely new set of people moving in to study the disaster after it has passed. These are usually scientists drawn not just from a range of pure science areas but even social scientists who may be interested in a disaster from the point of view of mass psychology, individual self interest, acts of heroism and what makes a common man do such significant feats—for instance, during an accident involving a school bus where a fully laden bus fell into the river Yamuna a bystander jumped in and pulled out as many as 28 children in a span of a few minutes unmindful of his life.

Apart from the human angle, the disaster is a living example of the worst that can happen say to a refinery, an oil tanker, a passenger plane which could never be simulated in any training programme. The scientists studying such accidents thoroughly would be able to teach the engineers and other safety officials on the various ways in which to secure a premise, manage a ship, avert a fire and generally be ready to handle a disaster if it should occur. One of the most thoroughly researched accidents in passenger shipping history, the sinking of the world's largest luxury liner, Titanic, has become a sort of benchmark for all the merchant shipping safety experts. The sinking of the world's biggest oil platform off the Brazilian coast is another modern day milestone in handling a potential disaster of truly gargantuan proportions. The sinking is also considered one of the best engineering challenges in the ocean ever undertaken in the maritime history of mankind. The series of oil spills, in its wake, has created a furor over single hull tankers, making the shipping trade scrap millions of DWTs and replace them with double hull tankers. The environmentalists like Green Peace have also been arguing in vain about the efficacy of continuing to sail the giant oil tankers carrying with them a constant threat of an accident, followed by massive oil spills and wiping out of precious marine life.

Post Disaster Follow-up

A lot has already been said about internal preparedness and learning from a disaster. But there is still the matter of handling the outside agencies which are essential part of any disaster management plan. These are usually the police, the health authorities, the government representatives, the social and environmental pressure groups besides the media. While the media has been discussed in detail, it is essential to focus attention on other aspects briefly in the post disaster follow-up scenario.

1. The police and fire service are two significant members of the government who should be in touch with always, whether during disaster or otherwise. In fact, when the disaster hits the first ones to appear on the scene would be these twin arms of the government. In the post disaster period, there should be enough feedback provided to these two organisations which in turn would help build mutual confidence and also help in building their own disaster response systems and policies.

   There should be mutual participation in seminars and workshops essentially aimed at understanding the disaster that had just passed and preparing for the worst. The learnings from these workshops should be propagated adequately.
2. Health authorities are another segment which is usually neglected by the companies until a disaster happens. It is essential to continue to keep the health authorities in touch with the happenings in the company in order to build confidence and rapport between the health services and the company representatives.

3. Other government and civilian administration relates to the officials such as customs, excise, and factories inspectorate, insurance and claims people, the legal people who would play a direct or indirect role in any disaster that may hit the company.
4. Social groups are more difficult to handle as there is no means of identifying these. The best way to manage this segment is to encourage community participation and social contact programmes on an ongoing basis.

Follow-up is an essential element in any professional management programme while in the case of a disaster or a major disaster, natural or man-made, it is all the more essential. Effective follow-up should be done so that many of the nuances which otherwise left out would have been learnt. The follow up should be systematic, first by learning from the disaster and then drawing up an effective post disaster management plan. The post disaster management plan need not be vastly different from the original disaster management plan, except that it should iron out any glitches that were encountered when the disaster was at hand.

CHAPTER 18

Managing Disaster Aftermath

In the aftermath of any disaster media would be on the alert even though normal routine there may be no visits or queries as during the peak of the disaster. This chapter helps to deal with the disaster Aftermath Action in Disaster Aftermath.

Action in Disaster Aftermath

In the disaster aftermath, the schedule for action should be as given in Table 18.1.

Table 18.1: Action in the Disaster aftermath

- Detailed documentation of the disaster.
- Debriefing of the disaster management staff.
- Media communications plan in the disaster aftermath.
- Promote growth trust, and healing.
- Revisit your corporate policy and legal procedures.
- Revisit your media management plan.

1. Documentation: Detailed documentation of the disaster is critical for two major reasons, one without quick and detailed documentation, many of the critical details of the disaster may be lost, the evidences destroyed, the people may get scattered, their memories stressed and the opinions become coloured. The detailed documentation is of three types.
   (i) Detailed account of the incident including the photographs, transcripts, messages exchanged during the disaster, television footage.

(ii) Interviews with the disaster management team by way of debriefing, other stakeholders and, in case possible, even some members of the media purely for internal research purposes.

(iii) A collection of media reports, television footage, interview transcripts, etc.

Such information carefully collated should be distilled and a working draft should be prepared for discussions by the top management. The working draft should be used to find out how the message was understood and communicated by the media to the people, a factor crucial in future disaster communication planning of the company. Any distortions should be isolated and studied carefully to determine whether the fault lies with the company's communication team or with that of the media.

Ask the following questions

(i) Was the disaster management plan developed with full knowledge of everyone affected by it?

(ii) Was there any internal dissension as the disaster continued?

(iii) Was the media satisfied with the communication plan?

(iv) What was the nature of media complaints?

(v) Was the legal procedures followed in the way the disaster was handled?

(vi) Are there any legal disputes in the aftermath of the disaster?

(vii) What is media response rate or in other words how often is media contacting after the disaster?

(viii) What was the involvement of other sister companies/agencies, any lessons learnt?

2. Debriefing of the disaster management staff is important to understand the nuances that the management may have missed in understanding the dimensions of the disaster and their effects on the company and the victims.

3. Media communication plan in the disaster aftermath would be different from the normal media plan and the learning during the disaster should be put to full use. The rapport established among the media members and the understanding of their requirements should shape the plan in the aftermath of a disaster. Besides, the communication plan in this case should achieve the purpose of building trust, growth and healing rather than merely informing and educating the people about the disaster at hand.
4. Promotion of growth trust and healing is a delicate process that could be built with great sensitivity and care. There should be specialised media campaigns and briefings to win trust of the community through their write-ups, features and other forum.
5. Revisiting your corporate policy and legal approaches would become necessary after any major disaster. The learnings should be absorbed with a positive attitude and the aftermath of the disaster and the corporate policy should be remodelled to suit the changing needs. The legal hurdles that one faced during the disaster should also be studied carefully to evolve a disaster management plan devoid of legal problems.
6. Finally, the overall corporate communications and public relations policy of the company should be revamped in the light of the recent disaster using the learnings from the disaster.

Disaster Communication Tool Kits

While the strategy in a disaster is to quickly adjust the company or community position from one of response and reaction to one of relative control, in the aftermath it should focus on taking proactive steps toward building trust, healing and a return to normalcy.

The aftermath of the disaster is quite important. The following point should be kept in mind in the aftermath.

1. Development of disaster response and prevention plans

2. The plans' goal should be to support company and the community.
3. The plans should provide strategies for informing all stakeholders within and outside the company and the broader community of the plans' purpose, process, and assignment of responsibilities after the disaster has passed. All staff must be aware of these plans and what they should do in the event of different kinds of Disaster.
4. Plans should be updated and practiced by all participants on a regular basis.

Following is a checklist for disaster communication aftermath:

1. *Policy and procedures:* Solid prevention programmes, thorough discipline codes and policies on threats and other breaches of security with procedures on what to do if they occur. It should be borne in mind that getting the policy right would depend upon how much learning has taken place from the just concluded disaster. This in turn would depend upon systematic debriefing etc., which we has been cited above. The new policy should have the following elements among other things
2. *Manpower training:* Human resource management policy should change vastly after any major disaster and even those not directly connected with the disaster should be apprised of the dimensions of the disaster and how it was handled.
3. *Communication plan:* The communication plan and communication architecture is also affected by the disaster. Short-term objectives and long-term objectives of the communication apparatus should be laid out using the learnings from the disaster. Mobil's stakeholders programme at Sydney harbour is a good example.
4. *Continuous monitoring and response system:* The disaster may have passed but years on end the after-effects

would continue which should be monitored and an effective system of responses built so that those interested in the disaster should be able to get correct and adequate information. For instance, even thirteen years after the Exxon Valdez disaster, the interest in it has not waned.

5. *Learning by the management:* The managerial decision making process, role and responsibilities should come under review after a devastating disaster.
6. *Operational plan:* The new operational plan should be comprehensive taking into account all possible disaster and the way of response by all the departments of the company including that of the communication section.
7. *Community outreach:* A concerted community outreach programme to build trust and confidence should become necessary after any major disaster.

Disaster communication in the aftermath of a disaster is special and it depends on how well the disaster that has just passed was understood by the stakeholders. Just the same way as extensive planning is done for preparing the disaster communication plan, even for the post disaster communication, a lot of planning is needed. Understanding of the disaster that has just passed would begin by debriefing the personnel involved in mitigating the disaster. Such information needs also to be documented well and stored. Thereafter it needs to be analysed carefully and a strategy for post disaster handling should be prepared.

CHAPTER 19

Epidemiologic Factors that Determine the Potential of Communicable Disease Transmission

The potential risk of communicable diseases after disaster is influenced by six types of adverse change. These are changes in preexistent levels of disease; ecological changes which are the result of the disaster; population displacement; changes in population density; disruption of public utilities; and interruption of basic public health services.

Changes in Pre-existent Levels of Disease

Usually the risk of a communicable disease in a Community affected by disaster is proportional to the endemic level. There is generally no risk of a given disease when the organism causes it is not present beforehand. Developing countries frequently have such poor systems for reporting communicable disease, however, that their national authorities lack adequate information about levels of specific organisms. Political pressure is nonetheless sometimes exerted for taking public health measures against diseases such as smallpox, cholera, yellow fever or other vector-borne diseases in geographic areas considered free of them by communicable disease specialists.

Relief workers can conceivably introduce communicable disease into areas affected by disaster. Diseases potentially introduced include new strains of influenza, foot-and-mouth disease, and those borne by insect vectors, particularly by *Aedes aegypti*. Also, nonimmune relief workers may be susceptible to endemic diseases to which the local population is tolerant or immune, and they may become ill.

Ecological Changes Caused by the Disaster

Natural disasters, particularly droughts, floods and hurricanes, frequently produce ecological changes in the environment which increase or reduce the risk of communicable disease. Vector-borne and water-borne diseases are the most significantly affected. A hurricane with heavy rains which strikes the Caribbean coastal area of Central America may, for example, reduce the number of *Anopheles aquasalis* hatched, since the vectors prefer brackish tidal swamps and increase A. *albimanus* and A. *darlingi*, which breed easily in fresh, clear water and overflows. The net effect of the hurricane on human malaria, of which both mosquitoes are vectors, would be difficult to predict. Rain from such a hurricane would also cause flooding of streams and canals which in rural areas are often the source of drinking water. Under some circumstances, a water-borne zoonotic disease, such as leptospirosis, may become more widely disseminated via water-contact or drinking from contaminated sources. There is evidence that the short term effect of diluting supplies of already contaminated drinking water with rain may, however, reduce the level of disease. The population may, moreover, avoid drinking water contaminated by flooding for a cultural/psychological reason such as the presence of animal carcasses.

Population Displacement

Movement of populations away from the areas affected by a disaster can affect the relative risk from communicable diseases in three ways. If the population moves nearby, the existing facilities and services in the receiving community will be strained. When resettlement occurs at some distance, the chances increase that the displaced population will encounter diseases not prevalent in their own community, to which they are susceptible. For example, nonimmunized, rural Andean populations brought together in camps after an earthquake may then be exposed to measles. Alternatively, displaced populations may bring the agents or vectors of communicable diseases with them. The latter concern frequently occurs when populations from low-lying coastal areas with malaria are evacuated further inland before a hurricane.

Population Density

Population density is a critical factor in the transmission of diseases spread by the respiratory route and through person-to-person contact. Because of the destruction of houses, natural disasters almost invariably contribute to increased population density. Survivors of severe disaster seek shelter, food and water in less affected areas. When the damage is less severe, crowding may occur when people move in with other families and congregate in such public facilities as schools and churches. The resulting problems most commonly mentioned are acute respiratory illness, and include influenza and non-specific diarrheas.

Disruption of Public Utilities

Electricity, water, sewage disposal and other public utilities may be interrupted after a disaster. In a village with no electric power and where there are promiscuous defecation habits and contaminated sources of water in normal times, very little (if any) additional risk from communicable diseases follows the disaster. However, in economically more developed areas the extended disruption of basic services increases the risks of food-borne and water-borne disease. Insufficient water for washing hands and bathing also promotes the spread of diseases transmitted by contact.

Interruption of Basic Public Health Services

The interruption of basic public health services like vaccination, ambulatory treatment of tuberculosis and programmes for the control of malaria and vectors are frequent, but often overlooked factors that increase the probability of disease transmission after disaster in a developing country. The risk of transmission increases proportionally to the extent and the duration of the disruption. An outbreak of communicable disease may, therefore, occur months or years after a drought, a famine or a civil disturbance. The interruption causing such an occurrence is usually the result of the diversion of staff and financial resources to the relief effort, beyond the critical period. In addition or in conjunction with this, the failure to reestablish resources at sufficient levels contributes to the interruption.

The Relative Risk of Communicable Disease after Natural versus *Manmade Disasters*

Manmade disasters fall into two categories. In the first are those that result from accidental destructive activity. Such events may be acute, as with airplane crashes, explosions, fires and intoxications, or they may be chronic processes like deforestation and the contamination of the environment. Accidental manmade disasters, which usually pose little, if any, additional risk of communicable disease to the community, are beyond the scope of this manual.

The second category consists of manmade disasters caused by warfare, economic or social disruption and civil disturbance. Warfare is frequently subdivided into the conventional type, including siege and blockade, and the nonconventional type, including biological, chemical (toxic gas) and nuclear warfare. Experience with the effect of nonconventional warfare on communicable disease is limited. Biological agents capable of producing epidemics that incapacitate military or civilian populations (e.g., anthrax and plague) are handled through taking the same public health measures as those used for naturally occuring outbreaks. Information about these is available elsewhere

The relationship of social disruption and conventional warfare to communicable disease is similar to that of chronic disasters such as drought. Warfare and drought are the most common causes of wide-spread serious malnutrition and famine. Communicable diseases, which have adverse nutritional effects in previously well nourished individuals, compromise malnourished patients further, and many, like measles, are more severe in extremely malnourished individuals. There is also anecdotal evidence that some parasitic diseases, like malaria, and viral diseases, like herpes, tend to reactivate during refeeding. Decision makers may not have political interest or may not be able to assist affected populations during wars and insurrections, unlike during drought where civil authorities usually support relief' efforts.

The six factors which contribute to the risk of communicable diseases after natural disasters mentioned earlier are generally valid in the event of conventional manmade disaster. Military activities, however, frequently involve movement through and extended stays in geographic areas which are not ordinarily inhabited by man. In the process, military populations may be exposed to a large variety of zoonotic and vector-borne diseases which are ordinarily of little concern to civilian relief administrators. Examples of such diseases are leishmaniasis, rickettsial diseases, and most arthropod-borne viral diseases. Military surgeons are aware of these risks and, thus, civilian physicians rarely become involved. The probability that these diseases will be spread to dependents and to the civilian population varies, but is quite low overall.

Post-disaster Experience with Communicable Disease

Historically, a variety of communicable dieseases have reached epidemic proportions after disaster or because patients are malnourished and thus more susceptible of many diesease agents. Indeed, until World War II more deaths during wartime or famine were caused by communicable disease than by hostile action or starvation. The diseases classically associated with war and famine and the most effective methods for controlling them are enumerated in Table 1. Human transmission of smallpox has now been certified to be global!! eliminated and several other conditions (i.e., louse-borne typhus, plague, and relapsing fever) have a severely limited geographic distribution, in remote and largely unpopulated areas.

World War II represented a transitional period for industrialized combatant countries. The five years of continual war and occupation had affected civilian populations in Europe surprisingly less than did warfare in previous conflicts. The most notable increases in disease levels were those of new cases of pulmonary tuberculosis, which rose steadily throughout Western Europe, and of reported cases of typhoid fever, the total of which doubled. Most seriously affected were displaced persons, encamped refugees and inmates of concentration camps. In marginally nourished and starving patients, typhus, dysentery, scarlet fever, and diphtheria caused sporadic outbreaks and many deaths.

Serious outbreak of communicable disease after disaster has not been documented in Western Europe, the Continental United States or Canada since 1945. This improvement is associated with generally improved sanitary conditions and with the disappearance of certain vector-borne diseases from many countries, as in the case of malaria, or the restriction of diseases to isolated areas after the development and usage of effective insecticides and pesticides. The immunization of susceptible populations with vaccines effective against diseases such as diphtheria, pertussis, tetanus, poliomyelitis and measles and the adequate treatment and interruption of transmission by antibiotics of diseases like typhoid, streptococcal diseases, and tuberculosis is also associated with the lack of serious outbreaks. In caring for populations affected by disasters in industrialized countries, physicians have observed apparent increases in nonspecific diarrhea, and influenza and minor respiratory infections. The magnitude of the problem created by these, however, is such that population density alone may adequately explain it.

The evaluation of recent experiences with communicable diseases in Latin America, the Caribbean and other parts of the developing world is complicated by several factors related to changing patterns of disease, development, and the public health infrastructure. Most important of these are the persistence of many serious communicable diseases; the decline of some serious communicable disease; a lack of base line surveillance data; the inadequate number of laboratory diagnostic facilities; and in adequate converage with vaccines.

Persistence of Many Serious Communicable Diseases

In spite of the rarity of documentation of outbreaks of communicable diseases after disasters in developing countries, there is a consensus that the probability of outbreak is

Table 19.1. Communicable Diseases of Public Health Importance Classically Associated with War and Famine, with Traditional Methods of Prevention and Control

Disease

A. ***Water and/or Food-Borne Diseases***
   Typhoid and Paratyphoid Fevers
   Food Poisoning
   Sewage Poisoning
   Cholera
   Leptospirosis

B. ***Person to Person Spread***
   Contact Diseases
   Shigellosis
   Nonspecific diarrheas
   Streptococcal skin infections
   Scabies
   Infectious hepatitis
   Respiratory Spread
   Smallpox
   Measles
   Whooping Cough
   Diphtheria
   Influenza
   Tuberculosis

C. ***Vector-Borne Diseases***
   Louse-borne typhus
   Plague (rat flea)
   Relapsing fever
   Malaria (mosquito)
   Viral encephalitis

D. ***Wound Complications***

Public Health Measures

a. Adequate disposal of feces and urine.
b. Safe water for drinking and washing
c. Sanitary food preparation
d. Fly and pest control.
e. Disease surveillance.
f. Isolation and Treatment of early cases (typhoid and paratyphoid fevers, cholera).
g. Immunization (typhoid fever and cholera).

a. Reduced crowding.
b. Adequate washing facilities.
c. Public health education.
d. Disease surveillance in clinics.
e. Treatment of clinical cases.
f. Immunization (infectious hepatitis).
a. Adequate levels of immunization before the disaster.
b. Reduced crowding.
c. Disease surveillance in clinics and community.
d. Isolation of index cases (especially smallpox).
e. Immunization of entire population (smallpox) or children (measles).
f. Continue primary immunization of infants (diphtheria, whooping cough, tetanus).
a. Disinfection (except malaria and encephalitis).
b. Vector control.
c. Disease surveillance.
d. Isolation and treatment (no isolation for malaria).

1. Tetanus
a. Tetanus toxoid immunization.
b. Postexposure tetanus antitoxin.

---

considerably higher in Latin America and the Carribbean than it is in the U.S.A. This opinion is based upon morbidity and mortality data in which patterns of many communicable diseases are at levels comparable to those in Europe and North America at the turn of the century. The most revalent of these diseases are acute respiratory infection, tuberculosis, diarrhea diseases of various etiologies and diseases which are preventable through vaccination.

Decline of Some Serious Communicable Diseases

In counterbalance to the high levels of most of the communicable diseases transmitted by person-to-person contact, in most of Latin America and the Caribbean the classical diseases associated with disasters have declined or disappeared. The Americas have also been spared the widespread severe malnutrition and recurrent famines which have afflicted Africa and Asia.

Lack of Baseline Surveillance Data

Lack of information regarding levels of communicable diseases between disasters in developing countries makes it extremely difficult for epidemiologists to confirm subsequent reported "increases" and to attribute them to an acute event. A medical team which moves into an area without previous health services or regular disease reporting may, for example, encounter clinical cases of typhoid fever or tetanus. When this happens it is frequently difficult for field workers or relief agencies to determine if an acute public health emergency exists or whether the true level of endemic disease is finally being appreciated.

Inadequate Laboratory Diagnostic Facilities

Documentation of communicable diseases such as typhoid or dengue fever is frequently frustrated after disasters in Latin America and the Caribbean when physicians rely exclusively on their clinical acumen to diagnose communicable diseases. This is the end result of medical curricula in which the effective use of the laboratory is not included, of poorly run microbiology laboratories in which the clinician or epidemiologist has little confidence, and of the policy of not providing adequate support to public health laboratories which are seen as too expensive, as using inappropriate technology, or as unnecessary to primary health care in developing countries.

Inadequate Vaccination Coverage

The probability of occurrence of vaccine-preventable diseases is related to the percentage of the population that has acquired natural immunity, and the percentage of unvaccinated susceptibles. Most of the vaccines in common use are directed against childhood diseases, such as diphtheria, pertussis, tetanus, poliomyelitis and measles. Indiscriminate or improvised vaccination programmes are neither feasible nor effective in the aftermath of disaster. Therefore, the extent to which the children have completed their primary series of vaccinations before a disaster will determine the likelihood of epidemic after a disaster.

CHAPTER 20

Post-Disaster Potential of Communicable Disease Epidemics

The preexistent level of disease in a community affected by disaster is one of six risk parameters. In theory, the absence in a country of a disease such as cholera eliminates the need for surveillance, but in practice, the need is not so simply perceived. Rumors and other unofficial sources of information frequently give rise to concern about cholera, plague, and other exotic conditions not otherwise believed endemic in an area. The epidemiologist cannot necessarily assume that because diseases have never been reported they do not persist in remote communities or in populations where there is no access to public health diagnostic laboratories. The recent discovery of an endemic focus of *Vibrio cholerae* in the United States is an excellent example of this point. If the patients in Louisiana had by chance been diagnosed after a hurricane or a period of flooding, public opinion would have accepted a cause-effect relationship without question.

A second consideration is the possibility that an infectious disease agent may be brought into an affected area by relief workers, or in transport vehicles or supplies. This may occur within a country or, more dramatically, from another country. The 1976 earthquake in Guatemala, for example, occurred during the winter influenza season in North America. Vectors and agents of communicable disease can also be introduced by transport vehicles (particularly the airplane) or in relief supplies. In Latin America and the Caribbean, the *Aedes aegypti* mosquito could easily be reintroduced into an area free of the vector by air or surface transport vehicles which originate in or pass through an infested area. When an explosive outbreak points to a common source of infection, epidemiologists should also consider the possibility that tinned or processed food used for relief was contaminated. Aftosa, or foot-and-mouth disease, is a prime example of a serious veterinary problem of public health nature that may be introduced via infected meat, contaminated relief supplies and the shoes of relief workers. A major natural disaster does not provide justification for abandoning such accepted public health precautionary measures as limiting the contact of patients with ill relief workers, and spraying aircraft or inspecting them at ports of entry.

Exposure of Susceptibles to Endemic Communicable Disease

There are three ways in which susceptibles may be exposed to endemic diseases which cause subsequent epidemics or increased levels of disease after disaster. Briefly, this occurs through the migration of rural populations to congested areas; the migration of urban populations to rural areas; and the immigration of susceptibles into areas affected by the disaster. Anticipating these problems and implementing preventive measures require an appreciation of the patterns of disease in the countries stricken by disaster.

Migration of Rural Populations to Congested Areas

In medieval times, the privileged classes tried to avoid the effects of epidemics by fleeing the pestilential cities. The present pattern of reaction to drought, civil disturbance, and many natural disasters is one in which populations congregate for food, safety and medical attention. In general, the more rural and isolated are such migrants, the greater is their susceptibility to common communicable diseases, particularly those transmitted by aerosol or person-to-person contact. Individuals from dispersed communities are also less likely to have received routine childhood immunization. When populations migrate from highlands to camps or population centers at lower altitudes, the risk of vector-borne diseases not transmitted at higher elevations is also added.

Migration of Urban Populations to Rural Areas

More rarely, urban populations may be forced by civil disturbance, an earthquake or a hurricane to move to a rural environment. In so doing they may be exposed to vector-borne diseases, in particular to malaria. The destruction of Managua by earthquake in 1972 was such an event in the Americas. The severity of chloroquine-resistant falciparum malaria among Kampouchean refugees is another recent example of acquisition of communicable disease through urban-rural migration. The refugees, first expelled from population centers to rural areas with low malaria indices, then migrated to the Thailand border through holoendemic areas.

Immigration of Susceptibles to Affected Areas

The poorly briefed or underprovisioned international relief worker is the most obvious type of susceptible entering an area affected by disaster. During the Nigerian Civil War a decade ago, this was a serious enough problem that the effectiveness of some foreign medical teams was jeopardized. Failure to appreciate the risk of malaria and/or unwillingness to take chemosuppressive drugs (e.g., chloroquine) caused several cases of the disease, which included cerebral malaria and one fatality. One group, assigned to Biafra, neglected to obtain prophylactic gammaglobulin, and before it could be flown in, members of the team were incapacitated by infectious hepatitis.

Established relief agencies have long been aware of the risk of disease which susceptibles incur, but they do encounter difficulty convincing skeptical, inexperienced and unsupervised volunteers of the dimensions of the problem. Ad hoc voluntary groups are usually established in the aftermath of a particular major disaster and are also formed in donor countries with special geographic interest in the affected nation. Organizers and their medical staff of ad hoc groups should consult the more experienced agencies or one of the excellent manuals about preserving the health of travelers to the tropics.

Increases in Levels of Endemic Communicable Disease in Local Populations

It must be appreciated that reports of communicable diseases should be expected to increase during medical relief periods in communities with high levels of contagious diseases. If medical services were not in existence before a disaster, instituting them afterwards will certainly increase the apparent levels of disease. Even when primary health services do exist before disaster, regular disease reporting is usually very incomplete. After a disaster, reports increase because the number of reporting units is augmented. The total population served may also be swollen by movement into the area. Clinicians used to practicing under other local conditions may be confronted with clinical syndromes with which they are unfamiliar, and try to make etiologic diagnoses without diagnostic laboratory support.

During an epidemic—defined as an unexpected number of cases of a communicable disease—it is extremely important to determine whether increases in disease are real or are only apparent. Except in encamped refugees, the precise figure of the total population at risk is rarely available for the calculation of reported case rates, which is the number of reported cases divided by total population at risk. Thus, it may be necessary to perform a rapid survey in the community to reach an approximation of how common a communicable disease is in the general population. Trends can be monitored by examining retrospective and prospective clinic reports of patients seen with the condition. However, even when evaluation is performed, it may be difficult to decide whether an increase in rates is significant enough to warrant taking emergency control measures or requesting additional medical supplies or staff.

Special Problems With Communicable Disease in Encamped Populations

Experience in both the historic and the modern eras has repeatedly shown that the threat of communication of disease is greatest among crowded encamped populations, and that the likelihood of a serious outbreak increases with time. The danger is rather independent of the natural or manmade disaster which produced the encampment. The preventive medical officer should, therefore, prefer to have affected populations return to their homes or be promptly resettled. When this is not feasible, housing the population in dispersed temporary quarters with unaffected kin, or in nearby communities, is preferable to instituting encampment. However, the relief administrator of: ten responds to the instinctive feeling that the situation can be better managed and the needs of those most affected by the disaster more efficiently provided when they are congregated.

When it is unavoidable to institute encampment for extended periods, the risks of communicable disease can be reduced through strict supervision of meticulous attention to sanitation. Civilian authorities often find it difficult to organize and then indefinitely sustain needed military discipline. If the camps are occupied by refugees or independent-minded citizens, they are likely to eventually rebel.

Communicable Diseases after Disasters

Even in very poor developing countries, serious outbreaks of communicable disease very rarely occur after natural disasters which do not involve the encampment of populations. Known exceptions to this include cases of leptospirosis, which increased in Brazil after flooding, the aggravation of an ongoing typhoid fever problem following hurricanes in Mauritius, and cases of food poisoning in both Dominica and the Dominican Republic. It is probably more likely that the diversion of scarce resources from normal public health activities to disaster relief, or subsequent economic problems aggravated by a disaster, will lead to epidemic long after the acute event, such as in the resurgence and subsequent failure to eradicate malaria from Haiti.

With this in mind, in the thirteenth (1981) edition of the American Public Health Association handbook entitled *Control of Communicable Diseases in Man* there is a consensus described that was reached by specialists in communicable disease, liaison representatives, and Pan American Health Organization/World Health Organization officials about the relative risk of individual communicable disease after disaster. This information is presented in a simplified form in Table 20.1. For a further discussion of each disease, the reader should consult the thirteenth edition or a tropical medicine text.

Table 20.1. Epidemic Potential of Selected Communicable Diseases Following Disaster in Latin America and the Caribbean

Disease	Disaster Potential Qualitative/Quantitative*		Geographic Areas at Risk
Amoebiasis	contamination water/food	?	cosmopolitan
Chickenpox- Herpes Zoster	overcrowding in emergency situations	3+	worldwide (infection nearly universal)
Cholera	contamination water/food, crowding in primitive conditions	1+	none
Diarrhoea, nonspecific	contamination water/food, crowding	4+	universal
Diphtheria	crowding of susceptible groups	2 +	universal
Ebola/Marburg Virus	direct contact with infected blood secretions, organs or semen. Possible by vector-borne/aerosol routes	?	Rhodesia, Kenya, Sudan, Zaire
Food Poisoning—Staphylococcus	mass feeding and inadequate refrigeration/cooking facilities	4+	universal
—Bacillus cereus	mass feeding and inadequate refrigeration/cooking facilities	3+	universal
Gastroenteritis — Epidemic Viral Gastroenteritis	contamination water/food crowding	?	universal
—Rotavirus Gastroenteritis	contamination of water/food, crowding	?	universal

Hemorrhagic Fevers of Argentinian and Bolivian Types	contamination of food	?	Argentina, Bolivia
Hepatitis Viral — Viral Hepatitis A	contamination of water/food, inadequate sanitary facilities	4+	universal
—Viral Hepatitis B —Viral Hepatitis, NonA, Non-B	improper sterilization procedures	4+	universal universal
Influenza	crowding	?	universal (pandemics, epidemics, localized and sporadic outbreaks)
Leprosy	interruption of case detection and therapy	4+	endemic
Leptospirosis	contamination of water/food, flooding of areas with high water table	?	worldwide
Malaria	availability of water for mosquito breeding	?	Tropical South America, Panama, and Haiti
Measles	introduction of measles to susceptible isolated population susceptible isolated population	4+	universal
Meningitis, Meningococcimia	crowding	?	endemic
Pediculosis	crowding, clothing	?	endemic worldwide
Plague	crowding, inappropriate rodent control, unhygienic conditions	?	endemic in certain areas of North and South America
Poliomyelitis	crowding nonimmune groups, contaminated food, inadequate sewage disposal	?	worldwide
Rabies	stray dogs	2+	worldwide

(Contd.)

Table 2. (*Contd.*)

Disease	Disaster Potential Qualitative/Quantitative*		Geographic Areas at Risk
Relapsing Fever	overcrowding. malnournishment, poor personal hygiene	2+	endemic
Salmonellosis	overcrowding, contamination of food in mass feeding, poor sanitation	3+	worldwide
Scabies	overcrowding	2+	endemic
Shigellosis	crowding, poor sanitation, malnournishment	4+	worldwide
Streptococcal Diseases caused by Group A (Beta Hemolytic Streptococci)	contamination of food	2+	common in temperate zones and semitropical areas
Tetanus	flood, hurricanes, earthquakes	3+	worldwide
Tuberculosis	crowding	1+	worldwide
Typhoid Fever	disruption of usual sanitary control of food and water	2+	worldwide
Typhus Fever (Endemic Louse-Borne)	unhygienic conditions , crowding	2+	endemic foci
Yellow Fever	availability of infected mosquitoes	?	enzootic in Northern South America and parts of Africa
Whooping Cough	crowding	2+	worldwide

*? Potential; 1+ rare; 2+ occasional; 3+ frequent; 4+ usual

CHAPTER 21

Disaster Response History in India

This chapter brings to light the manner in which India responds to the countless disasters is imperative to have a fair view of how things work in our country when disasters strike

Disaster: A Way of Life

Indian subcontinent has been wrecked by disasters from times immemorial and the region has been witness to every form of natural disaster from earth's quakes, floods, and cyclone and to hurricanes, landslides, severe droughts, with a single exception of volcanic eruption as there are no active volcanoes in India. The 2002 Gujarat earthquake has been the most recent reminder of the scale and enormity of havoc a natural disaster can cause and it is also a standing testimony about the nation's resilience and the people's industry in managing disasters of any kind. Even though organised response to disaster is of recent vintage with the government led initiatives having taken strong roots, the community participation, emergency preparedness at the regional and local level and high degree of responsiveness of all sections of the society have been the hallmark of disaster mitigation in the country. The vast coastline, dozen or so major rivers and the wide variety of geographical features coupled with the locational disadvantage of being a tropical country makes India a potential disaster zone from every angle.

Apart from natural disasters, India has had its own share of man-made disasters like industrial accidents the worst of which were the Bhopal gas tragedy, minor nuclear accidents at the Kaiga

Nuclear power plant and Kalpakkam N-power plant, refinery fires, coalmine accidents, series of train accidents involving high fatalities, air-crashes including the infamous mid-air collision at Charki Dadri described elsewhere in this document.

When disasters strike problems get compounded owing to our large population most of which is illiterate and nearly half of which is living below poverty line. The World Water Development report of the United Nations released in March 2003 argues that the poor actually pay more for water than the rich having access to protected drinking water and that floods affect the poor far more than those who are organised.

Media in India, like all other institutions and individuals, has complex attitudes when it concerns disaster, often treating natural disasters like any other news event, the greater the damage wider the coverage with little or no follow up or sustained campaign about disaster prevention. Not a single newspaper or news magazine has set aside special pages or sections for disasters despite their high frequency of occurrence and frightening proportion of damage both of human lives and property. Ironically even the educational system also does not incorporate any tangible disaster management or support studies in the schools or in colleges. There are no mock drills, no learning from the disasters just occurred and no emergency management plans involving the community.

From the disaster communication point of view there are mainly three sides to disaster management.

I. Prevention management
II. Damage limitation management
III. Effective follow-up management

Prevention Management

Prevention is about integrating broader tasks, including reducing risks from other environmental hazards, working with other local authorities, for instance in upstream watershed management, as well as with the National Red Corps or Red Crescent Society and non-governmental organizations, ensuring effective communication with local people and representing the priorities of its people in negotiations for funds with higher levels of government.

It is about building a network based on both active and passive communication methods and should involve all the disaster prevention and management agencies in its coverage.

Passive Communication Method

1. Taking stock of communication methods available
2. Periodic interchange of communication between authorities
3. Awareness through press reports
4. NGO based awareness programmes
5. Awareness through FM, television programmes
6. Awareness through programmes involving schools
7. Mutual exchange of experts from all disaster management agencies

Active Communication Method

1. Specialised user training programmes in disaster management
2. Specialised courses in engineering, medicine, urban arts fields in disaster management
3. Community based mock programmes
4. A highly evolved communication network and strategy
5. Periodic changes to the law including disaster adalats
6. Establishment of community command centres in prominent spots and giving adequate coverage to their existence so that everyone in the region can turn to the spot when disaster occurs. Such voluntary or sponsored command centres would be manned round the clock by citizens which may also create fresh employment avenues for some.

Damage Limitation Management

When the disaster strikes the following steps should be taken

1. Isolation of the spot of tragedy and demarcation of disaster limitation zone
2. Identification of agencies in the limitation zone
3. Firmly establishing chain of control and identifying the command centre in a predetermined spot

4. Leveraging all communication networks in the zone including (a) FM channel, (b) police radio, (c) VIP radio, (d) Pager messages, (e) Mobile telephony, (f) NGO networks, (g) ambulance networks, (f) press
5. Marshalling the help of doctors, volunteers, blood bank volunteers
6. Communication centre for next of victims

Effective Follow-up Management

During follow-up phase the following point should be kept in mind:

1. Gathering complete information relating to the tragedy
2. Total help to the victims of the tragedy and next of kin including (a) Immediate medical help, (b) Help for rehabilitation, (c) Help throughout the period of isolation, (d) Communication to next of kin, (e) Help with mortuary, (f) Timely payment of compensation, (g) Legal aid, (h) Leveraging the press and other communication methods to bring about awareness
3. Exchange of information along the passive network so as to further sharpen the active management techniques
4. Further strengthening the community command centres based on feedback Disasters are either natural, such as floods, droughts, cyclones, and earthquakes, or man-made such as riots, conflicts, refugee situations, and others like fire, epidemics, industrial accidents, and environmental fallouts like the oil refinery fires, oil spills, etc.

Indian Disaster Update

In India, floods recur annually during the monsoon season in different parts compounding existing problems and impeding reconstruction and rehabilitation. The eastern Indian state of Orissa, still recovering from the effects of the 1999 super cyclone, suffered the most from this year's flooding. An estimated 9.6 million people, including 2.4 million children, were directly affected by the floods. Close to 100 lives were lost, while over 250,000 houses and 239,000 acres of crops (valued at US$13 million) were damaged.

During flood, health becomes an increasing concern, as many water sources become contaminated or submerged, leaving no access to clean drinking water. According to the World Health Organization, the Government of Orissa reported 34,111 cases of diarrhea, including 33 deaths, between July 7 and August 14 of 2002. The population marooned in flooded areas was also susceptible to other diseases such as cholera, malaria, dengue fever, and dysentery.

In West Bengal, 400,000 persons were directly affected by the floods. While no death was reported, people lost their sources of livelihood. Extensive floods inundated cropland, damaging standing crops and other vegetation. Nearly 3 million people in the state of Bihar have been affected by floods as well, with 43 lives lost, 112,845 houses damaged, and more than 462,000 acres of crops damaged or destroyed.

In the state of Uttar Pradesh, more than 2 million people in 3,178 villages are affected. The death toll is estimated at 148. Floodwaters inundated about 655,000 acres of land. In the western State of Gujarat, heavy rains at the beginning of the monsoon season caused flooding in and around the city of Ahmedabad, and in two other districts. The rains came after a severe drought had already affected millions with food shortages.

Globally, natural disasters account for nearly 80 per cent of all disaster-affected people. The insurance industry estimates that natural disasters represent 85 per cent of insured catastrophe losses globally. According to the World Disaster report 1999 in 1996, 40 million disaster-affected people depended on humanitarian assistance, a 60 per cent increase over the average figure of 25 million in the 1980s. In the first half of this decade, over US$ 30 billion was spent on humanitarian assistance. The average cost of natural disasters over the past 25 years stands at over US$ 87 billion a year. The average amount spent on humanitarian response is US$ 3 billion a year. Compared to expenditure on disaster mitigation, the average annual global military spending is around US$ 780 billion.

The realities that confront disaster-affected communities in developing countries often challenge conventional Western academic definitions. In the absence of 'official' definitions, observations from the field suggest that disasters be classified under three broad categories: natural, human-made, and other disasters. Amongst these, there are the major disasters and the minor disasters. It is not just the damage-destruction potential that defines a disaster as major or minor, categorization under the former may just be a result of being comparatively well discussed and reported by the media. For a large number of people in several states of India, the distinction is academic: for them, most disasters are major and occur constantly. Yet another category, including situations such as a lack of rational policies to restrict the sale of hazardous and harmful drugs, free sale of tobacco and liquor, banned pesticides, and excessive displacement of people by development projects, consist of disasters caused due to negligence on the part of the policy-makers.

For instance, the continuing drought conditions in the southern states of Andhra Pradesh, Tamil Nadu and Karnataka got further accentuated owing to lack of preparedness of the states, which otherwise are considered prosperous and industrially forward. The tragedy of disasters is that those who are already vulnerable such as the poor and marginal farmers are the first ones to be affected by any kind of natural or man-made disasters. In the southern most districts of Tamil Nadu, for instance, the poor landless labourers were the worst sufferers when the continuing violence owing to caste politics took its toll whole of 2001 and 2002. In Andhra Pradesh, it is the poor cotton farmers who bore the brunt of the drought resulting in many suicides being reported from across the barren districts of central and north-western Andhra Pradesh.

Telling Contrasts

In the global debate about natural disasters countries like India and other south Asian neighbours are dwarfed even though in terms of actual death tolls and other damage the disasters may have caused more mayhem here than the places which continue to catch the headlines. For instance while the 1993 Marathwada earthquake in India left over 10,000 dead and the 2002 Gujarat earthquake also left a similar number dead, it is usually the Los Angeles earthquake of 1971 which is considered as a benchmark on any debate about devastating earth quakes. The actual death toll from this particular earthquake was merely 55. It should, however, be said that every single human loss should be considered as unacceptable.

Likewise, while the 1991 Bangladesh cyclone destroyed and damaged more than a million homes and totted up a damage bill of US$ 1.8 billion, the more talked about Hurricane Mitch in 1998 in the Honduras killed 5,642 people and destroyed about 100,000 houses. The 1996 cyclone along the east coast of Andhra Pradesh in India killed 1,077 people and damaged public buildings worth over US$ 139 million. In contrast, Hurricane Andrew that struck Southern Florida in 1992 killed 41 people and caused damage worth $20 million in Florida itself.

Disaster Response Networks

Indian disaster response system is elaborate and complex but quite practical. An elaborate administrative and financial management structure has been put in place with the hierarchy for decision-making going up all the way to the Prime Minister of India. The Department of Agriculture and Cooperation (DAC) in the Ministry of Agriculture, Government of India, is the nodal department for all matters concerning natural disasters relief at the Centre. The National Contingency Action Plan (CAP) facilitates launching of relief and rescue operations without delay. There are various committees at the national level for disaster management such as Cabinet Committee for effective implementation of relief measures in the wake of natural calamity; National Disaster Management Committee at the national level headed by the Cabinet Secretary who is in charge of various types of disasters and supporting ministries as members; Disaster Management Group reviews various measures required for dealing with a natural disaster, and coordinates activities of the Central ministries and the State Governments. A scheme called Calamity Relief Fund (CRF) has been constituted for each state with contributions from the Central and State Governments to undertake relief and rehabilitation measures. This enables the states to manage and provide for calamity relief on their own by drawing upon the resources available with the fund. In addition to CRF, a National Fund for Calamity Relief (NFCR) has been created to deal with hazards of rare severity which is managed by a National Calamity Relief Committee (NCRC).

Following are the institutional arrangements that are used for forecasting disasters and providing relief in case of their occurrence.

Indian Meteorological Department (IMD)

IMD provides cyclone warnings from the Area Cyclone Warning Centres (ACWCs). It has developed the necessary infrastructure to originate and disseminate the cyclone warnings at appropriate levels. It has made operational a satellite based communication system called Cyclone Warning Dissemination System for direct dissemination of cyclone warnings to the cyclone prone coastal areas. IMD runs operationally a Limited-area Analysis and Forecast System (LAFS), based on an Optimal Interpretation (OI) analysis and a limited area Primitive Equation (PE) model, to provide numerical guidance.

National Remote Sensing Agency (NRSA)

Long-term drought proofing programmes on the natural resources of the district have been greatly helped by the use of satellite data obtained by NRSA. Satellite data can be used very effectively for mapping and monitoring the flood inundated areas, flood damage assessment, flood hazard zoning and past flood survey of river configuration and protection works.

Warning System for Drought

The National Agricultural Drought Assessment and Management System (NADAMS) has been developed by the Department of Space for the Department of Agriculture and Cooperation, and is primarily based on monitoring of vegetation status through National Oceanic and Atmospheric Administration (NOAA) Advanced Very High Resolution (AVHR) data. The drought assessment is based on a comparative evaluation of satellite observed green vegetation cover (both area and greenness) of a district in any specific time period, with that of any similar period in previous years.

Flood Forecasting

Flood forecasts and warnings are issued by the Central Water Commission (CWC), Ministry of Water Resources. These are used for alerting the public and for taking appropriate measures by concerned administrative and state engineering agencies in the flood hazard mitigation. Information is gathered from the CWC's vast network of forecasting stations on various rivers in the country.

Cyclone Tracking

Information on cyclone is furnished on a real-time basis to the control room set up in the Ministry of Agriculture, Government of India. High-power Cyclone Detection Radars (CDRs) that are installed along the coastal belt of India have proved to be a very useful tool for the cyclone warning work. These radars can locate and track approaching tropical cyclones within a range of 400 km. Satellite imagery received from weather satellite is extensively used in detecting the development and movement of tropical cyclones over oceanic regions, particularly when they are beyond the range of the coastal radars. The existing mode of dissemination of cyclone warnings to various government officials is through high priority telegrams, telephones, telex and fax.

Indian Response Mixed

With all such trappings, Indian official response to disasters has been at best tardy even though on the ground a number of measures are believed have to been implemented like building of cyclone shelters, provision of public health centres, reinforcement of the public buildings along the coast, stockpiling of emergency rations, etc. Similarly, community participation and participation of local work groups and non-government organisations has been found severely wanting, if not absent, in many parts of the country. Missed opportunities and misplaced priorities have been the highlights of disaster response as an unstarred Rajya Sabha question 1998 shows. While the total financial allocation to states from Calamity Relief Fund during 1997-98 was Rs 1263.7 crore the actual release of funds was merely Rs 277.37 crore. Part of the reason for such poor response is the widespread inequality of income distribution and high degree of poverty in different parts of the country which makes the affected section without any recourse to funds as they have no means of actually seeking assistance owing to lack of education, awareness and inability to put together any coherent collective response to their own felt needs. Several states and regions in the country, such as Bihar, Orissa, Uttar Pradesh, Rajasthan, and several other pockets have higher levels of poverty than the national average. Poverty is also widespread in areas more prone to natural disasters—flood-prone areas such as north Bihar, east Uttar Pradesh, and north Bengal, and drought-prone areas such as Rajasthan, Marathwada, and north Karnataka.

While poverty is one of the key factors resulting in tardy implementation of any disaster mitigation and emergency preparation work, peculiar relationships and continuing animosity among the various workers are reasons for many of the major river water projects, which would have prevented large scale flooding, not being taken up. The fights over dams on the Cauvery river between Tamil Nadu and Karnataka, the continuing pressure from the environmental groups over an irrigation cum hydel project over the Narmada river, the aquaculture pressure groups that prevent bolstering of eastern coastal region against floods are factors that come in the way of disaster prevention.

Relief and Rehabilitation

Development is, by definition, a long-term process, and it has been occasionally argued that the immediate might sometimes be sacrificed in the interests of posterity. In most quarters today, the importance of providing immediate relief to the disaster-affected is a bedrock principle. In that sense, it is undeniable that following several considerable disasters in India, civil society and, to an extent, the State, have responded, occasionally swiftly and comprehensively, with rescue and relief operations.

Rehabilitation is part of Disaster Management, which is a larger strategic approach to disasters that transcends a reactive response. It has so far been virtually non-existent in India and is only now beginning to be accepted as an important area in the domain of public policy. It is small wonder, therefore, that while the Marathwada earthquake was endowed with a rehabilitation policy, those affected by the later Uttarkashi earthquake, or the even more recent Jabalpur earthquake were not so fortunate. The current tentative rehabilitation strategy at best limits itself to reconstruction and relocation of the affected populations, and even that is non-participatory and poorly implemented. Such measures almost always leave the affected communities as, if not more, vulnerable as they were and lead to both debilitating dependency and unfocused development. This does not imply that people comprehensively crumble under the impact of disasters. Contrary to portrayals in the media, they try to cope and such adversity often increases cohesiveness within the community.

The collation of knowledge and the management of its mobilization are, therefore, essential to the success of any programme for disaster mitigation, relief, or post-disaster rehabilitation. Programme implementation hinges upon the extent to which the key actors within the programme work out their respective mandates with integrity. The structure and process of decision-making, devolution of powers and responsibilities, extent of teamwork, flow of information and communication between and within various levels of the programme implementation apparatus, and personnel needs and strengths are some of the crucial variables in implementation.

Extensive and clear dissemination of complete information about all the components of the rehabilitation programme amongst all the key actors, especially the line department staff, is vital to effective implementation. In purely logistical terms, a disaster area is like a war zone. Since action is based on information, the lack of it can, and does, translate into serious mistakes in the field, spreading confusion and introducing ambiguity where there is none.

The rehabilitation policy must therefore be transparent, concise, and precise. It must necessarily incorporate within it a strategy for constant and wide-band dissemination of information regarding every aspect and component among key actors. The line department functionaries need to be continuously informed of any changes or additions to the policy or guidelines. If necessary, communication experts or consultants must be included in such endeavours.

In summary, this unit explains how disasters have been dealt with in India. The country being vast in size and geographically quite vulnerable to natural disasters, disaster management systems are strong and well entrenched. Even the communication aspect during disaster is also well developed. The media is very much aware of its role during any disaster and there has been fairly strong and consistent reporting of the Disaster, in whatever form it may hit, whether natural or manmade. Some instances of natural and some of man-made disasters have been cited in this unit.

Index

E

R

S